WILD **MALAYSIA**

WILD MALAYSIA

Geoffrey Davison · Junaidi Payne · Melvin Gumal
Photographs by Stephen Hogg and Cede Prudente

JOHN BEAUFOY PUBLISHING

Contents

These pages: Dawn sees the start of work for a traditional Semporna fishing community.

Page 1: Malaysia is a crucial territory for the conservation and survival of Orang-utans (Pongo pygmaeus).

Page 2: The Semporna Islands off the east coast of Sabah, formed from the rim of an ancient volcanic caldera, are fringed by immensely diverse coral reefs.

Foreword

The tropical rainforests in Malaysia have been around for almost 130 million years, covering much of the country's original landscape. In addition, the miles of coast are home to the world's richest marine biodiversity.

Malaysia embraces the best of both worlds with its coral reefs and tropical rainforests, making it truly a perfect destination for nature lovers. It hosts a huge diversity of plant and animal species, including a wide variety of birds – it is indeed a haven for birdwatchers.

Malaysia also hosts a diversity of national parks, including wetlands, wildlife sanctuaries and protected areas that are treasure troves of its natural heritage. Apart from being tourist attractions, some of these places are increasingly recognized for their significance for conservation. WWF-Malaysia plays a key role in ensuring that management plans are in place and endangered species are protected. From the unique Proboscis Monkeys, Orang-utans and Pygmy Elephants of Borneo, to the wild Tigers and Malayan Tapirs of Peninsular Malaysia, our forests are filled with a variety of mammals that are attractive, but also require our attention to conserve them.

In *Wild Malaysia*, you will explore the natural beauty and wonders of Malaysia. The indisputable dramatic landscapes, both in the sea and on the land, will inspire your spirit of adventure to take on a journey you will never forget. I commend the authors of this book for putting together such a vast amount of information, gleaned from years of field experience and complemented with stunning pictures.

I am confident that this book, produced in association with WWF-Malaysia, will contribute to the expansion of knowledge about Malaysia's national heritage, and at the same time inspire readers to conserve and preserve Malaysia's beautiful natural assets with its rich biodiversity. We all have a role to play to ensure that these old tropical rainforests and marine habitats are still around for future generations.

Have fun turning each page of this book and devouring the wilderness of Malaysia, and enjoy the delights that the country has to offer.

Dato' Seri Tengku Zainal Adlin
President
WWF-Malaysia

Opposite: Blyth's Hawk-eagle (Spizaetus alboniger) is found throughout Malaysia where forest exists at suitable altitudes in the foothills and mid-montane zone.

Introduction

Malaysia is a federation of 12 states, plus the federal territories of Kuala Lumpur (the capital) and Labuan (an island off northern Borneo). Ten of the states occupy the southern half of the Malay Peninsula, an appendage to continental Asia that reaches within almost one degree from the equator, while two states (Sabah and Sarawak) occupy the northern quarter of the great island of Borneo.

The Malay Peninsula and Borneo, together with Sumatra, Palawan, Java and Bali, form the key land areas on a broad continental shelf with shallow seas less than 100 m (325 ft) deep. Known as the Sunda Shelf, or Sundaland, this area has been repeatedly exposed by lowered sea levels on numerous occasions during the past couple of million years, leading to opportunities for exchange and spread of animals and plants from one land mass to another. It is a region with a complex physical, biological and environmental history, of which tantalizing evidence can still be traced in the existing rocks, reefs and forest.

It is sometimes claimed that this region contains 'the oldest rainforest in the world', with estimates of up to 130 or even 150 million years in age. This is a distortion of fragmentary fossil evidence that one or two plants similar to species found there today have been found in fine-grained sandstones from the late Jurassic period. In fact, much of the lowlands and even some of the key mountains were not in existence so long ago, and the land areas that did exist were far from their current positions. The drifting together, mutual distortion and partial anti-clockwise rotation of the Sunda Shelf has been a slow process resulting in the steady accumulation of plant and animal diversity to reach, perhaps, a peak before the arrival of modern man.

Changes in the past millennium have quickened and spread on a scale that is both exciting and tragic. The human population more than doubled between 1975 and 2010. Sleepy backwaters have become international trading and industrial hubs; removal of forests has created plantations for essential agricultural commodities driven by demand across the world. It has been said that 70 per cent of lowland forest has now been lost, and no single place is exempt from the pressures of tourism, economic development and insidious climate change. Ironically, the economic advances made possible by exploitation of the natural resources, with higher incomes and enhanced education, have led to heightened interest in nature and conservation. This is exemplified by a network of protected areas, some of the world's best examples of forest governance and world-class research institutions. Malaysia is a signatory to, and active negotiator in, the various international conventions and forums on forests, biological diversity and climate change.

Unconscious of such changes, the remaining wilderness of Malaysia on land and sea continues to support a vast array of plants and animals, amid exotic landscapes in the ever-moist, ever-humid climate. More than 1,000 species of butterfly have been recorded in Peninsular Malaysia. The total of moths is ten times greater. Key mountain ranges support different plants, many of them endemic. More than 8,500 plant species are known from Peninsular Malaysia, and the flora of Sabah and Sarawak is likely to be at least 50 per cent greater. Half the world's species of hard coral and possibly 2,000 fish species occur in Malaysian seas. Sandy beaches, chilly mountain tops, dark caves and peaty blackwater swamps provide the variety of living space to support what is still, in spite of human development, an immensely rich, wild Malaysia.

Many of the richest sites are contained within Malaysia's national and state parks, and these are made more resilient by a matrix of forest reserves intended for protection and production of forest products, and the conservation of water catchments. These parks are reviewed in the following pages.

Opposite: The dawn mist gradually lifts from a forest-lined river in rural Malaysia.

Key to Trail Maps

- feature
- town/village
- road
- river
- trail
- ▲ mountain/hill/pinnacle
- cave

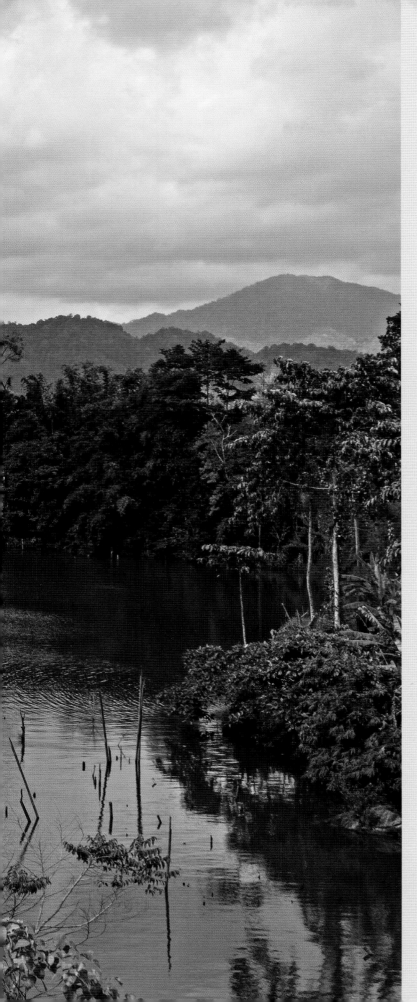

1
Peninsular Malaysia

Located on the Southeast Asian mainland, on a long peninsula bordered by Thailand to the north and nearly reaching Indonesia to the south, Peninsular Malaysia includes the federal territory of Kuala Lumpur, ten states and their surrounding islands. It covers 131,598 sq km (50,810 sq miles). Broad, low-lying plains on the east and west coasts, originally bearing lowland forest and a mangrove-fringed coastline, flank cool central hills rising to more than 2,000 m (6,550 ft) along the Titiwangsa Range. There is a rich flora and fauna with large Asian components and small Australasian components. Peninsular Malaysia accounts for about 80 per cent of Malaysia's population and economy. The west coast is the most developed. Key areas of interest include Cameron Highlands and Fraser's Hill (montane forest), Taman Negara (from riverine and lowland forest up to Peninsular Malaysia's highest peak), Batu Caves (limestone), major rivers leading to the west and east coasts, and the long sandy beaches and offshore islands of Terengganu and Pahang.

Left: Lakes, created by the need for hydroelectric power, have added to the landscape and the diversity of environments for wildlife in the forested foothills.

Significance

Taman Negara has been the biggest single protected area in the whole of Malaysia for more than 75 years. Because it is predominantly undisturbed, with a complete altitudinal sequence of forest from the extreme lowlands up to the peak of the highest mountain in the peninsula, the botanical diversity is enormous. Due to regional differences in the distribution of plant and animal species, no one area can protect everything in the country, but the conservation of Taman Negara goes a long way towards national conservation objectives. With other lowland protected areas in Krau Wildlife Reserve and Endau Rompin National Park, a fine cross-section of Malaysia's natural heritage is conserved.

Today, visitors to the park do research on the internet before their trips and comment on them afterwards. Two main factors seem to make a difference to their reactions to the park. One is the choice of tour operator, which is linked to the quality of accommodation, food and guiding (many visitors prefer to organize their trips independently). The other is the expectation of what may be seen. Those hoping for big mammals are almost inevitably disappointed. However, those who get onto the less-frequented trails and are prepared to look at the forest structure itself are likely to describe Taman Negara as truly magical. There is a vast range of species in the forest, and it has many hidden secrets – for instance minute features such as the range of textures on the bark of trees, and the microcosm of life on the surface of a single moss-encrusted leaf. There is also a huge range of continually changing sounds by night and day: calling barbets and screeching cicadas, the trickle of water and whisper of breezes in the foliage, the distant wailing of gibbons, and the chirps and rattles of a hundred lustful night-time frogs.

Taman Negara

The Gunung Tahan Game Reserve was created in 1925 in the northern part of Pahang, primarily as a response to interest in big-game animals such as Asian Elephants (*Elephas maximus*) and Seladang (*Bos gaurus*). It was not until 1938–1939 that heightened awareness of conservation led to the enlargement of the reserve in Pahang, and the creation of two adjoining reserves in the states of Terengganu and Kelantan, to create a single, huge protected area. Initially known as the King George V National Park; the 4,314 sq km (1,666 sq miles) of forest were later renamed Taman Negara (simply 'the national park' in Malay). In 1980 the park was consolidated under the National Parks Act.

Before there was overland access, the visitor facilities operated by the Department of Wildlife and National Parks were almost the only sign of a settlement in Taman Negara. These facilities have now been privatized and are operated by a hotel chain, while homestays and small lodges are managed by villagers and small companies on the opposite, eastern bank of the Tembeling River outside the national park boundary at Kampung Tahan and Nusa Holiday Village. Visitor numbers have shot up.

Large parts of Taman Negara are inaccessible to most visitors and require special permission – properly so in an area whose chief function is conservation. Over the past decade a number of research studies have focused on the role of Taman Negara in recreation and tourism, but there is still a huge amount to be learned about the plant and animal life of the remoter parts, and even the physical geography such as the stream systems. During the 1980s and '90s, ranger patrols mapped the occurrence of big mammals such as elephants, Malayan Tapirs (*Tapirus indicus*), Tigers (*Panthera tigris*) and Sambar deer (*Rusa unicolor*), and one of the most intensive studies of Tigers in the peninsula has been carried out here.

At one time up to 500 members of the Orang Bateq aboriginal group lived within Taman Negara, moving

in semi-nomadic style between fishing and hunting camps, and collecting rattan and other forest products. Their number within the park has declined with development and job opportunities outside the park, and improvement in schooling and living standards. However, some families do stay within the park.

Trails and treks

Kuala Tahan, the point of access to the park, though far inland, is only 120 m (395 ft) above sea level. Because of the low altitude and the river floodplains, several of the trails around the park headquarters make for easy walking over quite level ground. Inside the rainforest tall trees mask any distant view; only at Bukit Teresek, a small (333-m/1,045-ft) hill about 20 minutes' walk from the park headquarters, are there views over the Tembeling River and across the forest

Above: Tigers occupy huge forest areas, the range of any one male overlapping those of several females.

Top left: The lovely blonde colour phase of the White-handed Gibbon (Hylobates lar) is even more striking than its black counterpart.

Top right: Sambar deer are a key food resource for Tigers, together with Wild Boar.

Opposite top: The sluggish water of small creeks in the extreme lowlands provides an environment for frogs, freshwater fish and aquatic invertebrates, such as dragonfly larvae.

Opposite below: The Malayan Weasel (Mustela nudipes) is a rare sight, though it is seemingly widespread in lowland and hill forest.

in the other direction. This is one of the most common trails followed by park visitors, causing some trampling and trail erosion, but also leading to some of the wildlife becoming quite used to people. At one time this was a likely spot to see a Great Argus Pheasant (*Argusianus argus*), which is almost impossible elsewhere except at one similar site in Danum Valley, Sabah. Bukit Teresek is quite steep, and may be challenging enough for those not used to tropical forests, but the two-hour circuit gives a fair cross-section of experiences, and may inspire longer – but not necessarily steeper – exploratory walks.

A very different experience is offered by the Canopy Walk. This was 250 m (820 ft) long when it was first constructed in 1992, and was later lengthened to 510 m (1,675 ft); it is said to be the longest such walkway in the world. At up to 40 m (130 ft) above the ground, be prepared to face down any fear of heights – although with the crowns of so many trees around and even beneath you, and the ground itself sometimes not visible, you may not realize how high you are. The Canopy Walk is made of a rope network like a sling, extending up to chest height on both sides, with the

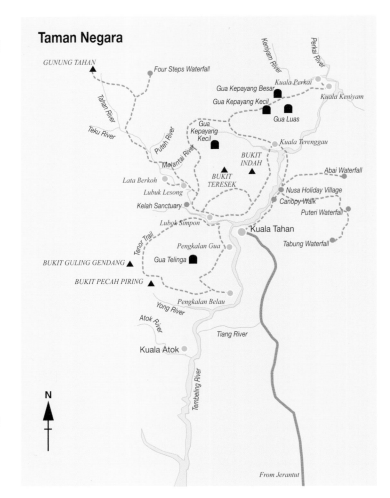

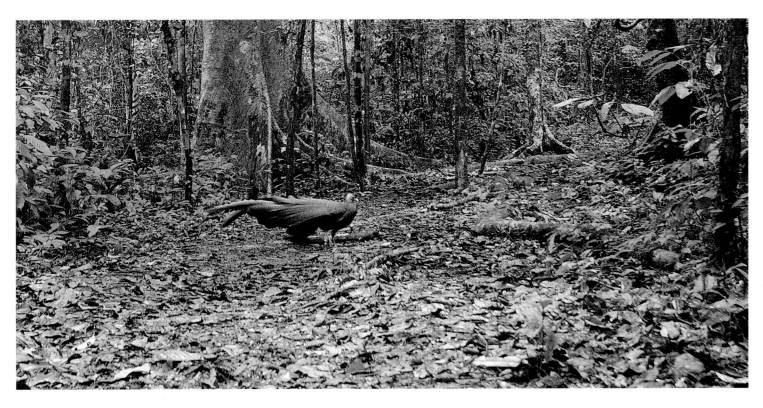

narrow metal walkway itself slung along the middle, and leading from platform to platform. Nine platforms at 50- or 60-m (165- or 200-ft) intervals make for stable viewing and resting points along the route.

It is best to visit the Canopy Walk in a small group rather than alone, and at a time when there are few other visitors. Early morning and during the declining light before dusk are usually the best times for seeing canopy-living birds, but there is always something interesting to see among the varied shapes and arrangements of leaves, the spiders, ants and bugs within the animal community, and the play of light amid the foliage. Even a visit during or after rain is not to be scorned (taking all due care in the frequently slippery conditions).

The walk along the Tahan River Trail can become the basis for a much longer trip; it is an out-and-back trail, not a loop, and the decision when to turn is up to you. Lubuk Simpon, a popular swimming spot, is 20 to 30 minutes away. Lata Berkoh, a stretch of the Tahan River with rugged boulders where swimming is possible, is 8 km (5 miles) from Kuala Tahan (by boat or on foot). It can form the destination for a long day-return trip, bearing in mind that walking in the forest may be slow, and rain is always a possibility – after all this is tropical rainforest. Leeches can be anywhere, and everywhere, especially after rain. It is a myth that they leave their teeth embedded if pulled off – it is subsequent scratching and infection of a bite-mark that can cause problems.

Scattered in parts of Taman Negara are caves in towering limestone outcrops. The small outcrop named Gua Telinga, near Kuala Yong south of Kuala Tahan, may be closed for safety reasons, but there are bigger, though more distant outcrops with impressive caves accessible from Kuala Terengganu (9 km/5½ miles up the Tembeling River) and Kuala Keniyam (25 km/15½ miles upriver). Even from these points the caves are still some hours' walk, so an overnight stay at one of the lodges may be needed. Another important but less visited outcrop is Gua Peningat, the tallest limestone hill in Peninsular Malaysia, accessible from the

Opposite below: During the breeding season a male Great Argus Pheasant will gradually clear away the fallen leaves from his display space.

Below: Spiders in the family Theraphosidae typically live in burrows or tree-holes and are seldom seen by day; this one may be an undescribed species.

western entrance to Taman Negara from Merapoh, near the border between Kelantan and Pahang.

On the map the mountains of Taman Negara form a broad, stubby letter H, with Gunung Tahan (2,186 m/7,170 ft) at the left of the middle stroke; the left-hand stroke of the H is formed by other mountains of the Tahan Range, and the right-hand stroke by mountains of the East Coast Range. Gunung Tahan is the tallest mountain in the peninsula, and a round trip from Kuala Tahan takes at least seven days (four out, three return), with all food and equipment carried. The challenge is only partly in climbing the mountain itself; the outward journey leads up and down over some 21 hills, followed by repeated crossing backwards and forwards through the Tahan River, before reaching Kuala Teku at the foot of the true climb. This is a trip often made by adventurous youth groups, but it is also quite feasible for fit adults prepared to rough it. There are a few technically difficult stretches, eased by steps and ropes, before reaching the open 'padang' of stunted elfin forest on the fourth day, just before the summit. This is the land of dwarfed rhododendrons, pitcher plants and montane birds.

It was partly demand for an easier route to the summit that led to the opening of park access from Merapoh, which can reduce the travel time to four or five days. Merapoh is still a much less frequented entry point, with fewer facilities than at Kuala Tahan, and less commercialization. Another entry point is from Kuala Koh in Kelantan (accessible from Gua Musang), and yet another is from the Terengganu side to the north-east; this trip involves crossing the Kenyir Lake from Kuala Berang, and is best suited to a short visit during a lake-based holiday, without a stay within the Terengganu sector of Taman Negara.

Birds

There are 380 bird species on the list for Taman Negara, 60 of which (including 16 babblers and six flycatchers) are confined to montane forest above 900 m (3,000 ft). Birdwatchers are keen to find the extreme lowland specialists, such as the Giant Pitta (*Pitta caerulea*), Large Frogmouth (*Batrachostomus auritus*), Malaysian Peacock-pheasant (*Polyplectron malacense*) and Short-toed Coucal (*Centropus rectunguis*). Storm's Stork (*Ciconia stormi*) is a possibility in flooded forest, along the river or in remote forest clearings, and the Blue-banded Kingfisher (*Alcedo euryzona*), Lesser Fishing-eagle (*Ichthyophaga humilis*) and migratory Masked Finfoot (*Heliopais personata*) are gems of forest-lined rivers. In principle there is much to be seen, but it is hard work finding birds among the dense vegetation. Sounds are a very important guide to what is around.

Fig trees (*Ficus* spp.) are a key food resource for many birds: 16 or more species of bulbul, together with hornbills, barbets and pigeons, can be seen at a favourite tree when it is fruiting.

Above: *Along forested rivers the Lesser Fishing-eagle can adopt a watch-and-wait hunting strategy.*

Top: *Dead-leaf camouflage and outline-breaking contrasts in colour of the Large Frogmouth help to confuse potential predators.*

Mammals

Various forest squirrels and other small mammals can also be seen on fruiting fig trees. The black Malayan Giant Squirrel (*Ratufa bicolor*) and the Cream-coloured Giant Squirrel (*R. affinis*) are both fig specialists. Civets and flying squirrels are possibilities for sighting at night. White-handed Gibbons, Siamang (*Symphalangus syndactylus*) and various monkeys (leaf-monkeys and macaques) also visit fig trees. The fruiting of fig trees is not easily predictable, as there are many species (100 altogether in the peninsula) and each has differing fruiting behaviour – some species fruit annually, some at intervals of three or five months, and others very seldom. Not all of the fig trees are attractive to animals.

The 120 mammal species in Taman Negara include some 40 or more bats, very few of which are reliably identifiable on the wing, and it is still possible to see the increasingly scarce Giant Flying Fox (*Pteropus vampyrus*). Most of the mammals are nocturnal, and a night walk with a reliable headlamp and an equally reliable guide can increase the chances of adding species to a list of mammal sightings.

Above: *A wide range of colour variation, some of it geographically determined, can be seen in populations of the Cream-coloured Giant Squirrel.*

Above left: *The Dusky Leaf-monkey (*Trachypithecus obscurus*) is one of two leaf-monkeys inhabiting the canopy of lowland forest.*

Fish

Because rivers form such a prominent feature of Taman Negara, it is not surprising that 108 freshwater fish species have been recorded, some of them important food fish in the big rivers, and many of them small, inconspicuous stream dwellers in the network of rocky or leaf-clogged forest streams. Lubuk Tenor, reached either by boat or by a very long (five-hour) walk, has been designated as a fish sanctuary for the famous Mahseer (*Tor tambroides*), which is protected in Taman Negara but was formerly a classic sports fish.

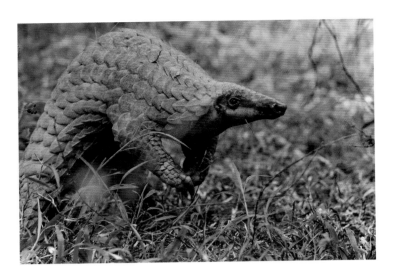

Plant life

The one thing that is impossible for visitors to miss is the plant life. More than 2,400 plant species are estimated to occur in Taman Negara, nearly a third of the total flora of Peninsular Malaysia, including at least 800 tree species.

Above: Susceptibility to flooding in forest near rivers is reflected in the presence of stilt roots amongst some of the trees.

Top: Sunda Pangolins (Manis javanica) occasionally blunder out of the forest into adjacent cultivation.

Opposite: Dawn viewing points along Girdle Road reveal the distant forested landscape along the Main Range and its foothills.

The area around the Tahan River is truly lowland forest, growing on the narrow alluvial floodplain, although the river itself is seldom in sight between the trees. Tall dipterocarp trees, the family of trees that form the bulk of the timber trade from forest elsewhere in Malaysia, belong to 30–40 different species. It is no use asking for the name of 'the tree with buttress roots', because many tree species have them – they are a common adaptation, improving the stability of very tall, shallow-rooted trees in the tropics. Some trees with stilt roots can also be seen; their roots project from a short distance up the trunk and arch down to the ground. *Dillenia* (*simpoh*) is a common genus of trees with stilt roots in this riverine habitat, but not the only one. The shrubby yellow-flowered *Dillenia suffruticosa* can be found in disturbed places along riverbanks, although it is not likely to be seen along the Tahan River. This runs through primary forest, where waterside trees such as the peeling-barked Pelawan (*Tristania*), the arching Neram (*Dipterocarpus oblongifolius*) and the lovely little orange-flowered Gapis (*Saraca declinata*) are characteristic.

Access

The most frequent access to Taman Negara is from the south. Visitors arrive at Kuala Tembeling, near the town of Jerantut, and proceed by river longboat up the Tembeling River to the settlement at Kuala Tahan. Depending on water levels in the river, this can be a fairly long but uneventful journey (three hours, considerably eased by bringing your own cushion), or it can include slow and difficult spots where the boat may have to be helped across shallow, stony rapids. Since the 1980s it has also been possible to travel from Jerantut overland to Kuala Tahan, and this can now be done by bus or private vehicle on paved roads. Some visitors experience both, going in by boat and coming out by bus.

Fraser's Hill

Fraser's Hill, perhaps the most famous birding location in the peninsula, is named after Louis James Fraser, who arrived in the Malay Peninsula following a rather abrupt and mysterious exit from the West Indies in 1883. He is reputed to have found tin ore in the mountains – superficially a rather unlikely place to prospect – and to have made a living by charging for horse transport over the Main Range, as well as by selling supplies to labourers. Opium and gambling dens are also said to have been on his agenda. He made another abrupt, and this time final, disappearance before the First World War.

At this time the route over the Main Range (now called the Titiwangsa Range) was not paved, and the additional 8-km (5-mile) way up from The Gap at 800 m (2,625 ft) to Fraser's Hill would have been little more than a trace through the forest. The road up was cut by prison labourers, its careful construction and narrow, contour-hugging approach accounting for there being relatively few landslips until at least the 1980s. Construction of some of the hilltop bungalows began at the time of the First World War, preceding the main development of Cameron Highlands – if not for that chance, Fraser's Hill might never have been opened – with the Rest House at The Gap being built in around 1926.

The small township is centred around the nine-hole golf course. This course was one of the first features to be created, by removing the forest and using water pumps to wash earth down into the valley to form the

level ground. The remaining colonial-style bungalows were completed between 1922 and 1930, spaced along the looping narrow road system, and another phase of building occurred in around 1970. A number of the bungalows are available for rent, either by the room or by a whole property. There are now also several hotel and apartment choices, including Puncak Inn at the town centre, Jelai Resort, Silverpark condominiums and Pine Resort.

Fraser's Hill is a cool, secluded getaway for both individuals and families retreating from the city bustle. Birdwatching along the little-used roads is usually good, and can be fantastic or occasionally a dreadful disappointment in poor weather. Botanizing along the roads and on the forest trails can reveal many fascinating and unusual plants, and spiders, moths, beetles and other creatures add to the level of interest.

At Fraser's Hill there is little by way of nightlife. If a visitor is not interested in seeking owls, moths and nocturnal crickets along the roadside, a leisurely dinner is possible at the Old Smokehouse. But most naturalists opt for an evening around the fire, an early night and a dawn start to nature watching.

Significance

Fraser's Hill is the best-known montane site for nature study in Peninsular Malaysia. Its proximity to Kuala Lumpur, easy access and relatively small area, with a good road network and accommodation on the spot, have all contributed to studies there. Being largely within the lower montane forest zone, Fraser's Hill supports a wide array of both lowland and montane plants and animals in a zone of transition between the two. There are many scarce species, such as the Trig Oak (*Trigonobalanus verticillata*), and there is high species diversity among many groups (for example figs, mistletoes and moths). Being near a saddle on a slight 'wriggle' within the overall north–south orientation of the Titiwangsa Range, Fraser's Hill has proved a superb spot for studies of bird migration.

Tracks and trails

The most comfortable way of exploring Fraser's Hill is by walking the quiet roads, as there is little traffic. The

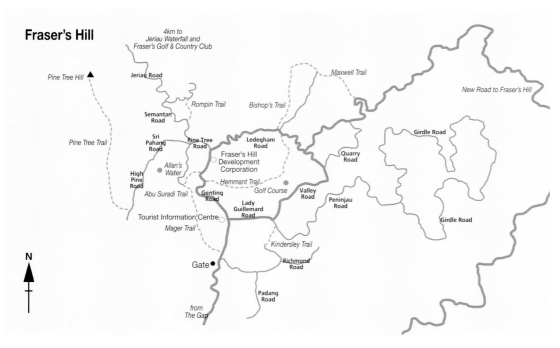

Fraser's Hill

4km to
Jeriau Waterfall and
Fraser's Golf & Country Club

Pine Tree Hill ▲

Jeriau Road

Maxwell Trail

New Road to Fraser's Hill

Rompin Trail

Bishop's Trail

Semantan
Road

Sri
Pahang
Road

Pine Tree
Road

Ledegham
Road

Girdle Road

Pine Tree Trail

Fraser's Hill
Development
Corporation

Quarry
Road

Allan's
Water

High
Pine
Road

Hemmant Trail

Golf Course

Valley
Road

Abu Suradi Trail

Genting
Road

Lady
Guillemard
Road

Peninjau
Road

Girdle Road

Tourist Information Centre

Mager Trail

N

Kindersley Trail

Gate

Richmond
Road

Padang
Road

from
The Gap

small section of Fraser's Hill within the state of Selangor (via Jalan Mager, first right turn immediately after the arrival gate) is quite undeveloped, with the least traffic, and can be good place to see owls. On the Pahang side, the Girdle Road (one-way traffic) can take half a day for slow birdwatchers and offers some good distant landscape views; there is a nesting colony of White-bellied Swiftlets (*Collocalia esculenta*) in an old garage beside the road. Another favourite route is from the town centre to Jalan Lady Maxwell – this takes you all the way around the old golf course and Silverpark Resort.

Right: The better marked of the forest trails at Fraser's Hill permit the viewing of plants and insects at close range.

Below left: The little used one-way road system doubles as a facility for birdwatchers along Lady Maxwell Road.

Below right: Fine details of bill and head shape distinguish the Malayan Whistling Thrush (*Myophoneus robinsoni*) from its close relatives.

In addition to the roads there are eight forest trails offering a range of challenges. Best known to naturalists are Hemmant Trail (running behind the old golf course), Bishop's Trail (virtually a continuation of Hemmant Trail across the road) and Pine Tree Hill Trail. Hemmant Trail is clear and wide, starts close to the town centre and is fairly level: it offers a good introductory walk. Bishop's Trail is narrow, and although it tries to follow the contour line there are a few slippery bits and boulder crossings. This is the classic trail used for locating Rusty-naped Pittas (*Pitta oatesi*).

By far the most challenging trail is that to Pine Tree Hill, beginning close to one of the high points at Fraser's Hill, at High Pines bungalow, and extending for 6 km (4 miles) through sometimes difficult terrain.

Above: *Semangkok Waterfall shows the typical form of streams at middle altitudes where flowing over granite bedrock.*

Left: *At Fraser's Hill the Malayan Striped Coral Snake* (Calliophis intestinalis) *is one of the most attractive, small but venomous snakes.*

Some extremely rare plants along the way will certainly be missed unless they are pointed out by a guide. Pine Tree Hill Trail requires an early start, and a return journey on the same trail, taking perhaps seven or eight hours to complete. The physical challenge detracts from birdwatching, but there are plenty of interesting plants, trees, fungi and other forms of life to see along the way.

The trails are mostly well marked, but can be obscured by recent treefalls, and there is always the possibility of rain or mist. People have been lost here, so before embarking on a trail walk it is sensible to let others know where you are going and when you expect to be back.

The Waterfall Road is a leisurely 5-km (3-mile) downhill stretch. Near the beginning is the justly famed town refuse dump, one of the best sites on the hill for birdwatching, although it is not for the faint-hearted. The remainder of the walk passes enjoyable forest landscapes, with Trig Oaks along the roadside. Siamang may be heard and perhaps seen in the mid-morning. After passing the entrance to the new golf course there is the possibility of a dip at the waterfall, although this is often crowded.

Birds

The Gap approximately marks the transition from lowland forest, so the remaining road to the top runs through lower montane forest with a different avifauna. From The Gap upwards just 270 bird species have been listed, of which 65 are montane forest specialists (the other five montane specialists in the peninsula are confined to higher altitudes not available at Fraser's Hill, or to one or two isolated peaks). This total includes all three of the birds endemic to the Main Range, the Malaysian Hill-partridge (*Arborophila campbelli*), Mountain Peacock-pheasant (*Polyplectron inopinatum*) and Malayan Whistling Thrush, and ten species that are confined to the mountains of the Sunda region (Peninsular Malaysia, Sumatra, Borneo,

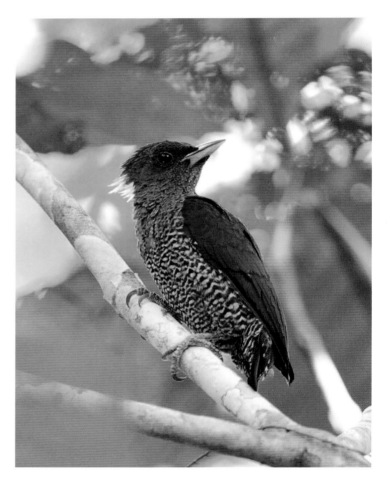

Above: *The Banded Woodpecker (*Picus miniaceus*) prefers secondary forest and the forest edge.*

Top: *Amongst the babblers of mountain forest, the Long-tailed Sibia (*Heterophasia picaioides*) is commonly seen.*

Opposite: *The Gap below Fraser's Hill is a known breeding site for Blyth's Hawk-eagle (*Spizaetus alboniger*).*

Java and Bali). The remaining 200 species comprise residents with a broad altitudinal range including both lowland and montane forest, some lowland birds that just creep above the boundary into the montane habitat along the road above The Gap, and many migrants.

Fraser's Hill happens to be at a slight east–west kink in the otherwise primarily north–south Main Range. As it is also bounded by higher ground to the north (Cameron Highlands) and to the south (Genting Highlands), local geography seems to make it a good site for migrants passing over the mountain range. Much of this migration is invisible to birdwatchers because it happens at night. In the 1960s and '70s, netting at one of the old telecommunications properties on the High Pines Road (now replaced by the Seri Intan bungalow) showed the great range of birds involved. Some 64 migrant species have been netted, together with locally resident birds making nocturnal dispersal movements (six pigeons and doves). Migrants include a few whose southwards terminus is the peninsula, but most populations winter extensively throughout Southeast Asia, not necessarily in forest.

The Malayan Whistling Thrush can be heard and seen from the road up as well as at Fraser's Hill itself, but great care is needed to distinguish it from the (now more common) local race of Blue Whistling Thrush (*Myophonus caeruleus*), which is minimally larger, with a more angular head and bill. The Malaysian Hill-partridge and Mountain Peacock-pheasant can both be lucky spots when wandering quietly along one of the forest trails, but some birdwatchers come to Fraser's Hill specifically to find the Rusty-naped Pitta. Although a resident form of pitta had been suspected since the 1940s, it was not identified until 1976 as an outlying population of the Rusty-naped Pitta, otherwise known from continental Asia and adding a resident bird to the Malaysian list. It is known from other mountain sites in the peninsula, but the forest trails at Fraser's Hill make this the most feasible site at which to see it.

Mammals

One of the magnificent experiences possible at Fraser's Hill is an encounter with a singing family of Siamang, the biggest of the gibbons. Their alternating booms and screams, along with cascades of shrieks and trills, are louder than any other sound in the forest and can never be forgotten.

Over the years White-thighed Leaf-monkeys (*Presbytis siamensis*) at Fraser's Hill have become considerably more tame than they used to be, with some troops showing indifference to people, walking in plain view along branches and overhead cables, and sometimes coming to the ground and even sitting by roadsides. This is a significant change in behaviour from their usual skittish fear of people and their machine-gun chatter of alarm when seen even from a distance, presumably influenced by the number of harmless visitors they encounter. Troops of the same species elsewhere, for example at Taman Negara,

remain much wilder. Over the years, too, it has become
clear that the leaf-monkeys in the central part of the
peninsula, including Fraser's Hill, all of which used to
be called Banded Leaf-monkeys, are a different species
from the true Banded Leaf-monkeys (*Presbytis
femoralis*) to the south in Johor and Singapore, and
perhaps also different from those to the north in
peninsular Thailand.

Further significant change has occurred among
Long-tailed Macaques (*Macaca fascicularis*). Not only
are they now present, and irritating, at Fraser's Hill
– where the possibility of some having been released
cannot be ruled out – but on the road up from Kuala
Kubu Bharu in the lowlands they can be a menace.
They have become thoroughly used to scrounging food
from passing cars, and any car that stops by the
roadside is likely to be surrounded by macaques
expecting handouts and snatching anything in sight.

Above: The Sunda Slow Loris (Nycticebus coucang) *is nocturnal and almost entirely arboreal.*

Above right: Fraser's Hill is enlivened by groups of the lovely White-thighed Leaf-monkey.

Below right: In montane forest lives a primitive insectivore, the Lesser Gymnure (Hylomys suillus).

Opposite top: Long-tailed Macaques have become extremely common and bothersome along the road leading to Fraser's Hill.

Opposite below: Southern Pig-tailed Macaques (Macaca nemestrina) *are stocky, powerful monkeys spending significant time at ground level.*

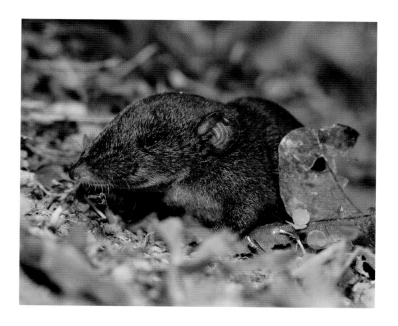

Insects

Associated with the plant life are butterflies and moths. The abundance of garden plants provides plenty of nectar for flower-visiting insects, so in sunny weather a good range of butterflies can be seen. Moths are perhaps best seen in the early morning, when they have settled on white walls lit during the night. There can be a very wide range of hawkmoths, and the total number of moth species is vast. The species that are abundant on any given night vary tremendously; sometimes there are big numbers of the Swallowtail Moth (*Lyssa zampa*).

Other significant insect groups at Fraser's Hill include grasshoppers and crickets, longhorn beetles and stick insects. Many others – such as ants, bees and wasps, and small beetles – can give hours of enjoyment as they go about their lives. Because this is a wildlife sanctuary, there should be no collecting of insects (or other forms of life) without a permit.

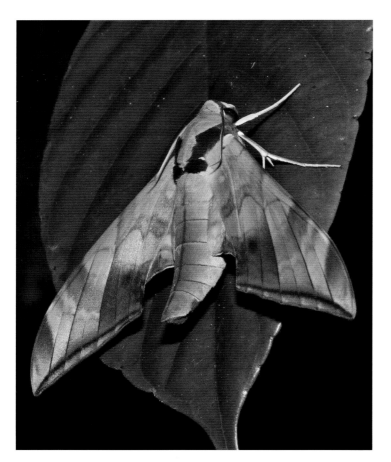

Plant life

Plants are an important part of the Fraser's Hill experience. The total plant list for the hill has reached a thousand species, some of which are exceedingly rare. One or two are known only from this locality and nowhere else in the world, even at other sites along the same mountain range. The Trig Oak is known only from Fraser's Hill, north Borneo and Sulawesi (Celebes); at Fraser's Hill it is known from the Jeriau Valley, where the distinctive coppicing trees have been planted along the verge of the Waterfall Road. A wild begonia (*Begonia fraseri*) is more widespread, near rocky streams in the forest, and several herbs of the African violet family (Gesneriaceae) can be found along the forest trails. Tree ferns, mushrooms and figs are other groups to look out for. The less active nature watcher may enjoy the planted gardens of horticultural interest around the older bungalows.

Access

Fraser's Hill is about 100 km (60 miles) from Kuala Lumpur. There is now no public transport. It is reached by car or taxi, a little over two hours' journey from Kuala Lumpur, by driving north either on the North–South Highway or on the old road towards Ipoh, turning off at Kuala Kubu Bharu to travel on the small road that winds up the western flank of the Main Range towards Raub. On reaching The Gap at 730 m (2,400 ft), it is another 8 km (5 miles) up the steeply winding one-way road to Fraser's Hill. Departure from Fraser's Hill is via another downhill one-way road. If either road happens to be closed due to repairs, a gated one-hour-up, one-hour-down system can be implemented.

Left: Many species of hawkmoth (Sphingidae) are attracted to lights from the surrounding forest.

Kuala Selangor Nature Park

Coastal hills have often provided strategic locations for settlements. A case in point is the hilltop at Kuala Selangor, Bukit Malawati, which was successively commanded in past centuries by Malay, Dutch and British forces. It has an all-round view of the sea, with the town to one side and the Selangor River curling away behind it, and cannon on the hilltop fort were able to control shipping, trade and taxes both coastal and riverine. Any traders slipping upriver past the fort might well be apprehended at Kampung Pelamun ('pirate village') a mile upstream.

Above: Daylight reveals the slim and ghostly outlines of Purple Herons (Ardea purpurea) *waiting at the edge of the lake.*

Encompassed in this same hilltop view today is the Kuala Selangor Nature Park, uniquely managed in a partnership between the Selangor State Government and the Malaysian Nature Society. Lying between the sea and the foot of the hill, approximately 290 ha (700 acres) of mangroves and secondary forest are protected within the park. The park provides an interesting view of the gradual transition from wet mangroves along the edge of the sea, which are inundated daily by tides, to the drier ground of the inland back-mangroves, where most water input is from rainfall.

Kuala Selangor Nature Park is open daily, with a small entry charge, and bicycles may be available for rental. At the entrance the visitor centre includes exhibits, an interpretation centre suitable for schools and small groups, and a shop. Observation towers, shelters, birdwatching hides and a boardwalk have been constructed, but these are high-maintenance structures within a mangrove environment, so it is best to check on arrival which facilities are available at the time. The park can be extremely hot during the day, with little or no shade out on the main trails around the lake and along the coastal bund (raised bank), so it is sensible to use sunscreen lotion and to wear a wide-brimmed hat.

There is a camping site in the park, but food is not available here – in part to avoid problems with waste disposal and with macaques. Across the river at Pasir Penambang are famous seafood restaurants, and a few kilometres away at Kampung Kuantan spectacular displays of synchronously flashing fireflies (*Pteroptyx tener*) can be seen; these are best at times of little moon, viewed from a boat poled gently along the smooth-flowing river.

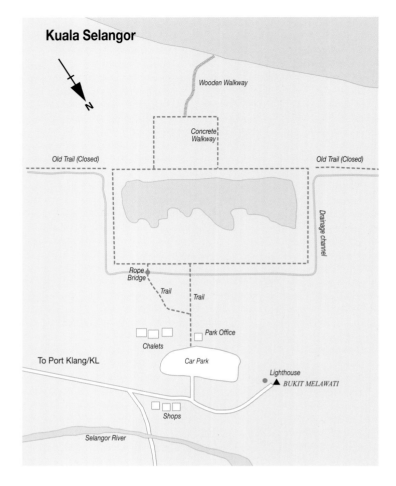

Significance

The mudflats along the coast of Kuala Selangor form part of the international chain of feeding and resting stations for migratory waders along the East Asian-Australasian migratory flyway. They are of key importance to the birds due to fragmentation of the chain by coastal development in various countries, which lengthens the distances that birds have to fly between staging posts. This is one of the few mangrove areas along the west coast that is still easily accessible to the public. The establishment of the nature park was a path-breaking example of collaboration between a government and a non-government organization in area management for nature conservation.

Tracks and trails

From the park entrance, with its visitor centre and exhibits, the main trail leads out to an area where camping and rental of A-frame chalets are permitted, through secondary forest towards the centre of the reserve. Three or four trail options are possible, allowing visitors to plan any length of walk, ranging from a few minutes to several hours in duration. A suitable day's programme can include a visit to the park in the early morning when it is still fairly cool, exploration of the hill and town for lunch or in the hot afternoon, and a return visit to the park in the evening. With several trails through differing environments available, and with the possibility of overnight accommodation in the park, other programmes can be devised to fully occupy a two- or three-day vacation.

Not least of the sights on Bukit Malawati are the introduced Rain Trees (*Albizia saman*), some of which were planted in the late 19th and early 20th centuries. Having survived decades of incoming coastal storms, some of these trees must be nearing their final years. They are now magnificent, with broadly spreading crowns of feathery leaves, their boughs providing fine monkey-travel routes, and their extensive roots

traceable for many metres across the shady grass lawns below. They provide a fine backdrop to the remains of two forts – cannon emplacements – the famous Altingsburg Lighthouse and the royal mausoleum where ancestors of the still-ruling sultans of Selangor are buried. From the old town, One Hundred Steps lead up the hill to the most popular tourism areas, with views across the estuary and out to sea. From there, another set of newly constructed steps can lead visitors back into the nature park.

Above: Purple Herons nest either on swampy ground or in adjacent trees.

Birds

The 10 ha (25 acres) of shallow lakes at the core of Kuala Selangor Nature Park were artificially created in 1986, to provide an alternative roosting site for waders at high tide, when these birds cannot feed on the mudflats along the shore. As this is primarily a roosting (rather than feeding) site, the fact that the lakes contain fresh or brackish water has little significance to the waders; what is important is the open habitat, with safe, secure islands for resting, sometimes in huge flocks. The islands and their scattered trees have also been a focus for efforts to conserve nesting herons and egrets, and an attempted reintroduction of the globally threatened Milky Stork (*Mycteria cinerea*).

Kuala Selangor is part of a chain of suitable feeding and resting spots for waders migrating along the west coast of Peninsular Malaysia. Of more than 200 birds listed for the park and its vicinity, virtually one-fifth are migrant waders (stints, sandpipers, plovers, godwits and their relatives). Past rarities have included Spotted Greenshanks (*Tringa guttifer*) and once a Spoon-billed Sandpiper (*Eurynorhynchus pygmeus*). Common Redshanks (*Tringa totanus*), among the most abundant waders to reach Kuala Selangor, originate from the Tibetan area, China, Mongolia and eastern Russia, some passing through and some over-wintering. A few may over-summer, and even those arriving for the non-breeding season sometimes retain partial breeding plumage. Mongolian Plovers (*Charadrius mongolus*) can also be abundant in the park, as can Pacific Golden Plovers (*Pluvialis fulva*), Whimbrels (*Numenius phaeopus*) and Curlew Sandpipers (*Calidris ferruginea*).

Right: One of the most abundant migrant waders along the west coast is the Common Redshank.

Opposite top left: The Intermediate Egret (*Mesophoyx intermedia*) is not as closely related to other egrets as its all-white plumage might suggest.

Opposite top right: Black-crowned Night-herons (*Nycticorax nycticorax*) occur in small numbers except at the very few known breeding colonies.

Opposite centre left: Bill and leg colours that change with the season make egret identification a challenge: is this the rather rare Chinese Egret (*Egretta eulophotes*), or another Intermediate Egret?

Opposite below left: Little or Striated Herons (*Butorides striata*) have a nearly worldwide distribution, with much geographical variation in plumage.

Between 60,000 and 120,000 waders have been estimated to pass along the coast each year, and a peak daily total of 8,000 at roost has been recorded at Kuala Selangor. Coastal development everywhere, including in both the breeding and non-breeding homes of these passing birds, poses conservation challenges and a struggle to maintain these past numbers. Nevertheless, searching bird by bird through a seething flock of waders, feeding out on the mudflats or scattered across the roosting grounds, is an exciting occupation that can turn up important rarities, as well as help to keep track of total numbers.

For anyone interested in waders or other migrants, the timing of a visit to Kuala Selangor is important. Just a few individuals of several species over-summer (for example Common Redshanks). Migrants typically

begin to arrive in August and September, build up numbers towards October, and may reach intermittent peaks through the non-breeding season before gradually declining in the early part of the following year. Even when numbers are low towards April and into May, the diversity of species can still be high as passage migrants of various species fly through en route to their breeding areas in the north. Differences between years can be significant, in terms of both the total number of birds recorded, and which species are the most abundant. Keen wader watchers may consider side trips to Sekinchan and Tanjung Karang along the coast a little to the north, to rice fields along the coastal road and inland and, if arrangements can be made (not easy), to the ash-disposal ponds at Kapar power station to the south.

At least 15 species of heron and egret have been seen at Kuala Selangor, as well as seven species of kingfisher, of which the most spectacular is the Stork-billed Kingfisher (*Pelargopsis capensis*). Within the mangrove forest the Mangrove Pitta (*Pitta megarhyncha*) is an internationally endangered species with a restricted range from Bangladesh to Sumatra, and is a proven nester at Kuala Selangor. Laced, Rufous and Common Flameback Woodpeckers (*Picus vittatus, Micropternus brachyurus* and *Dinopium javanensei*) occur, together with migrant Black Drongos (*Dicrurus macrocercus*) and possibly resident Ashy Drongos (*D. leucophaeus*), which are challenging to distinguish. Kuala Selangor is also one of the few sites in Peninsular Malaysia in which to seek White-breasted Woodswallows (*Artamus leucorynchus*).

Many common birds are easier to see around the margins of the lakes, where the trail along a raised bank allows views of Red Junglefowl (*Gallus gallus*), tailorbirds, bulbuls, magpie-robins, Olive-backed Sunbirds (*Cinnyris jugularis*) and many other birds. Abundant fig trees of various species attract a range of fruit-eating birds, and are interesting in themselves for their spectacular aerial root systems.

*Above right: Various nectar-feeding birds, such as this female Brown-throated Sunbird (*Anthreptes malacensis*), are attracted to the bright red flowers of* Lumnitzera littorea.

Centre right: The most abundant sunbird in mangroves and in gardens is the Olive-backed Sunbird.

*Below right: The Oriental Magpie-robin (*Copsychus saularis*) is a good example of the spread of mangrove birds into gardens and cultivation.*

*Opposite top: *Periophthalmodon schlosseri* is the biggest of at least 13 species of mudskippers in the mangroves.*

Opposite below: A tangle of stilt roots creates a vast number of physical niches for surface-living organisms, with differing tidal conditions, temperature, shade, humidity and other variables.

Water wildlife

Within the park a coastal bund, originally created to protect the low-lying town from flooding, now separates the mangroves, which are strongly influenced by every tide, from the more inland, drier back-mangroves and subcoastal forest. In the mangroves life is everywhere. The roots and lower parts of tree trunks are encrusted with Mangrove Oysters (*Crassostrea gasar*), while winkles live on the bark and foliage, and Telescope Shells (*Telescopium telescopium*) on the mud below. At low tide various crabs can be seen moving about on the mud: male fiddler crabs are the best known and most entertaining, ready to retreat back into their burrows at the slightest disturbance, but emerging to feed, court females and threaten their rivals with a wave of one big, colourful claw.

All of these and other water wildlife can be seen without leaving the public trail. Mudskippers are one of the great attractions, seen in the mangroves and along the edges of the lake. Four of the world's 34 species are present, ranging from tiddlers to big adults more than 25 cm (10 in) long. The males of the biggest species

– grey with bright blue-green spots, their wet bodies glistening in the sun – can be seen raising their sail-like dorsal fins in aggressive display, and chasing one another across the mud. At high tide they may be found resting out of the water, frequently clinging to a mangrove root.

In spite of the regular tides washing across the mud, the surface of the ground within the mangroves is not level. Besides the litter of twigs and fallen trees, and winding tidal channels, mounds of mud can be seen. These are formed by Mud Lobsters (*Thalassina anomala*), which are rarely seen but always evident from these rough, sturdy constructions up to nearly 1 m (3 ft) tall.

Mammals

On the inland side of the bund is a tidal drain and it is here, or in the mangroves or out in the shallow lake, that Smooth-coated Otters (*Lutrogale perspicillata*) can occasionally be seen. They sometimes occur as a pair, but are more often seen in a family group including well-grown young from a previous litter – up to ten or

a dozen individuals altogether. As well as fish, the otters may take a wide range of molluscs and crabs. Other mammals in the park area include Plantain Squirrels (*Callosciurus notatus*), an array of fruit bats (including those that pollinate the mangrove trees) and insectivorous bats, and the Short-tailed Mongoose (*Herpestes brachyurus*).

Silvered Leaf-monkeys (*Trachypithecus cristatus*) are one of the famous attractions of Kuala Selangor, where they live at high density within the mangroves and the subcoastal vegetation. Troops of 10–15 animals are dominated by an adult male, and include various females, younger and subordinate males, and juveniles. Babies clinging to their mothers are a magnificent bright orange all over; the bright colour gradually fades as they become independent, with the pelage turning to the typical smoky-grey tipped with silver that gives the species its name.

At least six troops of Silvered Leaf-monkeys enter the town and park-like grounds of Bukit Malawati, where they encounter visitors to the hill fort. It is astonishing to see how tame some of the leaf-monkeys have become, even sitting on visitors or taking food from the hand. The leaf-monkeys are natural vegetarians, feeding on the foliage and green propagules of mangrove trees; they have a multiple stomach like that of a cow in which bacteria break down the plant cellulose. As in the case of cattle, eating artificial sugary foods should lead to excessive fermentation and bloat, yet these tame monkeys at Kuala Selangor accept all manner of foods that should be highly unsuitable.

Long-tailed Macaques are also common at Kuala Selangor – primate ruffians mixing with their more aristocratic leaf-monkey cousins. Like them they live in troops, but these are often larger and have more than one adult male, are boisterous and indulge in all sorts of social and anti-social behaviour. These are not animals that the more cautious visitor should engage with too closely. If in doubt, one might consider that the adult males have long, sharp canines, and these are not designed purely for appearance.

Right: The orange infants of the Silvered Leaf-monkey delight visitors to Kuala Selangor.

Below right: Figs of various species provide a staple food of primates such as the Long-tailed Macaque.

Opposite: Groups of Asian Small-clawed Otters (Aonyx cinereus) are curious and intelligent, and may investigate anything new within their territory.

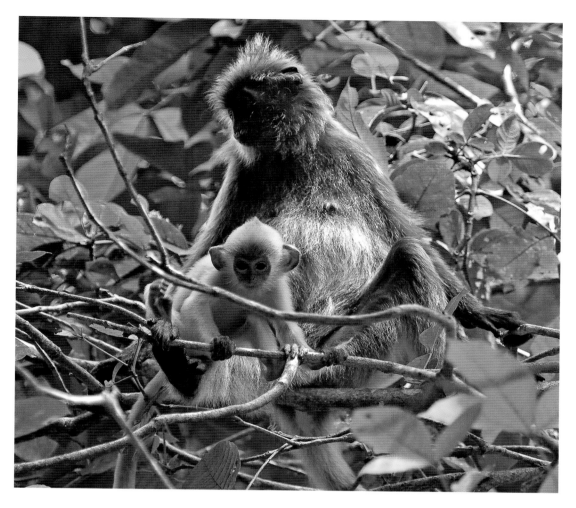

Access

Kuala Selangor is 70 km (44 miles) west of Kuala Lumpur (up to two hours by bus) and 45 km (28 miles) from Kelang (up to one hour by bus). A taxi or private car may be faster and more convenient. The nature park is signposted to the left, just before reaching Kuala Selangor town, at the base of Bukit Malawati. There is space at the nature park for buses, cars and motorcycle parking. The park, Bukit Malawati and old town are within walking distance, but hot weather or heavy rain can make walking an ordeal. The park and visitor centre are open daily. Enquiries can be addressed to the Malaysian Nature Society.

Kuala Selangor

Having paid and passed through the Kuala Selangor park-arrival building, with its sales and exhibition area, the early-morning visitor emerges onto a grassy, tree-lined path where the traces of a dawn mist still linger.

The short trail leads directly towards two shallow lakes, and on the way it is pleasantly overhung by fig trees. Column-like roots extend down from the branches; some are a hand-span in diameter, while others are mere threads, festooning the branches and not yet long enough to reach the ground below. From their leaves it is evident that there must be at least two types of fig tree here, for some have simple oval leaves, while others have diamond-shaped leaves as though someone has taken a pair of scissors and snipped the leaf-tips neatly into shape.

One of the trees is fruiting. Soft red figs, each about the size of a fingernail, are pattering to the ground as a Plantain Squirrel bounces along the smaller branches. There is a burst of sound as an unseen Pink-necked Green-pigeon (*Treron vernans*) takes off; then another and another. The birds must have been very quiet as they deliberately picked off the figs one by one, concealed by their green plumage matching the foliage, until they were disturbed by the squirrel. Now a group of Long-tailed Macaques is heading towards the fruiting tree.

On reaching the lakes the canopy opens up to the brilliant sky. The early-morning mist has been burned off by the sun, the day is heating up and the overnight dew on the long grass is diminishing. Pushing past the vegetation, you can enter the low, wood-built hide that looks out over the shallow water. Excavated in 1986 to a depth of just a few centimetres, the lakes show patches of mud and sand, and clumps of tangled greenery.

A little patch of sand appears to be moving some way off. A look through binoculars shows that it is actually a group of Mongolian Plovers, shuffling forwards as they feed. Their grey-brown backs are the same colour as the sandy patch they are on. Now that you have seen them your eyes begin to pick out other birds – a flock of Common Redshanks, bigger than the plovers but further off across the lake, and a single Whimbrel.

The sky is not empty either. Two raptors are very high up, making use of the rising thermals now that the day has warmed up. At first they appear to be different species, but using binoculars again reveals that they are both Brahminy Kites (*Haliastur indus*), one with the rufous plumage and white head of an adult, the other a less richly coloured juvenile. While looking at them through the binoculars, more black specks are suddenly noticed against the blue. Very much higher there are other birds: swiftlets, then higher again soaring raptors so far up – well over 1,000 m (3,250 ft) – that they are almost impossible to identify, but likely to be Oriental Honey-buzzards (*Pernis ptilorynchus*) on migration. Here they can pass across the Melaka Straits to Sumatra, or continue down the coast another 65 km (40 miles) to Cape Rachado, where they will find the narrowest possible sea crossing. Thousands of them will do so in October.

Bringing your eyes down to lake level again you can see other migrants. One or two Yellow Wagtails (*Motacilla flava*) are feeding on areas of bare mud, and across to the left there is the call of a Brown Shrike (*Lanius cristatus*) setting up its wintering territory. Migrant populations of both these species arrive in Peninsular Malaysia from several different parts of mainland Asia. It takes some careful observations in the field, and book work later, to identify the exact subspecies.

Having cleaned up on the other birds at the lake, it is time to head around the boundary trail to pick up some of the residents. In the low mangrove trees and lantana shrubs there are tailorbirds and bulbuls. A long way ahead, straight along the grassy trail, a couple of Red Junglefowl cross the open ground ahead. However, we are off to see if we can pick up an elusive Mangrove Pitta, potentially the bird of the day.

Opposite, clockwise from top left: *Adult and immature Brahminy Kites make use of thermals to gain height; the Black-shouldered Kite (*Elanus caeruleus*) is an open-country raptor that seeks prey by hovering; this race of Brown Shrike winters well to the west of its main continental breeding range; the curved bill of the Whimbrel is used to probe in soft mud.*

Endau Rompin National Park

Endau Rompin National Park consists of 488 sq km (188 sq miles) of forest, covering part of Rompin District in the state of Pahang, and part of Endau District in the state of Johor. Each of these districts is the catchment of a river, the Endau and the Rompin, after which the park is named. Difficult decisions had to be made in the 1970s and '80s over the relative merits of development and conservation. Following the Malaysian Nature Society's major expeditions to Endau in 1985–1986, and to Rompin in 1990, a happy outcome was achieved by the state governments to protect this large and ecologically valuable forest area.

Significance

Three things set Endau Rompin apart: its bizarre hilltop forests, its waterfalls and its rivers. The park has many distinctive features, including the state of the forest. Although some of the forest on the outskirts of the park was logged selectively in the 1970s and '80s, there is much pristine forest in the park's core. The sandstone hills with their flat tops and steep sides, including cliffs clothed by forest, are another feature. They have led to the creation of waterfalls, which gradually erode the sandstone. When trekking in the forest, eyes on the ground or on the immediately enclosing vegetation, it is often difficult to get a true impression of the landscapes, but at Endau Rompin river journeys open up the landscape to view. The flora includes endemic plants and others that show links with Borneo; it is of abiding interest, with many of the species differing from those seen further north.

The hills themselves appear very odd: when observed from a distance, for example during a boat ride upriver, they may be seen to have flat tops and steep sides – just like the hills in cowboy films, except that they are clothed in forest. These are sandstone plateaus with the soft rock strata still lying undisturbed in their original horizontal form, but deeply cut away by old river systems. The flat hilltops accumulate water – hence the presence of swamps – while the soil layer is very shallow. Only palms, and a few trees whose roots are lucky enough to find deep cracks in the closely underlying sandstone, can survive. The soils are not only thin but poor, so palms send their roots into decaying tree stumps, and trees send their surface roots zigzagging up palm trunks, burrowing about among the nutritious leaf litter trapped in crevices up the trunk. Where the ground is swampy, pitcher plants can be found – this plant group is well adapted to living on poor soils and supplementing its diet with insects.

Besides the hilltop swamp at Gunung Janing, other places with strange vegetation types include Padang Temambung (a naturally stunted hilltop patch turned to grassland by the shallowness of the soils and the activities of the Wild Boar, *Sus scrofa*). On the Pahang side of the park the plateau of Gunung Keriong supports extremely dense, tangled vegetation, with many interesting swamp-living plants to be seen only by visitors prepared for a risky scramble up the surrounding cliffs.

As the swamps are on hilltops they are entirely dependent on rainfall, not springs. They are therefore vulnerable to droughts, and their condition, whether full of water or dry as a bone, can change fast.

Where rivers do tumble down the hillsides, the rock strata are cut into steps. This feature accounts for the second of Endau Rompin's big hits: the waterfalls. Each of the access points to the park has key attractions, the best known being the giant waterfall at Buaya Sangkut, upstream from Kuala Jasin. At the Selai entrance to the park is the bathing point known as Takah Melur, and on the Pahang side accessed from Rompin is the Seri Mahkota waterfall, with a cave-like cleft between the sandstone strata behind the waterfall.

Opposite: The main ridge of Gunung Janing provides a sweeping backdrop to the curves of the Endau River.

Because of the large area of undisturbed forest catchment, and the sandy rather than muddy soils, the water in the streams and rivers is typically very clear and excellent for bathing. However, the riverbeds are strewn with boulders in places, currents can be fast and turbulent, and heavy rain can swell rivers very fast. These are risks anyone must keep in mind. Deep pools sometimes form a home for big fish, and at Takah Melur schools of fish follow swimmers in the hopes of a food handout. Three beautiful waterfalls occur on the same river, Takah Pandan, Takah Beringin and Takah Tinggi (an alternative name for Takah Melur), of which the first has a 50-m (165-ft) free fall.

An amusing feature at Upeh Guling rapids, within walking distance of the park headquarters, is the cauldron-shaped holes worn into some of the riverside rocks. Where a stone has been caught up in a natural crevice, its constant rattling and whirling round and round by floodwaters has gradually enlarged the crevice and rounded it out. Some of these holes in rocks are now big enough to sit in, forming curious natural jacuzzis.

The residents of Kampung Peta in Johor are of an ethnic group known as the Jakun, with features of their own language heavily mixed in with Malay. They have close cultural ties to the forest, and have many tales explaining the origins of the rivers, plants and animals. Any visit to Endau Rompin is enriched by striking up a conversation with the locals. Kampung Peta is well integrated into the modern economy, but forest produce can still be a significant part of the residents' livelihoods. Tourism is also important to them; some work as park staff, and others as guides and boatmen.

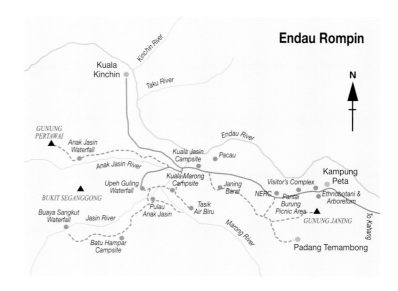

Tracks and trails

From the visitor complex at Kuala Jasin there is a range of different trails on offer, some running over fairly level ground through logged forest, and others challengingly steep.

Gunung Janing is the closest hill to the visitor centre, a steep climb through forest that at first is interesting but not unusual, but gradually transforms through the appearance, then the total dominance, of a single species of fan palm. *Livistona endauensis* is named after its locality, and the plateau on top of Gunung Janing is home to a fan-palm forest. It is known locally as *sabun* (soap) because the dead leaves on the sloping ground slip away beneath your feet like a rug on a polished floor. Another oddity of Gunung Janing is the freshwater swamp located on top of the hill, a habitat one would normally associate with low-lying places, but here set hundreds of metres above the valley.

From the park headquarters at Kuala Jasin, some of the best features of the rivers and their waterfalls are reachable within two or three hours. The trek to Upeh Guling rapids, with its water-worn rocks, can be a good picnic expedition. Just below the rapids is a small island, occasionally scoured by floods, which bears unusual plants including the 'fossil fern' *Dipteris conjugata*, here growing at unusually low altitudes; normally it is a mountain plant. Batu Hampar is another waterfall that is readily accessible by foot. Buaya Sangkut, by far the largest and most impressive of the waterfalls accessible to most visitors, is best

tackled on a one-night camping trip, so as to enjoy the falls on afternoon arrival and again the following morning. Examples of particularly clear water can be seen upstream of Kuala Jasin, and at Kuala Marong (a little stream entering halfway on the walk to Upeh Guling), although a large campsite, wooden shelters and toilets have now been built there.

Above: Although well camouflaged against the leaf litter, the Giant Frog (Limnonectes malesianus) is vulnerable to predators such as snakes.

Opposite: Differences in hardness of the sandstone strata account for the development of series of rapids on many of Endau Rompin's rivers.

All of these journeys take in river crossings, some of which include ropes or wooden handholds. These crossings should be treated seriously, as should bathing in any of the rocky, unpredictable rivers. At all three entrances to the park, however, there are safe spots allowing beginners to lounge on the riverbanks, paddle and enjoy the sun on boulders. There are a few sandy and gravel patches, and river boulders are excellent lookout spots for seeing and photographing some of the sky-blue, scarlet or iridescent green dragonflies and damselflies.

Birds

More than 250 bird species, about 40 per cent of the Peninsular Malaysian total, have been seen within the park. The large area of available forest makes it important for big birds living at low densities, such as the seven species of hornbill. The extent of forest is important not only in supporting sufficient hornbill numbers, but also in enabling them to move long distances between fruit sources. This is also true of Green Imperial-pigeons (*Ducula aenea*), for which Endau Rompin is a stronghold, and other lowland forest pigeons.

Further importance is given to Endau Rompin by the extreme lowlands with forest over alluvial terraces close to the rivers. Although such specialized habitats are small, they support Grey-breasted Babblers (*Malacopteron albogulare*) and other restricted range species. In addition, the rivers support a range of kingfishers, of which the scarcest may be the Blue-banded Kingfisher.

Above: Not necessarily associated with water, the Oriental Dwarf Kingfisher (Ceyx erithacus) is the smallest of the forest kingfishers.

Opposite, top: Deep blue crown and wings characterize the Blue-eared Kingfisher (Alcedo meninting).

Opposite, below left: The Emerald Dove (Chalcophaps indica) is a forest-dwelling, ground-feeding pigeon, extending into plantations and gardens.

Opposite, below right: Migrant Ruddy Kingfishers (Halcyon coromanda) occur in lowland forest, in contrast to the mangrove-living resident population.

Mammals

Endau Rompin was originally created in part to conserve the very rare Sumatran Rhinoceros (*Dicerorhinus sumatrensis*). Studies in the 1970s showed this to be one of its remaining strongholds. The rhinos have proved virtually impossible to conserve – boundaries to the area are too leaky, the animals must always have been at low density, requiring very large forest areas no longer available to them, and budgets have always been a challenge. There may be no rhinos left, but other big mammals are still present. The most likely to leave traces seen by visitors are elephants. Their dung and footprints may be seen during the drive into Endau Rompin, as can traces of their feeding

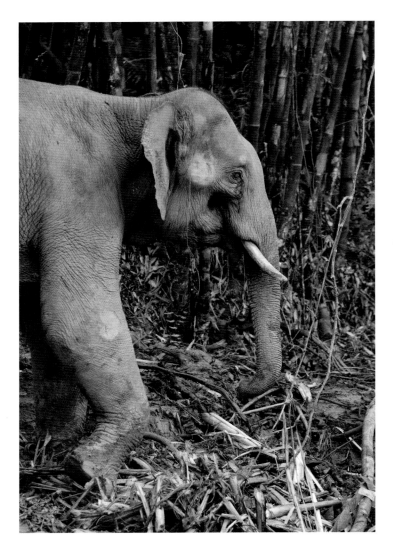

snouts and tusks. Both species of pig can leave conspicuous wallows, as well as areas of churned-up ground where they have been feeding.

Roots are eaten by pigs, and pigs are eaten by Tigers. It is hard to see Tigers anywhere, but at Endau Rompin it is still possible to walk out onto one of the earth roads in the early morning and to see pugmarks, perhaps mingled and overlapping with the tracks of wild pigs, where a Tiger has been walking during the previous night. The tracks of a Leopard (*Panthera pardus*) are also a possibility. All in all, 95 mammal species have been recorded in the park area – including some exceedingly rare bats – and Endau Rompin is the most important protected area for mammals in the southern part of Peninsular Malaysia, especially for elephants, Tigers, Malayan Tapirs and Bearded Pigs.

Plant life

The oddly specialized fan-palm forest and the swampy vegetation on hilltops, ranging from forest to scrub to open reedbeds, are two of the key habitats for plants. The impoverished fan-palm forest contains a significant number of trees of the mango family (Anacardiaceae), noted for their irritating sap. The swampy forest patches contain a weird array of plants. These include pitcher plants as well as other plants, which live in association with ants – for example the Monkey's Head (*Hydnophytum formicarium*) and Giant Hoya (*Hoya mitrata*).

In the extreme lowlands of the alluvial terraces, a number of the tree species reflect botanical links with Borneo rather than with the rest of Peninsular Malaysia, for example the white-flowered *Dillenia albiflos*, and the recently discovered *Dipterocarpus tempehes*. The riverbanks are important refugia for waterside plants, of which the feathery leaved *Phyllanthus watsoni* is one.

Additionally, communities of herbs along the rivers and in the spray zones of waterfalls, on cliffs and boulders in the forest, contain some unusual and

where they have pulled up rattans or gingers; even a sighting is not impossible, dense though the forest is. Big herds cannot be expected, but small parties led by old females tend to follow open, forest-lined trails, rivers or previously used paths through the forest.

Wild pigs are typically common in the rainforest, and the ubiquitous pig of the forests of Asia is *Sus scrofa* – the same as the Wild Boar of Europe, and the ancestor of domestic pigs. At Endau Rompin, however, there is a second species as well, the Bearded Pig (*Sus barbatus*), also known from Sumatra and Borneo. This is a bigger animal, higher in the leg, with a longer jaw and heavier head. If merely glimpsed in the forest it might not be possible to tell the difference between it and a Wild Boar, but the Bearded Pig has paler hair, and males have great bushes of blond hair around their endemic plants. *Begonia rajah* has been found in the western part of Endau Rompin – it is one of only three populations scattered in unexplained isolation in different parts of the peninsula.

Access

There are three main access points to the park: from Kahang to Kampung Peta in Johor; from Segamat to Selai in Johor; and from Kuala Rompin to Sungai Kinchin in Pahang. Of these, the access via Kampung Peta is by far the most used, leading to the visitor complex at Kuala Jasin where there are family chalets, standard chalets and dormitory accommodation.

Travel arrangements must be made well in advance, not least because each of the three access routes includes travel on dirt tracks with wooden bridges. For most overseas arrivals this means making arrangements through a tour company, or liaison in advance with the park office. Visitors to the park via Kampung Peta must first register at the office in the town of Kahang (on the road between Keluang and Mersing), before the two-hour, 56-km (33-mile), four-wheel drive entry on tarmac and dirt roads passing through oil-palm plantations and logged forest. Visitors coming to the Selai entrance must register at the park office in Bekok town, near Segamat, before the one-hour, 30-km (19-mile), four-wheel drive entry on partly surfaced roads, and check in at Kampung Kemidak ranger post. From Rompin at least 26 km (16 miles) of the journey is on dirt roads.

Opposite: *The movements and feeding of Asian Elephants encourage the growth of bamboo within the forest.*

Below: *A very long snout and the abundance of facial hair are sufficient to identify the Bearded Pig.*

Endau Rompin

So you thought it would be easy? Gunung Janing, close to the main visitor facilities at Endau Rompin, is not very high but it is one tough climb. The unusual profile of the hills here, getting steeper and steeper towards the top before emerging onto the summit plateau, makes the climb hot, sweaty work. In addition, the fallen leaves of the Endau fan palms can make the climb surprisingly slippery, even in dry weather. In fact, the drier the leaves are, the more likely they are to slide away beneath your feet.

You may not even notice the tall trunks of the fan palms themselves, if you are concentrating on your foothold and the trail in front of your nose. However, as you approach the summit you may feel a sighing breeze that rustles the leaves. Looking up to see what has caused it, you suddenly find yourself standing among the column trunks of an almost pure palm forest.

It might not be wise to camp here. Of the few trees that are not palms, some are Rengas Trees (*Swintonia malayana*), members of the mango family. Like the mango, this tree has irritant sap to which a percentage of people react badly. Walking around in the forest is generally no problem at all, but if you accidentally touch or rub against the broken or cut wood of this tree, you may find yourself bearing a nasty skin rash over the next few days.

Apart from the breeze the forest is very still. The fruits of the Rengas Trees are small, red-winged nuts, containing the same unpleasant resin as other parts of the tree, and are not generally eaten by animals. The fan palms have tough leaves and sharp spines along their bases, so travelling through the canopy is not easy for monkeys and squirrels. You will not see many mammals here.

This certainly does not mean that a visit to this place is dull. A morning mist drifting between the palm trunks provides an extraordinarily romantic fairy-tale scene. Sun shining through the leaves above creates a bright light green that is quite unusual in the ordinarily dark rainforest. Roots snake across the fibrous red surface of the ground, from palm to tree-trunk and from tree-trunk to palm, each plant seeking nutrients where it can.

Then there is the swamp. It is not large, but it is a big surprise. Given that water flows downhill, swamps should be at the bottom of a hill, not the top. It is only because of the level or even slightly hollowed summit to this clay-and-sandstone plateau that water can accumulate, and reeds and swamp-loving orchids can grow beneath the palms.

Returning to camp downhill, it is necessary to be even more cautious than on the way up, as light fades towards the end of the afternoon. The risk of sliding down the slope is greater, and no one wants to hit a boulder or a tree. By the time you have reached the lower part of the slope, where the going is easier again, bats are out. Bicolour Roundleaf Bats (*Hipposideros bicolor*) and the closely related Intermediate Roundleaf Bats (*H. larvatus*) are out in numbers; there could be many other species, too, but they are almost impossible to tell apart in flight.

Now, in mid-February, it is still light after 7.30 in the evening. On reaching the trail at the base of Gunung Janing the light is fading fast, and a group of frogwatchers from camp has gone down to the edge of the river to try its luck.

Frogs are indeed beginning to call in the gathering darkness, but their calls – if, indeed, all the calls belong to frogs – are only a general guide to their positions along the riverbank. The frogwatchers are wearing small headlamps, and cast their beams here and there. Soon enough, one of them picks up the reflected light of an amphibian eye. Striped Stream Frogs (*Hylarana signata*), like little black, red and yellow jewels, call at the edge of the water. A huge Blyth's River Frog (*Rana macrodon*), sits on top of a boulder at the edge of the river. As one of the frogwatchers stealthily approaches, she sits motionless; then, suddenly, she is off with an enormous leap and a splash into the river. There is no hope of seeing her again. It is time to get back to camp for dinner.

Opposite from top: Three frogs of the lowland rainforest, separated by their habits: the clambering White-lipped Frog (Hylarana raniceps); the terrestrial Blyth's River Frog; and the riverside Striped Stream Frog.

Cameron Highlands

Three small towns form the nucleus of Cameron Highlands. In sequence Ringlet, Tanah Rata and Brinchang, they are progressively larger, more varied and at higher altitude. Due to their situation, Tanah Rata and Brinchang are generally more popular than Ringlet, but for some Ringlet is intrinsically more appealing precisely because of its position, although it has far fewer facilities. Surrounding the towns on the hill slopes and in the valleys are important agricultural areas for the production of vegetables, flowers and fruits, and beyond this are the forested slopes and mountain tops, which include Cameron Highlands Wildlife Sanctuary.

Cameron Highlands was declared a wildlife sanctuary in 1962, and it covers 649 sq km (251 sq miles). This represents 90 per cent of the Cameron Highlands administrative district. Much of the area is still forested; nevertheless, areas continue to be cleared for agriculture, housing, hotels, road building and small-scale industries, making environmental care a contentious issue at times.

The variety and extent of highland agriculture make Cameron Highlands very different from any other site in Peninsular Malaysia. Once an extensive highland area had been identified by the British surveyor William Cameron in the 1880s, it took another 40 years before an agricultural experimental station was set up, and from 1926 onwards zones were mapped out for agriculture, housing, recreation and administration. Only after completion of the road in 1931 could the main settlements be established, and tea plantations laid out.

The road leading up from Tapah is an experience in itself. Once very winding, some of the more challenging bends have now been smoothed by flyovers cutting corners across valleys, which have the advantage that wildlife can pass below them without hindrance. Halfway from Tapah to Ringlet is the impressively big Iskandar waterfall. Along the road are aboriginal settlements hidden in the forest, and at the

right season the Semai and Temiar people sell very tasty durians at roadside stalls. When durians are not available there may be bananas, and a variety of village fruits including mangosteens.

The opening of several road-access routes has expanded visitor numbers to the area, while increased demand for fresh vegetables and fruits to supply lowland towns has put pressure on land for agricultural development. All of these factors have led to environmental management challenges that the authorities have had to address as best they can. Soil erosion and the use of chemicals are part of the picture. It is therefore important for visitors interested in nature to pitch expectations reasonably and to get away from the busier roads, and the fruit and flower farms, in favour of the less-frequented trails. Visits should be timed to avoid public holidays and school vacations. Bearing those caveats in mind, Cameron Highlands are well worth an extended visit, taking several days and nights to experience the range of features. Not least, they give an excellent overview of the social, physical and economic geography in the highlands, with nature as a bonus.

Significance

Overall, Cameron Highlands present a very different atmosphere from that of any other site in Peninsular Malaysia. The bulk of the district lies between 600 and 2,000 m (2,000–6,500 ft), so that the weather, although warm by day, is typically chilly by night, and mists and drizzle are frequent. The widespread agriculture creates views that are not replicated elsewhere, and the forest trails give rather easy access to rocky waterfalls and high mountain peaks. No other mountain site in the peninsula has such a large human population (although this is widely dispersed, in comparison with the dense mega-resort atmosphere of Genting Highlands outside Kuala Lumpur).

Cameron Highlands are famous for their tea estates, and the two best known are at Sungai Palas at the foot of Gunung Brinchang, and the Boh Plantation just above the town of Tanah Rata. The Boh Plantation supports a small nature-stay and education centre operated by the Malaysian Nature Society, and the tea-processing factory is open to the public, with guided tours on certain days.

Tea bushes used for leaf production are maintained at about waist height by continual trimming, with a narrow footpath between every second row of bushes. Nowadays some clipping is automated, with a mechanical trimmer being passed over the tops of the bushes, but better quality tea is obtained by hand picking as this avoids the mixing in of twigs. Hand picking can be done efficiently by using a plastic can sawed in half, with wooden handles attached, and wielding the two halves like clappers; but the very best tea is made from just the top two leaves of the shoot, picked off with the fingers. The eventual prices of the tea differ according to the specialist effort required, as hand picking the very tips is slower and more skilled work than other types of picking.

The resulting landscape of the area is unique: hillsides blanketed by very smooth arrays of bushes, the parallel pathways showing up from a distance, with occasional shade trees (often Australian grevilleas) planted sporadically, and wilder vegetation left only in the steep, inaccessible gulleys and along ridge tops to prevent erosion. Listening to the tea pickers setting out before dawn, and seeing them working the rows as the sun rises beyond the hills to burn away the early morning mist, is most evocative.

Chrysanthemums and roses are two of the most popular flowers grown in Cameron Highlands, often now under plastic roofing so that they are protected from damage by heavy rain. Orchids and other flowers are also produced. These are supplied to local and overseas markets, together with a range of vegetables such as tomatoes, lettuces, cabbages and many other types of produce. The result is a daily procession of lorries bringing produce down from the highlands, mostly to Tapah whence they can go on to Ipoh, Kuala Lumpur and Singapore.

Strawberries, passion fruits, tree tomatoes and grapefruits are among the other well-known products. Many can be found in local shops, in Brinchang and Tanah Rata, or at roadside stalls, in particular near Ringlet dam. The main agricultural areas are located at Kea Farm, Kampung Terla (fruits, flowers and vegetables), Ringlet (many fruits) and Tringkap (mostly vegetables).

Left: Vegetables such as cabbages grown in the temperate highlands provide a huge export market in the region.

Opposite: Neatly trimmed tea bushes form a smooth green carpet draped across the slopes.

Tracks and trails

Close to the towns are various walking trails; maps can be obtained in some of the local shops in Tanah Rata and Brinchang. The trails are numbered and signposted, and several form loops, making circular walks. Parit Falls is just outside Tanah Rata, and requires a very easy, short stroll on a paved path. Other trails lead to scenic spots, waterfalls, mountain peaks and aboriginal villages.

Among the eight highest mountains in Cameron Highlands are Gunung Brinchang (2,031 m/6,663 ft), Gunung Beremban (1,840 m/6,040 ft) and Gunung Irau (2,091 m/6,860 ft). Gunung Brinchang has a radio and television relay station at the summit, beyond which is largely undisturbed forest with no marked trails. The paved road reaches the radio station, making this the highest road in Peninsular Malaysia. With a map and due care it is possible to take a challenging hike back through the forest to Palas Estate and Brinchang town.

If mist and clouds permit, an observation tower near the summit can provide spectacular landscape views into the distance. Gunung Jasar (1,696 m/5,564 ft) is better marked and still provides lots to see along the way, including tall lower montane forest with plenty of epiphytic ferns and wild flowers.

Anywhere on walks through the forest, the interesting plant life forms the basis of the visitor's experience, with butterflies, birds and other small wildlife as the seasoning.

Birds

The relative ease of reaching high-altitude forest with roadside views has made Cameron Highlands a favourite among bird and butterfly watchers, but birdwatching is safer along the forest walks than along the roads. Of the 74 bird species in Peninsular Malaysia confined to montane forest, all but one or two have been recorded here. In addition, there are many forest species that occur over a wider range of lowland and montane forest, as well as birds of open country, and aerial swifts, swallows and raptors.

Cameron Highlands is good for barbets such as Black-browed and Golden-throated Barbets (*Megalaima oorti* and *M. franklinii*), and for a few species, like the Chestnut-tailed Minla (*Minla strigula*) and Rufous-bellied Niltava (*Niltava sundara*), which do not occur at Fraser's Hill. Now that the Brown Bullfinch (*Pyrrhula nipalensis*) is no longer found at Fraser's Hill, this is the

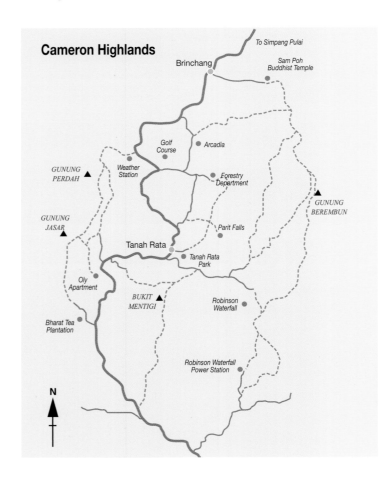

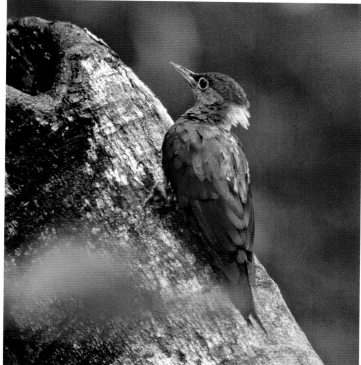

best peninsula site to seek it in. The Grey-headed Woodpecker (*Picus canus*) is found only here and on Gunung Tahan in the peninsula.

Along streams the Slaty-backed Forktail (*Enicurus scistaceus*) can be seen at Parit Falls and above Robinson Falls, while there are also two species of whistling thrush, the Malaysian and the Blue (*Myophoneus robinsoni* and *M. caeruleus*), which are hard to tell apart.

Right: Because of land use change, birds such as the Peaceful Dove (Geopelia striata) have been able to extend their range up into cleared land in the mountains.

Above left: The call of the Fire-tufted Barbet (Psilopogon pyrolophus) is astonishingly similar to the sound of a buzzing cicada.

Above right: On the journey towards Cameron Highlands, a stop along the forested roadside could reveal the Crimson-winged Woodpecker (Picus puniceus), primarily a lowland bird.

Opposite top: Frogs, frogspawn and tadpoles are the main food items of the Red-sided Keelback Snake (Xenochrophis trianguligera).

*Right: Streams around Cameron Highlands are well known for attracting Rajah Brooke's Birdwing (*Trogonoptera brookiana*).*

*Below: The Blue Glassy Tiger (*Ideopsis vulgaris*) is very common throughout Peninsular Malaysia at all altitudes.*

*Opposite: Sightings of the Grey-bellied Squirrel (*Callosciurus nigrovittatus*) are confined to the forest and the forest edge.*

Butterflies

With its wide range of habitats, including different forest formations and open country with varied crops, Cameron Highlands has a long butterfly list. Rajah Brooke's Birdwing still occurs near streams, although it has been seriously over-collected in spite of legal protection. As is the case with birds, there is a significant number of montane specialists, including members of the jezebel genus *Delias*, the hedge blues *Celastrina*, the forest punches *Dodona* and the awls *Hasora*; but these are mere examples.

Mammals

Mammals are harder to find than birds and butterflies. In the forest edges there are likely to be various squirrels, of which the very small Himalayan Striped Squirrel (*Tamiops mcclellandii*) is one of the most attractive. A feature of Cameron Highlands is the presence of a mole: following name changes, this is now known as Kloss's Mole (*Euroscaptor klossi*). Although its natural habitat is within the forest, its burrows are hard to

detect among the leaf litter, but can be seen more easily in the flower gardens and tea plantations.

Plant life

All the road routes up to Cameron Highlands begin in the lowlands, in areas of widespread plantation agriculture. As a road climbs increasing areas of logged lowland and hill forest can be seen. These are gradually modified by slope, increased cloud cover and lowering temperatures as you ascend, to lower montane forest from about 1,220 m (4,000 ft), and upper montane forest from something above 1,525 m (5,000 ft). These limits are very approximate: the transitions are blurred, not sharp, and are lower on exposed ridges than in sheltered valleys. On the highest points upper montane forest becomes stunted by local conditions (exposure and shallow soils) into an elfin forest hardly much above head height, in which the gnarled and knotty trees are festooned with mosses and lichens. Gunung Brinchang offers the best chance of seeing this forest up close.

The lower montane forest is dominated by laurels and oaks that are not readily recognizable to the non-botanist, but acorns of varied sizes, shapes and spikiness can be found on the forest floor. Birds' Nest Ferns (*Asplenium nidus*), and other look-alike species in the same genus, occupy the bigger crotches and boughs. In damp spots beside the path there may be Golden Balsam (*Impatiens oncidioides*), while the pink-flowered Cameron's Balsam (*I. sarcantha*) is confined to rocks along streams. Various ornamental begonias are known, including the Fleshy-fruited Begonia (*Begonia tricornis*) – one of the few begonias recorded as being eaten by people – as well as the Hairy Begonia (*B. decora*), Peacock Begonia (*B. pavonina*), and others each requiring a specialized habitat. Among the climbers there may be lipstick plants (*Aeschynanthus* spp.), related to one of the commonly cultivated houseplants.

At higher altitudes rhododendrons start to move in. At least three species can be anticipated, ranging from shrubs growing on rocks or as epiphytes, to free-standing gnarled trees. They include Jasmine-flowered,

Wray's and Robinson's Rhododendrons (*Rhododendron jasminiflorum, R. wrayi* and *R. robinsonii*). Flowers of the Malayan Rhododendron (*R. malayanum*) are usually deep red, while others range from white through pink to apricot and yellow.

Although it is tempting to take home some of these plants, they are doubly protected by virtue of living within forest reserves that are also gazetted as wildlife sanctuaries. Furthermore, they have very specialized needs, and usually die within days of being brought down to the hot, relatively arid lowlands. The curious Coral Plant (*Balanophora multibrachiata*), with small cream flowers on a scarlet dome, although simple to remove, depends for its survival on tree roots – it is a parasite – and cannot be grown independently.

Access

Cameron Highlands can be reached by road from Kuala Lumpur north to Tapah, 138 km (86 miles), then using the 65-km (41-mile) road to the highlands that was created in the 1920s; or from Penang or Ipoh via Simpang Pulai; or from Gua Musang in Kelantan using a road constructed in the 1980s. The best transport is by long-distance taxi or by car, which makes travel within the highlands much easier than do other forms of transport. Long-distance coaches leave from Pudu Raya bus terminal in Kuala Lumpur. Bus services running from Penang, Ipoh, Kuala Lumpur and Singapore pass through Tapah. The most recent access route is from Raub or Kuala Lipis in Pahang, via a new road to Sungai Koyan up the Bertam valley to Ringlet.

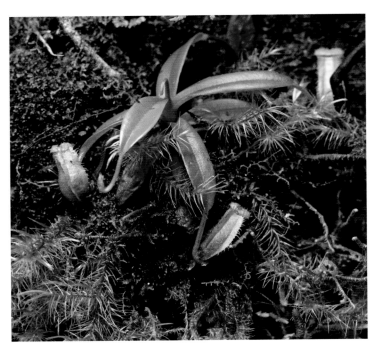

Above right: The naming of orchids may depend on details of their pollinia and other flower structures impossible to see when they are growing up in the forest canopy.

Below right: Even when they are very young and no higher than the surrounding moss, pitcher plants (Nepenthes spp.) may already have functional insect-catching pitchers.

Batu Caves

By no means the wildest of places in Malaysia, Batu Caves are now almost enveloped by the urban sprawl of Kuala Lumpur. They have experienced removal of cave earth, blasting and quarrying, loss of surrounding forest, and encroachment to their foot by roads and housing. Yet they exemplify the value of limestone outcrops throughout Malaysia for their historical and archaeological value, as well as for their highly specialized flora and fauna. There are more than 400 such outcrops in Peninsular Malaysia – particularly in the northerly states of Perak, Kelantan, Perlis and Kedah – and many others in Sabah and Sarawak. Each one has special features.

Karst landscapes are landscapes lacking a coherent directional drainage system, and around the world many such landscapes consist of limestone because of its porous nature. The porosity of the stone causes erosion by seepage, and chemical and physical wearing away of the limestone internally – it is predominantly this that accounts for the abundance of limestone caves. Sinkholes, hidden valleys, lost rivers, the sudden collapse of underground caverns, and pinnacles of standing rock that have resisted erosion are characteristic of such landscapes.

The limestone of the Batu Caves outcrop was formed beneath the sea more than 400 million years ago, but is thought to have undergone two main periods of uplift, about 300 and again about 200 million years ago, with associated pressure metamorphosing the limestone into marble. The caves may well have begun formation before the outcrop was exposed on land, and would have been largely created in their present form while the water table in surrounding land (now totally eroded) remained high. It was this erosion of everything around it except the hill itself that has now left Batu Caves as such a prominent feature of the landscape.

Lying 13 km (8 miles) to the north of Kuala Lumpur city centre, Batu Caves are the best known of all caves and limestone outcrops in Peninsular Malaysia. They are approximately 5 km (3 miles) in circumference and 274 m (899 ft) in height.

Significance

While Batu Caves are not the largest of the cave systems in the peninsula, they are impressive within, and harbour bats that pollinate fruit trees and mangroves over a wide swathe of countryside. The limestone massif dominates the landscape north of Kuala Lumpur, and within the cave deposits are fossils from the Early and Late Pleistocene ages. These include the only fossil record of Orang-utans from Peninsular Malaysia. Endemic species of plant, and of snail and other invertebrate, occur on the limestone.

Above: The seemingly burdensome shell of the Cave Snail (Subulina octona) is actually extremely light and fragile.

Batu Caves are the most significant of Hindu religious sites in Malaysia. The Hindu festival of Thaipusam falls at the full moon in the tenth month, Thai, of the Tamil calendar. This corresponds to late January or early February. The day before a vast procession bearing a statue of the Lord Murugan with his two consorts, on a wood and silver chariot, leaves the Sri Maha Mariamman Temple in the centre of Kuala Lumpur and makes its slow progress to Batu Caves. There it is carried up the 272 steps to the Temple Cave. That night many devotees, who have already prepared for a month beforehand by fasting or by subsisting on an entirely vegetarian diet, with abstinence and prayers, bathe in the river at the foot of Batu Caves, under the light of the full moon. Many, particularly children, have their heads shaved. Already, some will be in an ecstatic frenzy.

Worshippers perform Puja (an act of respect) by breaking a coconut as an offering in front of an image of Lord Murugan. Other offerings may be of flowers and fruits. Many devotees perform tasks of thanksgiving in return for good fortune, or carry out acts demonstrating a high degree of religious devotion. The most demanding include piercing of the ears, piercing of the cheeks and, as a repentance or thanksgiving or petition for a favour, the bearing of a Kavadi. The Kavadi is a tray spanned by a wooden arch, decorated with peacock feathers, coloured paper, streamers, ribbons and flowers, bearing bowls of milk and offerings of flowers, fruits or sugar. It is carried on the shoulders, often with painful supports in the form of metal rods, spikes or hooks inserted into the flesh. Some devotees may carry a Kavadi all the way from the Sri Maha Mariamman Temple; others may bear one up the steps to the main Temple Cave, where the milk and other offerings are poured down at the feet of the shrine. The chariot bearing the image of Lord Murugan then makes its return journey to Seri Maha Mariamman Temple. It may halt at one or two places during the heat of the day, and finally reaches the temple at night accompanied by torches borne by the huge procession.

Although this is the greatest procession of the Hindu year, and has been celebrated at Batu Caves since at least 1892, the caves are considered a religious place throughout the year, with charitable foundations providing schooling and other social support. The huge, gold-painted image of the standing Lord Murugan, completed in 2006, is nearly 43 m (140 ft) tall. Along the cliff to the left is a 15-m (50-ft) image of Hanuman.

Trails and climbs

For visitors to Batu Caves, access to the crowning vegetation on top of the hill is difficult and possibly dangerous, as the foot of the hill is largely cleared, replaced by development or has sheer cliffs. There are access points from the rear of the hill, but these are not widely known. Rock climbers and abseilers have developed routes on the north-east side beginning near an area known as Damai Caves, and there are now more than 160 known climbing routes. It is not wise to attempt these unless you are accompanied by a knowledgeable guide. Disabling or fatal falls are possible on the treacherous limestone with loose rock, hidden sinkholes and chimneys. Still, those who do get well up onto the bulk of the hill are provided with a deeply instructive view of unusual vegetation, with

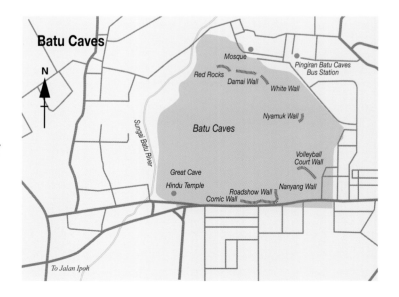

large and minuscule snails, spiders and colourful but scarce flowers, as well as views of the surrounding country and the city of Kuala Lumpur.

The Temple Cave is reached by the main staircase of 272 steps. The cave has an extremely high ceiling and sheer walls, and opens out beyond to a skylight and open area formed by the long-ago collapse of a portion of the cave roof. Here it is possible to see a large dripstone column formed by the downwards trickling and evaporation of water, super-saturated with calcium carbonate so as to leave the fine crystalline deposit. The entire floor space is covered by cement, and religious items may be seen here and there. Because it is in heavy public use, there is rather little by way of cave fauna in the Temple Cave.

The Dark Cave is completely different. This is a series of chambers known as Caverns A, B, C, D and E, linked at a central nexus known as the Great Room, which is more than 110 m (340 ft) high. Within the length of the Dark Cave, many of the classic geological features can be seen. These include hanging stalactites, standing stalagmites and thin curtains of flowstone

that have covered part of the walls or that hang alone. In some places stalactites have grown all the way down to the floor; in others a growing stalactite has joined with a stalagmite immediately below it to form a broad dripstone column or pillar.

Cave life

All the main features of the caves owe their existence to water, which physically and chemically erodes away some portions of the limestone and deposits it elsewhere in the cave system. This movement of materials provides physical space for various animals in the caves, and the water itself is also a resource for animals, but by far the most important driver of the cave ecosystem is the import of nutrients from outside the cave.

It is the bats that bring in most materials to a cave. Of more than a dozen species now recorded roosting within Batu Caves, only the Cave Fruit Bat (*Eonycteris spelaea*) is really abundant. This is the bat that has

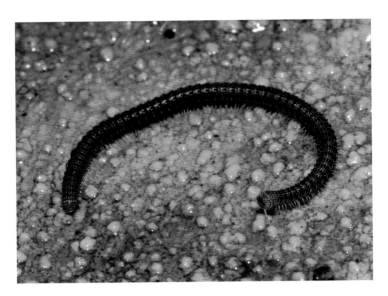

become famous as an example of ecological connectivity. The bats are able to fly the 70 km (44 miles) nightly to mangroves along the coast in order to feed on nectar and pollen from the blossoms of mangrove trees and, when durian trees are flowering, they are one of their important pollinators, too. As these are not echolocating bats, but rely on sight, at Batu Caves they roost mainly within Cavern A, closest to the entrance, where it is not completely dark.

The bats are the main providers of guano, which supports a huge community of cockroaches and other cave animals. Most abundant now are invasive forms of domestic cockroach not native to the caves, but there

are also cave cockroaches (*Pycnoscelus striatus*). They feed voraciously on guano and any other material on the cave floor. Millipedes, beetles, cave crickets, caterpillars and flies are all to be found in or close to the guano layer.

The guano feeders themselves support communities of predators and parasites. They include ichneumonid wasps, trapdoor spiders, assassin bugs and Long-legged Centipedes (*Scutigera decipiens*). Furthermore, there are vertebrates such as the Asian Giant Toad and Asian Common Toad (*Bufo asper* and *B. melanostictus*), and the Cave Racer (*Elaphe radiata*), a pale-coloured snake that is able to climb up the vertical walls and overhangs to prey on bats roosting in the cave roof.

Many differences have been noted in the fauna using the various caverns, depending on factors such as darkness, moisture, and number and species of bat providing the main nutrient input. Beyond Cavern A,

for example, the Long-legged Centipede, the Long-legged Cave Cricket (*Diestrammena gravelyi*) and cave slaters (*Armadillo intermixtus*) can be found. In Cavern C trapdoor spiders (*Liphistius batuensis*) unique to the Batu Caves outcrop build silk-lined tubes on the walls of the cave; each tube is closed by a loosely hinged door with tripwire threads radiating from the entrance. When a victim brushes against one of these threads, the spider can rush out and seize it.

Above: The nymphs of common bush crickets go through several moults before reaching adulthood.

Opposite top: Inside the cave, the Cave Millipede (Plusioglyphiulus grandicollis) *feeds on grass and organic growth on the substrate.*

Opposite below: Outside the cave, the Giant Millipede (Julus *sp.)* feeds on algae and mosses growing on decaying wood.

Opposite: The Asian Giant Toad is found both inside and outside caves, and grows impressively big.

Below: A predator on bats and swiftlets, the Striped Cave Racer (Elaphe taeniura) is an expert at climbing vertical and even overhanging rock faces.

Plant life

The loss of forest vegetation around the foot of the limestone outcrop, on the mineral soils of the level ground, has placed heavy constraints on conservation of the flora of the hill. Not only have the humid, shady natural conditions that should prevail been replaced by direct sunlight and desiccating heat, but the sources of propagules and replacements, the large majority of species and populations that would once have surrounded the hill, have been stripped away. Any plants now growing on the hill are left to fate as isolated populations with little chance of replenishment from outside if any of them should be locally extinguished.

The plant life of limestone outcrops is a fascinating subset of the Malaysian flora. It includes a selection of species typically found in lowland forest, and a selection of plants that are able to grow on limestone and not elsewhere; each limestone hill also has some endemics exclusive to it. Trees grow in the forest over limestone, but few of them are the dipterocarps characteristic of the lowland forest, and very big trees are scarce. The families of African violets (Gesneriaceae) and begonias (Begoniaceae) are particularly known for limestone endemics confined to single hills, or sometimes to a few hills scattered many kilometres apart. Batu Caves and the next nearest limestone outcrop at Bukit Takun together support 11 endemic plant species, of which at least five are rare or endangered. The balsam *Impatiens ridleyi* is one of those confined to Batu Caves; the milkweed *Hoya occulosa* is one of the endangered species.

Access

Batu Caves are fairly easy to reach by car or taxi from Kuala Lumpur, lying only 13 km (8 miles) north of the city. Depending on traffic, the journey may take 30 to 60 minutes. Public buses are challenging. There is a train service to Batu station, but it is then necessary to walk to the caves across busy roads. Entrance and car-parking charges are collected at the foot of the caves. Access to the Dark Cave is controlled, partly for visitor safety and partly to protect its abundant cave fauna, as well as the limestone formations. Tour companies and guides should be able to arrange a tour, but visitors arriving on spec are not allowed entry. The shortest distance from the entrance (at a point halfway up the main staircase) to the furthest end of Cavern C is some 800 m (2,600 ft), and including side branches the system is well over 1,000 m (3,280 ft) in length.

Pulau Redang and the Terengganu Coast

Nine islands, of which Pulau Redang is the largest, make up the archipelago whose waters comprise the Pulau Redang Marine Park. The archipelago lies approximately 45 km (28 miles) off the coast of the eastern state of Terengganu. This was one of 22 marine parks set up around the coasts of Peninsular Malaysia, whose management and enforcement have now been transferred to a new Department of Marine Parks Malaysia. In addition, the Terengganu State government initiated a Pulau Redang Setiajaya Cooperative in 1989, to encourage socio-economic development programmes that would benefit the island, businesses and residents.

Of the nine islands, only Pulau Redang itself has resort facilities. There is also simpler chalet accommodation, and bathing facilities, picnic spots and barbecue pits have been created at selected points. A visitor centre was opened in 1990, the first at any of the marine parks, on the small island of Pulau Pinang south of Pulau Redang; a jetty facilitates boat landings, and there is a small park-entry fee. An exhibition caters to visitors, while research and educational facilities are used by students and university staff.

There is a single village on Pulau Redang; its former economic basis was fisheries, but job opportunities in tourism have become increasingly important. Most visitors stay at one of the two or three main resorts on the east coast, facing out towards the South China Sea, about 3 km (2 miles) from the airstrip that bisects the island. There is also accommodation on some other islands in the group, for example at Pulau Lang Tengah.

Right: The nutrient-poor sands along the coast of Terengganu make agriculture challenging for the local residents.

Previous pages: Centuries of on-shore winds and waves have built up a sand dune system round the mouth of the Setiu River, behind which are successive phases of swamp forest.

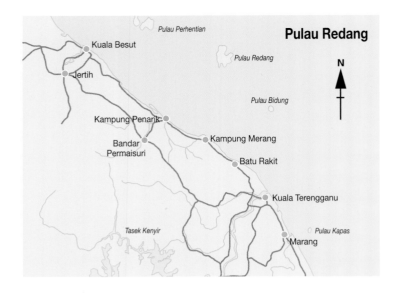

Pulau Redang

N

The marine park administration in fact covers three separate island groups: the Pulau Redang group, the Pulau Perhentian group to the north and Pulau Kapas to the south. The towns and especially the smaller villages along the Terengganu mainland coast are well worth exploring; this region is strong on handicrafts and homemade snacks and delicacies.

Around the Redang group the boundaries of the marine park were set by drawing a line that links the points 3.7 km (2 nautical miles) from the shores of Pulau Redang, Pulau Pinang, Pulau Lima and Pulau Ekor Tebu. The waters are extremely clear, and inshore, where they lie over a bed of nearly white sand, their appearance can be like pure turquoise. Sandy coves and bays are interspersed between rocky headlands, the largest of them being Teluk Dalam to the north; another important bay is Chagar Hutang close to the northernmost tip of the island.

The activities considered to be compatible with the conservation objectives of the marine park include camping, swimming, snorkelling and diving, underwater photography and boating. On land there is jungle trekking and climbing, photography and birdwatching. These are additional to the typical seaside holiday pursuits of sunbathing, picnicking and barbecues, and beach games. Picnic tables and barbecue pits are available at some sites. The resorts can give advice on dive equipment, and there are dive shops that can rent equipment to those who do not bring their own. The marine-park management has provided mooring buoys for boats over the more popular reefs, to avoid damage from anchoring by snorkelling and diving boats.

Significance

Pulau Redang is generally considered to be one of Malaysia's best dive sites for the overall good condition of its reefs, the range of species and colour variety of corals hard and soft, the very high diversity of associated fish and invertebrates, and the visibility of some big fish such as groupers. Good underwater visibility cannot be guaranteed, but it is the norm.

Corals and fish

The corals are generally better developed off the northern and eastern sides of the islands, and off the smaller islands they tend to be better than off Pulau Redang itself. The main island can thus form a base for less location-dependent activities such as swimming, camping and barbecues, and forest walks, combined with day trips out by boat to specialist sites for the divers and snorkellers to experience the array of marine life. The range of habitats includes shallow coral-reef flats where coral gardens may be dominated by stagshorn corals (*Acropora* spp.), and moderate to deeper slopes below 10 m (32 ft) where there are many-branching corals (*Porites* spp.) – in which the blue, red, yellow or striped Christmas Tree Worms (*Spirobranchus giganteus*) prefer to build their calcareous tubes – mushroom corals (*Fungia* spp.), brain corals (*Symphyllia* spp.) and barrel sponges (*Xestospongia testudinaria*).

Even at the marine park jetty on Pulau Pinang it is possible to see a range of reef fish. Jacks and trevallies should be abundant. Fish feeding is not explicitly prevented by the park regulations, and many visitors

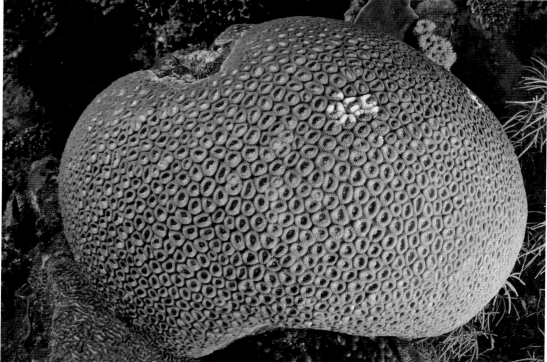

Above: Stagshorn corals of the genus Acropora *show the greatest diversity in growth forms of any coral genus.*

Left: The corals popularly known as brain corals have a massive growth form resilient against wave action, and are mostly in the family Faviidae.

Turtles

Chagar Hutang is the best-known turtle-nesting beach on Pulau Redang, and has been declared a turtle sanctuary; it is probably now the largest turtle 'rookery' in Peninsular Malaysia. The vast majority of turtles found here are Green Sea Turtles (*Chelonia mydas*), and several hundred nestings per year occur on this beach. Very occasionally there is a nesting by a Hawksbill Turtle (*Eretmochelys imbricata*). Nestings occur at night, and the beach is closed to visitors so as to avoid disturbance to any nesting turtles.

A female turtle can lay 100 to 120 eggs, over an hour or more, in a pit dug above the high-tide mark and carefully covered over and tamped down before she returns to the sea. Incubation takes in the region of 55 days, depending on the temperature (this is pretty constant at the depth at which the eggs are laid, but it is influenced by the shade of trees overhead and by the weather), and clutches are susceptible to predators such as monitor lizards, as well as to fungal infections and the possibility of waterlogging by prolonged rain. If all goes well the hatchlings emerge at night in order to enter the sea under cover of darkness, but even then they have to run the gauntlet of predatory crabs along the beach and predatory fish in the shallow waters near the shore; few survive.

Volunteers and staff from the Turtle Research and Rehabilitation Group have been working since 1993 to ensure that nesting success is maximized. Wherever possible nests are left in place, and protected from predators by pinning over the sand a wide mesh mat that enables young turtles to emerge but prevents monitor lizards from digging down. On average, more than 20,000 hatchlings have been produced each year.

This is in marked contrast to the fate of some turtle rookeries on the mainland coast of Terengganu. North of Dungun, the stretch of beach for about 6 km (4 miles) at Rantau Abang was famous for the numbers of Leatherback Sea Turtles (*Dermochelys coriacea*) that came to nest, mostly from June to September. They have now virtually gone, in spite of nearly 40 years of

find this a high point of their visit. However, there is no feeding of large predatory fish such as sharks, or of groupers. The reef at the front of the marine-park centre is a good place for snorkelling. Diving off the eastern slope of Pulau Pinang reveals large numbers of wrasse, parrotfish, triggerfish and damselfish, and there is an impressive outcrop of the Blue Coral (*Helipora coerulea*).

Above: The Pink Anemonefish (Amphiprion perideraion) *is in the same group of sea anemone inhabitants as the clownfish.*

Opposite top: Female Green Turtles come ashore at night to dig a nest and lay eggs in soft sand above the high tide mark.

Opposite below: Hawksbill Turtles can be identified by their beak shape, colour pattern on the head and flippers, and overlapping scutes on the shell.

effort in relocating nests in protected areas, and releasing hatchlings straight into the sea. Human enthusiasm for eating turtle eggs, plus accidental by-catch of young turtles in fishing nets and deaths from consumption of floating litter, are among the reasons for the decline.

However, other turtle-conservation centres exist along the coast of Terengganu, including one at Setiu concentrating on both marine and estuarine turtles, and another at Ma' Daerah near Paka and Kertih that is closed to the general public. At the Setiu river estuary, not only are there nestings of Green Sea Turtles and others along the beaches fronting the sea, but also Painted Terrapins (*Batagur borneoensis*) living most of their lives within the river come out to nest on the same marine beaches. The terrapins are relatively small but spectacular animals – the males change colour during the breeding season so that the head

becomes silvery-white, with a scarlet stripe from the snout to the top of the head.

Hawksbill Turtles still occur in small numbers on some beaches at any time between January and September, with a peak around May. Green Sea Turtles nest a little later, between March and December, with a

peak around August. On Pulau Redang, although Chagar Hutang beach is closed to the public, there is a possibility of sighting turtles on other beaches, at Teluk Dalam, or at Pasir Mak Kepit, Pasir Bujang or Pasir Mak Simpan. If a turtle is encountered it is important to keep well back, and to avoid using a torchlight or camera flash so as to prevent disturbing her before or during laying. Although public access to Chagar Hutang is restricted, it is permissible to snorkel offshore, and anywhere around Pulau Redang there is a chance of seeing a turtle while swimming or diving.

Birds

There are no seabird colonies on Pulau Redang, but where there are sheltered clefts in the granite cliffs above the zone of sea spray, there are small nesting colonies of Black-nest and White-nest Swiftlets (*Aerodromus maximus* and *A. germani*). The nests, made from solidified saliva, are used to make bird's nest soup and fetch a high price; good practice is to remove them only after the young have fledged. The relatively small numbers of swiftlets here and their poor accessibility, in comparison with what can be produced in the factory-like system of an artificial swiftlet house on mainland Terengganu, makes this practice less financially attractive nowadays than it used to be.

Of at least equal interest to birdwatchers are the mostly open-country and coastal forest birds such as the Pink-necked Green-pigeon, as well as Olive-backed Sunbirds (*Cinnyris jugularis*), Purple-throated Sunbirds (*Leptocoma sperata*) and Brown-throated Sunbirds. At the top end of the size range is the White-bellied Sea-eagle (*Haliaeetus leucogaster*). Migrants have been recorded, such as the Grey Wagtail (*Motacilla cinerea*), Yellow Wagtail and Forest Wagtail (*Dendronanthus indicus*), and Asian Brown and Blue-throated Flycatchers (*Muscicapa dauurica* and *Cyornis rubeculoides*). Rarer migrants could be revealed by future observations.

Mammals

Because it is a small island well offshore, Pulau Redang supports a rather small range of terrestrial mammals such as Long-tailed Macaques, Lesser Mousedeer (*Tragulus kanchil*), Plantain Squirrels and Common Treeshrews (*Tupaia glis*). The most noticeable of the six bats recorded here may be the Island Flying Fox (*Pteropus hypomelanus*), with a wingspan of about 1 m (3 ft).

Plant life

These east-coast islands are predominantly granite; they are exposed to heavy weather during the annual monsoon in around October to February, with strong winds. With exposure to strong waves, the areas of mangroves are small and confined to sheltered inlets. Despite this, the area of mangroves at the mouth of Sungai Redang is one of the largest on any of the east-coast islands.

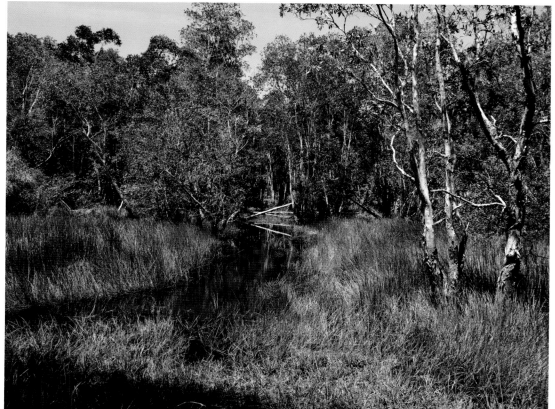

Above: Gelam *(Melaleuca kajuputi) forest, growing on swampy ground behind the coast, is a source of aromatic oils.*

Left: Small creeks meandering between the Gelam trees at Setiu harbour an array of freshwater fish species able to tolerate acidic conditions.

Opposite: Lesser Mousedeer occur on the mainland and on many offshore islands.

Pulau Redang consists of two main ridges running approximately north–south, with the airstrip also running north–south on the low-lying ground between them, approximately on the alignment of Sungai Redang. As they are the most exposed, the peaks of the two main ridges bear stunted vegetation, limited by both the prevailing north-east winds and the shallow soils. There are pitcher plants, a range of orchids and a relatively impoverished total flora. Lower down the slopes and near human settlements the vegetation has been strongly influenced by introduced plants such as fruit trees and cultivated sago, and by grazing by goats and other domestic animals.

Above: A very fast runner, the Butterfly Lizard (Liolepis belliana) occurs on the sand dunes and beaches, and is partly herbivorous.

Access

There are flights to Pulau Redang from Kuala Lumpur and Singapore, and most visitors stay at the Berjaya or Laguna Island Resorts; other places include Redang Kalong, Mutiara and Amannagappa Resorts. A public ferry goes from Kuala Terengganu (Shahbandar jetty), and another from Merang jetty 32 km (20 miles) north of Kuala Terengganu, to Kampung jetty on Pulau Redang. Some of the resorts operate their own ferries from Merang jetty, too (not to be confused with Marang, south of Kuala Terengganu). Pulau Perhentian is normally reached from the small town at Kuala Besut, and Pulau Kapas, much closer inshore, is reached from Marang town (not to be confused with Kampung Merang).

Langkawi

Traditionally there are said to be 99 islands in the Langkawi group, situated about 51 km (30 miles) off the north-west coast of Peninsular Malaysia. The islands are closest to the tiny mainland state of Perlis, but belong to the larger state of Kedah, and in 2008 they were given the official name 'Langkawi, Jewel of Kedah'. They are close to the climatic transition between the ever-wet equatorial tropics and the slightly more seasonal regime of peninsular Thailand and continental Asia; they have a distinct dry season from December to February.

The three biggest islands in the group are Pulau Langkawi itself (320 sq km/123 sq miles), Pulau Dayang Bunting and Pulau Tuba. Other substantial islands of interest include Pulau Singa Besar to the south and Pulau Langgun to the east.

The harbour at Kuah, the main town on Pulau Langkawi, is now dominated by a huge concrete image of a Brahminy Kite, alluding to a possible origin of the island's name in the Malay term *lang* (eagle). An alternative derivation could be from the Sanskrit word *langka* (island), by way of the name for the ancient Malay kingdom of Langkasuka. The Langkawi group has a rich and exotic history, with many legends. Local place names are unusual, and cultural aspects of the islands are well worth investigating. Although some of the tiny village streets have disappeared, the culture and environment have so far stood up remarkably well to the development of an airport, resort accommodation on both the north and south coasts, and duty-free status since the mid-1980s.

As a rapidly developing tourism destination, Langkawi is provided with many resorts, hotels and restaurants. The wide range of activities includes swimming, snorkelling and scuba diving, kayaking, mangrove river cruises, caving, sailing, island-hopping tours, jet skiing, birdwatching and jungle trekking, as well as golf and go-karting. Attractions include an aquarium, a crocodile farm, an art gallery, a museum and demonstration rice fields. Each of these of course has a different appeal, but for the naturalist it is still possible to escape to less-frequented parts of the main island, or to get away to one of the smaller islands by boat for a completely undisturbed time with nature.

Significance

The geology of Langkawi is varied and unusual. In 2007 a major part of Langkawi was designated a Geopark by UNESCO. On the west of the main island is Gunung Machinchang, a 778-m (2,322-ft) peak with some of the oldest known rock formations in Malaysia. This is now known as the Machinchang Cambrian Geoforest Park.

The highest peak on Langkawi is Gunung Raya at 881 m (2,890 ft). There is a recreational forest park at Lubuk Sembilang near the base and a narrow road to the peak, so a leisurely stroll or a vigorous workout are options while birdwatching, with views out across the island and the sea beyond.

The Langkawi group is one of two Malaysian archipelagos (the other is the Semporna Islands in Sabah) showing intertidal erosion of limestone. In the old volcanic Semporna Islands this is erosion of surrounding coral rock, where an intertidal notch eroded in the rock is topped by an overhanging 'visor' and followed by a low-tide platform up to 30 m (100 ft)

wide. In the Langkawi group the rock is ancient Palaeozoic crystalline limestone. Many of Langkawi's limestone islands have steep sea cliffs that continue below sea level; intertidal notches are cut into them, but there is no low-tide platform. At both places the rock between high and low tides is eaten away not simply by the action of the sea, but by chitons and bivalves (*Lithophaga* spp.) rasping away at rock-inhabiting algae, and by the boring sponge *Cliona*. The notches can be up to 4 m (13 ft) deep.

Langkawi offers the unusual experience of limestone cliffs rising within mangroves, particularly on the east side of the main island. This area is now

known as the Kilim Karst Geoforest Park. A boat tour into the mangroves presents a fascinating way to get close to the otherwise inaccessible cliffs, and at night it reveals the extra attraction of fireflies.

The limestone in Langkawi is bunched towards the eastern flank of the main island, and on Pulau Langgun and Pulau Dayang Bunting. It is of two main periods: most is Lower Devonian to Ordovician (400–450 million years old), dark grey and crystalline with many impurities. On the western margin of this limestone are much smaller outcroppings of Permian age (about 250 million years old), white to light grey, purer and more finely crystalline. In mainland Perlis and Kedah the sequence is reversed, with ancient Ordovician limestone on the west and younger Permian limestone on the east. This shows where domes of successively younger limestone have been eroded away over vast landscapes that are hardly imaginable today.

Nor is this the complete story. On the north side of the island can be found examples of black-sand and white-sand beaches. On the south side of Langkawi is a fine example of a tombolo, a sand bar connecting the main island to a small off-lier, walkable at low tide. On Pulau Tuba there is a limestone arch over the sea, through which a boat can pass. On Pulau Dayang Bunting ('Island of the Pregnant Maiden') there is a brackish lake within a limestone valley. This forms the third component of the UNESCO designated site, the Dayang Bunting Marble Geoforest Park.

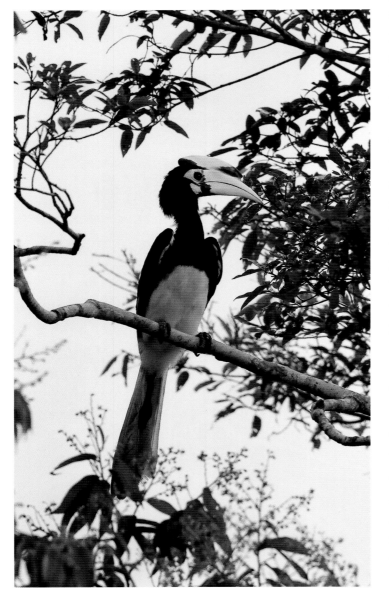

Trips and climbs

One way to see the area is by hiring a boat to circuit the island (this can be a full-day trip) and viewing the coloured crags from the sea. The crags are mostly sandstone, metamorphosed under heat and pressure to quartzite, whereas the lower parts of the hills are mudstone and shale. Another way to become familiar with the hills is to hire a guide to take you across part of the range from north to south. This can be a very

tough journey and must not be undertaken alone, but it allows intimate exploration of the forest. A third way is to take the spectacular cable-car journey to the peak, which opens up majestic photographic possibilities.

The Langkawi Cable Car route was completed in 2003. It begins at the Oriental Village, a cluster of 30 buildings portraying Malaysian and Oriental architecture, near Burau Bay. The route is in two parts, a first stretch of 1,700 m (5,577 ft) from Base Station to Middle Station, and a further 400 m (1,312 ft) to Top Station. At the top is the elegant crescent-shaped Sky Bridge spanning 125 m (410 ft), completed in 2005. The steepest part of the cable route is nearly 45 degrees, and the total height climbed is some 700 m (2,295 ft). In clear weather the views can be magnificent.

Within walking distance of the Oriental Village and the start of the cable-car Base Station is the Seven Wells Waterfall.

Above: Female (above) and male (below) Oriental Pied Hornbills may extend their courtship into aerial displays.

Left: Oriental Pied Hornbills are typical of coastal forest, islands and forest edge vegetation in the lowlands.

Birds

Being on the verge of the climatic transition to the semi-evergreen tropics of continental Asia, Langkawi sees the beginning of a transition in the avifauna, too. Among the birds not encountered further south are the Brown-winged Kingfisher (*Pelargopsis amauroptera*) and Mountain Hawk-eagle (*Spizaetus nipalensis*). Over the past decade the hawk-eagle has been added to the resident Malaysian fauna of Gunung Raya, and the slopes of Gunung Raya have also become known as a hornbill-watching site, with groups of up to 100 Great Hornbills (*Buceros bicornis*) present if trees are in fruit. Wreathed and Oriental Pied Hornbills (*Rhyticeros undulatus* and *Anthracoceros albirostris*) can also be seen on Langkawi.

Right: Bees, wasps and dragonflies form key prey items for the Bue-tailed Bee-eater (Merops philippinus).

Above: The Red-wattled Lapwing (Vanellus indicus) is often betrayed by its loud piping cry and its distinctive appearance.

Opposite: The impressive wingspread of a juvenile White-bellied Sea-eagle reveals a very different parti-coloured pattern from that of the grey and white adult.

The Plain-backed Sparrow (*Passer flaveolus*) has previously occurred as far south as Kuala Selangor, but is easier to see here. On the opposite mainland there are more species: the Great Eared Nightjar (*Eurostopodus macrotis*) and Lineated Barbet (*Megalaima lineata*). Gunung Raya is a well-known birdwatching site, and migrant shorebirds are sometimes present in Burau Bay. In spite of being an island group, with fewer species than equivalent areas of habitat on the mainland, the total bird list for the Langkawi archipelago exceeds 220 species.

The rice fields in various parts of Langkawi, particularly near the village of Padang Matsirat, can be good for egrets and a selection of waders, including Pacific Golden Plovers, Wood Sandpipers (*Tringa glareola*) and Red-wattled Lapwings. There may also be wagtails, shrikes, warblers, bee-eaters, swallows and other migrants.

One of the tourist attractions of Langkawi, acted out by boat operators, is the feeding of Brahminy Kites by throwing offal into the sea. Although this practice may be frowned upon by purists, it certainly produces spectacular results. There are few records of seabirds, but not many people go birdwatching at sea, so surprises can happen. At least coastal raptors such as Brahminy Kites and White-bellied Sea-eagles are near certainties. There can additionally be bonuses such as sightings of dolphins.

Access

Langkawi can now be reached by air from Kuala Lumpur, Singapore and other airports in the region (Penang, Hat Yai and Phuket). The main ferry service is from Kuala Perlis on the mainland to Kuah; other boats operate from Kuala Kedah and Penang, and from Satun on the coast of Thailand. There is no public transport within Langkawi, but it is possible to get around by hired car, taxi, bicycle or motorcycle. The main settlement, the town of Kuah, is located on Pulau Langkawi and can be reached by ferry from Kuala Perlis.

2
Sabah

Located in the northeastern quadrant part of Borneo, with Sarawak to the south-west and Kalimantan, Indonesia, to the south, Sabah covers an area of 73,631 sq km (28,430 sq miles). The capital is Kota Kinabalu. More than three-quarters of the human population inhabits the coastal plains, while the interior is sparsely populated in a scatter of small towns. The most prominent mountain range is the Crocker Range, with mountains from 1,000 to 4,095 m (3,280–13,432 ft) high. Mount Kinabalu, the highest mountain between the Himalayas and New Guinea. Kinabalu Park (hill and montane forest) is a World Heritage Site due to its rich plant diversity and unique geography and climate. The Kinabatangan River (disturbed forest over river floodplains) runs through central Sabah to the Sulu Sea, and is the second longest river in Malaysia at 560 km (348 miles). Other key wildlife regions include Maliau Basin (an extraordinary forested sandstone amphitheatre), Danum Valley (lowland forest), Tabin and Sepilok (dipterocarp forest and mangroves), as well as important islands and coral reefs along and beyond the coasts.

Left: A view of the Trus Madi mountains eastwards across the Tambunan valley from the foothills of Crocker Range National Park.

Kota Kinabalu

In 1899, with the construction of a railway already underway from the town of Weston in the south of Sabah, the British North Borneo Company decided that the northern coastal extension would need to end in a deep-water port. For its location, the company chose a small Bajau fishing village opposite Gaya island. This site was traditionally known as Api-api, the Malay-language name for one of the species of mangrove tree (*Avicennia alba*) that lined the mouth of the Likas River. The term *api-api* (fire-fire) in turn derived from the tiny flickering lights of the fireflies that lived in the mangrove trees. South of this mangrove area was a long hill that was later called Signal Hill by the British and is now known as Bukit Bendera. At its base is a sandy beach, which is now covered in the roads and shops of downtown Kota Kinabalu. The British

administration named Api-api Jesselton, and it was renamed Kota Kinabalu in 1967.

Offshore islands

Off the west coast of Sabah, the South China Sea covers a part of the Sunda Shelf, an extension of mainland Southeast Asia that includes Borneo island, which was exposed as dry land during the Pleistocene ice ages. Only about 20,000 years ago (recent in geological times) sea levels had fallen by as much as 100 m (330 ft) below present levels. The depth of the sea off western Sabah is now largely less than 100 m, which is shallow in the global context, and there are several islands located within Malaysian waters. Some can be visited on day trips or for one or two nights from Kota Kinabalu.

Attractions of the islands include diving, snorkelling, beachcombing and the presence of several bird species confined mainly to offshore islands, including scrubfowl (*Megapodius* spp.) and imperial-pigeons (*Ducula* spp.). The most readily accessible islands off Sabah's west coast are within Tunku Abdul Rahman Park, all within half an hour's boat ride from Kota Kinabalu city. The park, established in 1974, consists of five islands with adjacent marine waters and coral reefs, covering a total area of about 5,000 ha (12,355 acres). A part of the largest island, Gaya, is privately owned, and there are villages over the water on the side facing Kota Kinabalu. A tropical storm named Greg swept through Gaya island in the early hours of 26 December 1996, toppling most of the large trees. Sapi island is an offshoot of Gaya and, along with Manukan, is the most popular with local and foreign visitors. The quietest islands in the group are Mamutik and Sulug, both with the least disturbed corals.

Significance

Urban and expanding, with a burgeoning human population, Kota Kinabalu not only retains examples of natural habitats, but also provides a base for day trips to several diverse places of interest to naturalists.

Trails and trips

Starting from the steps at the north end of Lorong Dewan or from the Atkinson clock tower – built in 1902–1905 and the oldest remaining building in Sabah – you can walk up Signal Hill, where a mix of trees and strangling figs provides habitat for common wild birds and a few mammals. On the east (inland) side of Signal Hill is the Kota Kinabalu Wetland Centre and Bird Sanctuary, a 24-ha (59-acre) patch of regenerating mangrove, and the only remaining patch of the extensive mangrove that once existed to the south and north of the city. The site was designated a bird

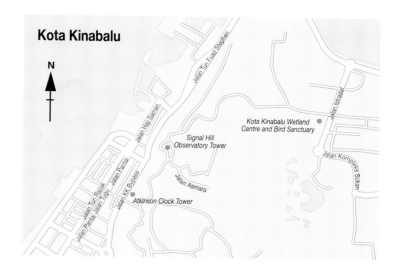

sanctuary in September 1996, as a refuge and breeding site for several species of heron and egret, and to help foster a better understanding and awareness of the value of wetlands. Wildlife in the sanctuary can be viewed from a boardwalk.

On the inland side of the coastal highway heading northwards from the city, beyond the northern tip of Signal Hill, is Likas lagoon, an example of the way wildlife habitats can be created by human developments, in this case inadvertently. The lagoon is a tract of freshwater runoff from inland that became trapped by the construction of the coastal highway, and is managed as a repository for excess water during heavy rainstorms. It has become shallow through settlement of sediments, creating a gradation of swamp covered by sedges, grasses, shrubs and small trees, to deeper open water.

Two hours by road to the south of Kota Kinabalu is the Klias Peninsula, where you can view wild Proboscis Monkeys (*Nasalis larvatus*), fireflies and, sometimes, flying foxes from a river boat, leaving the city after lunch and returning to town by ten at night. Also to the south of the city are options to engage in white-water rafting on the Padas River, or to visit Kawang Recreational Forest. Other possible day trips from Kota Kinabalu, both to the north of the city, involve white-water rafting on the Kiulu River or watching waterbirds on Tempasuk Plain, an inland wetland plain near the small farming town of Kota Belud.

Right: Velvet-fronted Nuthatch (Sitta frontalis), a rare and rarely seen bird that has a distribution from the coast to mountain ranges, usually seen searching for insects in tree bark.

Below right: Female and young of the Proboscis Monkey, a unique primate found only in Borneo, with small populations along the main rivers of the Klias Peninsula.

Opposite top: White-bellied Sea Eagle, commonly seen in pairs near the coast and islands off western Sabah, soaring above land or sea, but young individuals like this one venture inland.

Opposite below: Long-tailed Macaque, a monkey of coastal and riverine forests; a small group lives on Signal Hill.

Animal life

Bulbuls, pigeons, Plantain Squirrels and a troupe of Long-tailed Macaques can usually be spotted on Signal Hill. From the top of the hill views can sometimes be obtained of Brahminy Kites, or even pairs of White-bellied Sea Eagles, which live along the coastline. Kota Kinabalu Bird Sanctuary was known from the 1970s up to the early '90s as a breeding site of the Black-crowned Night Heron and Rufous Night Heron (*Nycticorax caledonicus*), birds that roost during the day and fly at dusk to feed at night. Around the time of the sanctuary's establishment, the night herons seemingly abandoned it as a breeding site, probably due to disturbance as the result of an attempt to build an illegal settlement within the mangroves.

The sanctuary is best treated not so much as a place to see wild birds, but as a location to visit in the early morning or late in the afternoon when temperatures are relatively low, and the mangroves can be seen from inside and below. You can enjoy the characteristic mangrove sounds, notably the monotonous calls of the

Above: Striated or Little Heron, the most common bird of the mudflats in western Sabah, where it feeds on crabs and fish.

Top left: Female fiddler crab (Uca spp.), a crustacean of inter-tidal mudflats that feeds on detritus filtered from mud and sand.

Above right: Cinnamon Bittern, one of two resident bittern species of the coastal swamps and irrigated rice fields of western Sabah.

North Borneo Coastal Cicada (*Ayesha serva*) and the popping of pistol shrimps (*Alpheidae*), and sights like hermit crabs and mudskippers. Any sighting of birds can be viewed as a bonus.

Likas lagoon is a stop-over point for migrant wader birds, which move to the tropics during the northern winter. Resident species that can be seen at the lagoon include the Little Egret (*Egretta garzetta*), Purple Heron, Little Heron, Cinnamon Bittern (*Ixobrychus cinnamomeus*), Wood Sandpiper (*Tringa glareola*) and White-eyebrowed Water Crake (*Porzana leucophrys*), while migrants include Red-necked and Black-winged Stints (*Calidris ruficollis* and *Himantopus himantopus*), and the Grey-tailed Tattler (*Tringa brevipes*).

In the coastal vegetation characterized by casuarina trees (Casuarinaceae) at Tanjung Aru, along a tiny stretch of sandy coastal plain on the south side of Kota Kinabalu, can be found Blue-naped Parrots (*Tanygnathus lucionensis*), Pied Trillers (*Lalage nigra*), pigeons and sunbirds. The small tracts of mudflats off Kota Kinabalu are the habitat of the Pacific Reef Egret (*Egretta sacra*), curious in being nowhere common, and in being represented by two phases, or colour forms, within a single species, one white, the other grey-black. A little further out to sea you can see several species of tern, lighter and more graceful equivalents of the gulls that would be seen on the coasts of temperate regions of the world.

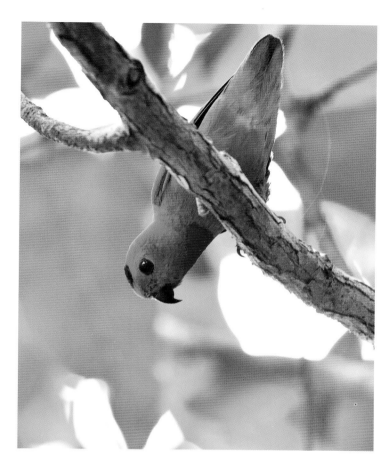

Plant life

Plants of interest on Signal Hill include several species of fig, Tembusu, known locally as Tempasuk (*Fagraea fragrans*), and the Nibung Palm (*Oncosperma* spp.). Ten species of mangrove tree occur in the Kota Kinabalu Bird Sanctuary, and these can be viewed from a wooden boardwalk.

Apart from on Signal Hill and in the mangroves, the most common tree species around Kota Kinabalu, as well as on most coastal hills to the north and south of the city, are imports of the 1960s from northern Australia: Tan and Black Wattles (*Acacia auriculiformis* and *A. mangium*), and hybrids of the two, which have spread to cover most hill slopes and reclaimed land due to their tolerance of very poor soils, dry spells and fire. The seeds of these trees have been spread largely by noisy flocks of Philippine Glossy Starlings (*Aplonis panayensis*), some of which can be seen and heard roosting in the trees in the centre of Kota Kinabalu at dusk. Although viewed with distaste by some naturalists, these trees and the starlings have contributed to a natural restoration of tree cover on many coastal hills in the west of Sabah, where previously there was mainly *Imperata* grass and a few native Kulimpapa (*Vitex pinnata*) trees.

Access

Kota Kinabalu has the second busiest airport in Malaysia, served by over 25 daily flights from Kuala Lumpur, as well as several international destinations; it is only ten minutes' drive from the city centre.

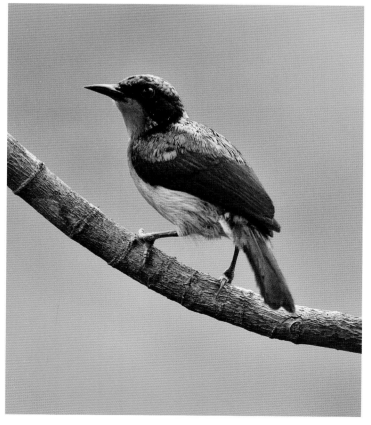

Left: Male Brown-throated Sunbird, a common nectar-feeding bird of the gardens and coconut groves of Sabah's west coast mainland and islands.

Above left: Blue-crowned Hanging Parrot (Loriculus galgulus), the smallest Malaysian parrot species, unique for its ability to rest and sleep hanging upside-down.

Mount Kinabalu and the Crocker Range

The first person known to have reached the highest point of Kinabalu (Low's Peak, today ascended daily by climbers) was an ornithologist, John Whitehead. The unfortunate earlier pioneers Hugh Low and Spenser St John inadvertently reached a slightly lower peak in 1858. From January to April 1887, an era when collection of wildlife specimens was not only acceptable, but indeed necessary in order to be able to describe and name 'new' species, Whitehead obtained 300 bird specimens from Mount Kinabalu, 18 of which were new to science.

During an even more gruelling return visit between January and May 1888, Whitehead reached Low's Peak on 11 February, with four local Dusuns and two Kadayans. Having collected not only birds but also other vertebrates and invertebrates, these two expeditions were regarded by Whitehead's scientific contemporaries in Europe as among the most successful scientific expeditions of the era.

Mount Kinabalu was established as a national park in 1964, with the name amended in 1984 to Kinabalu Park. Mount Kinabalu occupies the southern end of a much bigger, 766 sq km (295 square mile) tract of tropical rainforest within the park. Named after William Crocker, governor of North Borneo in 1887–1888, the Crocker Range of forest-covered mountains forms a backbone along the west side of Sabah rising to approximately 1,500 m (4,920 ft) for most of its length. Much of the Crocker Range was established as a park in 1984, but the same area had originally been established as a protected forest reserve in 1968 to limit cultivation and development on the steep slopes, and to protect the quality of water flowing into rivers on the west-coast plains and in the interior. The Crocker Range was designated as a UNESCO Biosphere Reserve in 2014.

Significance

Geologically, the Crocker Range mountains are thick layers of deformed sedimentary rocks. Mount Kinabalu is a great mass of granite that has been pushed up through the Crocker Range. With its highest peak at 4,095 m (13,435 ft), Kinabalu is the tallest mountain between Myanmar (Burma) and Papua New Guinea. The top is bare granite, while the lower slopes are covered in farms and settlements. In between there is a variety of natural tropical rainforests, the individual differences of which are linked to local differences in soil, temperature, light and exposure to wind. The Crocker Range is the main water-catchment area for western Sabah, supplying clean water to both the coastal plains and inland valleys.

Above: The top granite zone of Mount Kinabalu seen from the ultrabasic zone.

Opposite: Vegetation at the upper montane zone of Mount Kinabalu, including wild raspberries (Rubus *spp.).*

Following pages: An iconic view on the granite dome top of Mount Kinabalu, with the Summit Trail route marked with white rope.

Trails, trips and climbs

The major and favourite trail runs from Kinabalu Park headquarters, located at 1,564 m (5,130 ft), to the summit peak. There is also a network of trails through the forest around the park headquarters. An alternative route exists through the lower montane forest to the summit, starting at Mesilau, located at about 2,000 m (6,560 ft), and joining the old Summit Trail just above Layang-Layang at 2,700 m (8,858 ft). Mount Kinabalu has the world's highest 'Via Ferrata', a mountain route made up of a network of iron rungs, rails and cables that allow access to very steep areas.

The annual Mount Kinabalu International Climbathon originated in 1984 as an internal competition to improve response to visitor rescue efforts, and became an international challenge in 1988. One of toughest mountain races in the world, the route covers 21 km (13 miles) and an ascent of 2,250 m (7,382 ft) with a qualifying time of four hours. The record completion time, up and back down again, is just over two hours and 42 minutes, a feat that seems incredible to even the fittest of 'normal' climbers.

On the south-east side of the park is Poring, at 400 m (1,312 ft). It is best known for its natural

sulfurous hot-water spring, channelled into baths that provide a welcome relief after climbing the mountain. Nowadays Poring has a great scarcity value in being one of the most accessible natural dipterocarp forests on the western side of Sabah. Forest trails also exist at Sayap, Monggis and Serinsim 'substations' on the northern fringes of Kinabalu Park. In the middle of the park lies Mount Tambuyukon (summit 2,579 m/8,461 ft), the third highest mountain in Borneo, formed of ultrabasic rock, and visited very rarely even by keen botanists and mountaineers.

A way to see the traditional land use of native people on the lower slopes of Mount Kinabalu is to visit the village of Kiau, which is accessible by rough road off the highway from Kota Kinabalu to Kinabalu Park. This site is of historical interest, having been the last inhabited stop for the early climbers of the mountain before the Second World War, and the place during that period where foreign climbers sought the most experienced guides and porters.

Before the Second World War, people from the inland Dusun communities had to walk over the

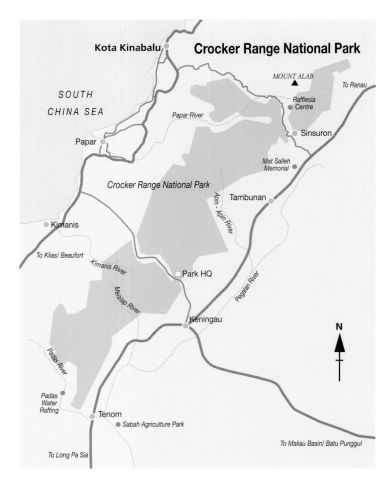

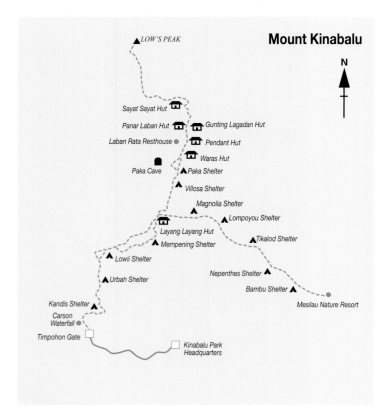

Crocker Range mountains down to the coast to trade or barter salt for forest products. Serious trekkers, who are happy to spend several days camping and moving from site to site daily, can recapture the feel of that past era by walking over the Tambunan–Penampang part of the Crocker Range on trips of three days or more, following a route often called the 'salt trail'.

An extraordinary feature at the southern end of the Crocker Range is the Padas Gorge, where the Padas River cuts through the mountains from the interior of Sabah. With access provided by a remarkable railway laid in 1903, and still subject to occasional collapses during periods of very heavy rainfall, Padas Gorge represents one of the prime locations for white-water rafting not only in Sabah, but in the entire Southeast Asian region.

Opposite: The splendour of Mount Kinabalu in close-up, where the upper forest gives way to bare granite.

Tambunan is the name of a small town and a unique, broad valley landscape at 600–700 m (1,968–2,297 ft), dominated by wet-rice fields, some of which are carved as terraces on the eastern foothills of the Crocker Range. Above the rice fields, on the lower slopes of the Crocker Range and – to the east – the Trus Madi mountain range, are great groves of bamboo interspersed with rubber gardens. Stream water here is clean, coming from these two mountain ranges on the west and east side of the valley. A unique culture has developed here, self-sufficient in rice, some of which is turned into rice wine, along with the use of bamboo for fencing, roofing and construction of small houses in the rice fields, and as pipes for channelling water from forest streams. Trus Madi peak, to the south-east of Tambunan town, is an outlier from the Crocker Range; at 2,649 m (8,690 ft) it is the second highest mountain in Borneo.

Driving southwards from Tambunan, the landscape changes gradually from the fertile rice fields, through a jumble of steep valleys, to Keningau. Here is another and different sort of inland plain, one that is characterized more by pale-coloured, sandy soils and deposits of gravel, pebbles and boulders that have tumbled down from the Crocker Range over geological time scales. Further south Tenom, a small town and agricultural region 300 m (984 ft) above sea level, was the first part of Sabah's interior to be opened up and developed with rubber and other crops. The main stimulus was the arrival of the railway, built along the Padas Gorge in the early 1900s.

Tenom has fertile soils and a climate characterized by moderate rainfall throughout the year, and temperatures lower than those of the west-coast plains. Sabah Agriculture Park (formerly Tenom Agricultural Park) is hardly wild, but offers a convenient way to see a remarkable variety of native and exotic tropical plants in one place. Hundreds of tropical crop species, fruit trees, orchids and ornamentals can be seen within the space of a few hours. The park is an extension of a government agricultural research station, developed in the 1970s, which focused on crop diversification rather than on just one or a few conventional species. On fine days outstanding aerial views of the Crocker Range can be obtained from daily scheduled flights from either Lahad Datu or Tawau; these pass quite low over the middle part of the Range to Kota Kinabalu.

Birds

Three of Borneo's most colourful mountain bird species, Whitehead's Broadbill (*Calyptomena whiteheadi*), Whitehead's Trogon (*Harpactes whiteheadi*) and Whitehead's Spiderhunter (*Arachnothera juliae*), were discovered by John Whitehead and named after him by museum colleagues. All three were subsequently found to occur on other high mountains of north-western Borneo.

About 326 bird species are currently known from the Mount Kinabalu area, of which around 40 are seasonal migrants and 23 are endemic to Borneo. Visitors to the Kinabalu Park headquarters can expect to see noisy groups of the Chestnut-capped Laughingthrush (*Garrulax mitratus*), the diminutive Black-capped White-eye (*Zosterops atricapilla*), the solitary, raucous Malaysian Treepie (*Dendrocitta*

occipitalis), and the Mountain Tailorbird (*Orthotomus cuculatus*) and Scarlet Sunbird (*Aethopyga mystacalis*). At higher altitudes along the main trail, from 2,500 m (8,202 ft) to the uppermost vegetation, the Mountain Blackeye (*Chlorocharis emiliae*), Kinabalu Friendly Warbler (*Bradypterus accentor*) and Mountain Blackbird (*Turdus poliocephalus seebohmi*) can be seen.

Above: *Indigo Flycatcher (*Eumyias indigo*), a common bird of the forest edge on Mount Kinabalu.*

Top left: *Whitehead's Spiderhunter, a nectar-feeding bird of the upper forests of the Crocker Range and Mount Kinabalu.*

Centre left: *Chestnut-hooded Laughingthrush (*Rhinocichla treacheri*), a prominent, noisy bird that feeds on fruits and insects in the Crocker Range and Mount Kinabalu forests.*

Below left: *Mountain Blackeye, the most common bird of the very highest vegetation of Mount Kinabalu.*

Opposite: *Whitehead's Trogon, a rarely seen bird of the damp, dark forest valleys on Mount Kinabalu and the Crocker Range.*

Mammals

Mount Kinabalu provides habitat for one assemblage of mammal species that comprises essentially lowland species, and another which consists of species that have evolved to live in highlands. At around 1,700–1,800 m (5,577–5,905 ft), the two assemblages overlap. Small mammals adapted to mountains are the ones most commonly seen by visitors. They include the Bornean Mountain Ground Squirrel (*Dremomys everetti*), Brooke's and Jentink's Squirrels (*Sundasciurus brookei* and *S. jentinki*), and Mountain Treeshrew (*Tupaia montana*).

Plant life

After its imposing physical presence – and the fact that the mountain is often wet, misty, windy and cold – the most prominent feature of Mount Kinabalu is its diverse flora. One of the botanical pioneers of Mount Kinabalu, Miss Lilian Gibbs of the British Museum, visited the mountain in February 1910, starting by railway train from Jesselton, proceeding south through Padas Gorge to Tenom, then by horse to Tambunan, then northwards on foot. Apart from collecting more than 1,000 plant specimens, and from being the first woman to ascend to the Kinabalu peak, she made a basic classification of the vegetation types. In 1914 she listed 203 plant species from Mount Kinabalu, but by 1989 American researcher John Beaman had listed almost 4,000 from the same general area. The Sabah Parks authorities suggest that perhaps an additional 2,000 plant species exist in the other mountains, hills and valleys within the park.

Many eminent botanists have tried to create a simple classification of Mount Kinabalu's vegetation zones for the layman. In practice, however, this has never really been possible, in large part due to the enormous numbers of species within various plant groups, ranging from tiny herbs, ferns and mosses, to pitcher plants, shrubs, orchids and other epiphytes, to

trees. In turn, the diversity of plants and vegetation structure, along with shifts in climate and vegetation zonation up and down the mountain during the Pleistocene ice ages, have resulted in a diversity of animal life.

On the lower slopes of Mount Kinabalu, up to around 1,000 m (3,280 ft), most of the original vegetation has been cleared, either to grow hill rice on a fallow system, or to plant crops such as rubber and vegetables. However, to the east and north of Mount Kinabalu, and most accessible at Poring, there are tracts of original hill dipterocarp forest up to and beyond this altitudinal zone. From 1,000 to 1,800 m (3,280–5,905 ft) is the lower montane forest. Kinabalu Park headquarters nestles in the lower montane forest zone, a forest dominated by Bornean species of oak, myrtle, laurel and conifer. These plant families are typically associated with northern-hemisphere temperate and Mediterranean climates, but their species diversity is highest in the hills and mountains of Borneo. At 1,800–3,200 m (5,905–10,500 ft) is lower stature mossy forest, where mosses drape tree-trunks and branches.

Between the sedimentary rocks of lower slopes and the granite peak is a narrow intervening layer of ultrabasic rock, at around 2,750–3,000 m (9,022–9,842 ft), with its own type of scrub forest. Above 3,000 m (9,842 ft) is the granite dome of Mount Kinabalu, with dwarf scrub forest. Above 3,700 m (12,140 ft), cold winds and rain frequently lash the mountain top, which is almost devoid of plant life.

The name Poring refers to the giant-stemmed *Gigantochloa levis* bamboo, which is locally common here. The bird life here is different from that at higher elevations on Mount Kinabalu. An aerial walkway in the Poring forest allows views from within and above the tree canopy. Two species of the extremely rare *Rafflesia* genus occur in the Poring region.

Sabah Agriculture Park offers a chance to see an example of the massive, parasitic *Rafflesia* flower, when no plants in bloom can be found in the wild in the Crocker Range or near Poring. The species at Tenom is *Rafflesia keithi,* and it is special in representing the successful outcome of a project to inoculate the host vine, *Tetrastigma*, with *Rafflesia* seeds obtained from Poring, as a conservation measure for the *Rafflesia* species. The Tenom Park managers waited nearly ten years between the inoculation and the first flowering of a *Rafflesia* in 2004.

Opposite: Bird's Nest Ferns are prominent epiphytes on the trunks and branches of tall trees in the upper dipterocarp forests of Mount Kinabalu and the Crocker Range.

Below: The flower of Rafflesia keithii, *with the newly opened inflorescence at its centre and a blackish flower bud to the right.*

Access

Visitors can reach Kinabalu Park headquarters within two hours of Kota Kinabalu, by bus, taxi or through a tour operator.

Four roads cross west to east over the Crocker Range. The northernmost road is a part of the Kota Kinabalu to Sandakan highway, which passes the southern slopes of Mount Kinabalu, and the entrance to Kinabalu Park. The southernmost road traverses a low pass at the narrow end of the Range, and skirts the northern fringes of the Sabah Forest Industries forest concession.

The middle two roads over the Range (Penampang to Tambunan, and Kimanis to Keningau) pass through tracts of natural highland dipterocarp and montane forest inside the Crocker Range National Park. The Penampang to Tambunan route was the first motorable road to be built over the Crocker Range, and passes through the Rafflesia Forest Reserve, where the flowers of *Rafflesia pricei* can sometimes be seen. The Kimanis–Keningau road was built over the Crocker Range in the mid-1970s as a means to extract logs from the interior of Sabah down to the west coast. A small park headquarters is situated on this route, not far from Keningau town.

Above: *The flower and bud of* Rafflesia pricei *in the Crocker Range.*

Top: *Lower montane forest on the slopes of Mount Kinabalu, characterized by frequent rainfall, palms, epiphytes and a dense ground cover.*

Opposite: *Mangrove forest on the southern fringes of Sepilok Forest Reserve, with dipterocarp forest on the dry land ridges and Sandakan Bay in the distance.*

Sandakan and Sepilok

Sandakan is the name of a town, a bay and a peninsula. The precise origins of the name, said to mean 'to be pawned' in the Suluk language, and human settlement of the area are unknown. The first known written record came from the English adventurer John Hunt, who either visited or obtained contemporary information on Sandakan in around 1812 during his trade-seeking tour of the southern Philippines and eastern Borneo, and who recorded that the Sulu sultan Sharaf ud-Din appointed his son to govern the settlement of Sandakan from 1791 to 1808 (quoted in James Warren, *The Sulu Zone, 1768–1898: The Dymanics of External Trade, Slavery and Ethnicity in the Transformation of a Southeast Asian Maritime State*, 1981). Sandakan had a

chief named tuan Abandool and a hundred Islams and there are many orang idan [natives] in the interior parts. Its annual products, when the Sulo people come over in numbers and chuse to exert

themselves are 50 piculs [about 3 tons] of white birds' nest, 200 piculs [about 12 tons] of black ... 3 piculs [about 180 kg] of camphor ... 3 piculs of wax ... pearls ... and tripang [sea cucumbers].

In 1879, William Pryer landed on the western side of the mouth of Sandakan Bay, as newly appointed 'resident' employed by the founders of the North Borneo Chartered Company to develop eastern Sabah. An energetic visionary, Pryer imagined that a century hence, the perimeter of Sandakan Bay would be a metropolis, supported by agriculture in the hinterlands. Early British administrators realized that as agricultural expansion proceeded, forests would disappear from the Sandakan region, bringing the need for a specific forest area to be allocated to provide wood supplies long-term for Sandakan town. Thus, Kabili-Sepilok Forest Reserve (usually known just as Sepilok) was established, a part in 1931, with an extra area added in 1938, to supply wood to Sandakan, then the capital of British North Borneo. Logging in Sepilok was done by what would now be called sustainable

timber production, using axes, manpower and a narrow-gauge railway. Timber extraction from Sepilok ceased in 1957, and the status of the area changed for research and conservation.

By 1970, as Sabah's timber boom was well underway and many people saw how rich they could become by obtaining a licence, buying a bulldozer and cutting down large trees, Sepilok came under threat. The threat was averted by providing the interested party with an alternative logging site.

As the years went by, Sepilok Forest Reserve became isolated by farm and plantation development. Road access to what is now the rehabilitation centre was completed in 1976, and soon after Sabah's first active inbound tour operator opened for business. The last visit to the western edge of Sepilok by a wild elephant herd from the Segaliud River occurred in

1980. As Sandakan's human population expanded, the town's water supply, derived from boreholes, became inadequate; in 1981 it was proposed that additional boreholes had to be opened to boost supplies, and plans were made to drill 17 new holes inside Sepilok. Fortunately an alternative option was proposed, of piping water in large quantities directly from the Kinabatangan River, and the threat was averted. By 1982 Sepilok had become cut off from all the forests further inland, although mangrove-forest connection is maintained around Sandakan Bay.

The 1970s to the early '80s was the peak of Sabah's logging era, when millions of massive logs of dipterocarp trees were brought annually to the 'log ponds' in the sea off Tanah Merah. Some were brought out of the forest on trucks, but most were floated or barged by sea from the coastal lowlands to the north and east. Looking down from Trig Hill above Sandakan town, you could see the logs, ranging from 50 cm to 2 m (1½–6½ ft) in diameter, lined up like so many matchsticks, before being loaded on to a never-ending queue of ships from Japan. Some species of dipterocarp logs are 'floaters', and they were preferred at that time due to their ease of transportation by water, and used mainly to make plywood. 'Sinkers', the dense hardwood characteristic of other species, had to be tied to floaters.

Significance

Sandakan is the Malaysian town that is the closest in the country to the greatest diversity of readily accessible wildlife habitats. Sepilok has lowland dipterocarp forest, an important Orang-utan (*Pongo pygmaeus pygmaeus*) rehabilitation centre and the world-class Rainforest Discovery Centre. Within an hour's drive of Sandakan town there are mangrove forests and Proboscis Monkeys. Further afield are islands where marine turtles lay their eggs, as well as the lower Kinabatangan floodplain and limestone caves (see page 109).

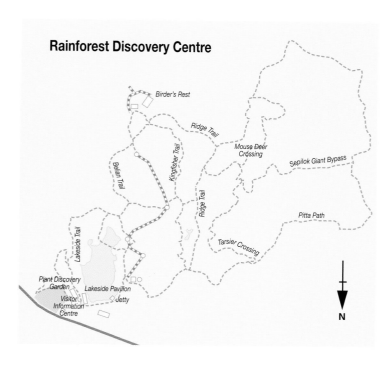

Rainforest Discovery Centre

Birder's Rest

Ridge Trail

Mouse Deer Crossing

Sepilok Giant Bypass

Belian Trail

Kingfisher Trail

Ridge Trail

Pitta Path

Lakeside Trail

Tarsier Crossing

Plant Discovery Garden

Lakeside Pavilion

Visitor Information Centre

Jetty

N

is reached by walking from the bus stop along a path that bypasses the Restricted Area. There are additional trails of up to 2 km (1¼ miles), and some visitors walk a 5-km (3-mile) trail from the Orang-utan centre to the mangrove forest on the south side of Sepilok Forest Reserve, with the most scenic section being a stretch along a sandstone ridge. To learn about the forest and stay away from day-trip crowds, the Rainforest Discovery Trail, Plant Discovery Garden and Canopy Walkway offer an alternative choice.

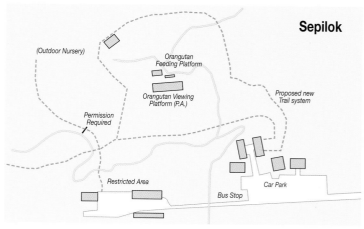

Sepilok

(Outdoor Nursery)

Orangutan Feeding Platform

Proposed new Trail system

Orangutan Viewing Platform (P.A.)

Permission Required

Restricted Area

Car Park

Bus Stop

Trails and treks

A short boardwalk from the main entrance to Sepilok leads to the Orang-utan rehabilitation centre feeding platform. The Bornean Sun Bear Conservation Centre

Left: Part of a dipterocarp tree, showing the characteristic one-seeded, winged fruits that are blown off by wind when ripe, and spin away from the parent tree.

Opposite: Lowland dipterocarp forest in Sepilok Forest Reserve, showing mast flowering of the dipterocarp trees in early 2014.

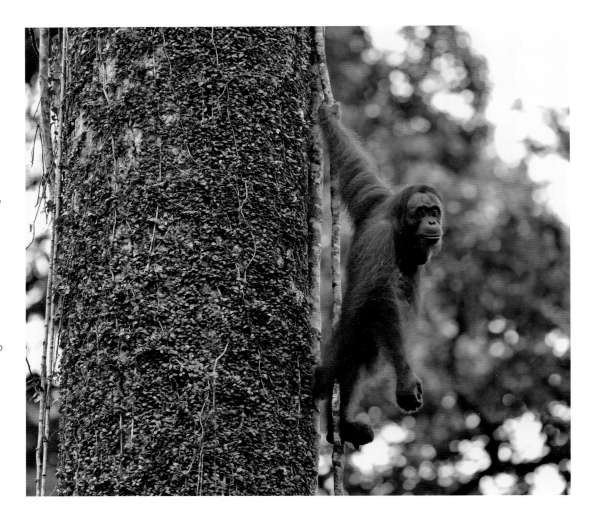

Right: A young mature male Bornean Orang-utan hangs from a liana in Sepilok Forest Reserve.

Opposite top: Orphaned juvenile Orang-utans do not climb instinctively – they tend to stay on the ground and in the absence of a mother, seek the company of other orphans.

Opposite below: Orang-utans' intelligence enables them to do things that other wild mammal species cannot – in this case, to use a bunch of leafy twigs as a shelter from rain.

Orang-utans

Sepilok became famous for its Orang-utans, but the link between the two is largely historical rather than biological. World Wildlife Fund (WWF), the international conservation organization, was founded in 1961 to help save endangered species. In 1962 WWF sent Barbara Harrisson to British North Borneo to investigate the status of Orang-utans. She reported that they were endangered (in fact, at that time they were not), and that the main threat to their survival was the capture of young animals as pets (which in fact was trivial at the time). During her return visit two years later to the recently independent Sabah, and in collaboration with the Assistant Chief Game Warden, Stanley De Silva, the Sepilok Orang-utan rehabilitation centre was established as a place to receive and train pet Orang-utans for a life back in the wild. Sepilok was

chosen because in 1964 the site was considered quite remote, yet only just beyond the end of the main road out of Sandakan.

Starting in the early 1980s, the availability of regular and moderately priced air routes from Europe all the way to Sandakan, coupled with road access to Sepilok, increasingly drew tourists to visit the Orang-utan rehabilitation centre. The nature-tourism element of Sepilok had never been planned by anyone in the early years, but as the popularity of the site grew the government authorities realized that Sepilok was not only an unintended tourism icon, but also presented a convenient way to attract and maintain interest in nature conservation, both globally and locally. As early as 1980 the first nature-education centre had been established at Sepilok, with assistance from the government of Canada.

The first part of 1983 brought the brunt of a major

El Niño drought to eastern Sabah. There was almost no rain between August 1982 and May 1983, and Borneo experienced the worst drought since 1915–1916. Sepilok saw not only the first recorded case of big dipterocarp trees gregariously shedding their leaves, but also a boost in the number of Orang-utans being brought in, emaciated and dehydrated, just as the big wave of oil-palm plantation establishment was underway in eastern Sabah.

By the mid-1980s the role of Sepilok as a permanent Orang-utan centre had thus been established by historical events and trends. Young Orang-utans were coming in steadily as plantation expansion proceeded. Sepilok was advertised globally as a reason to visit Sabah, and Orang-utans became Sabah's second big global icon after Mount Kinabalu. Now, in the 21st century, the number of Orang-utans brought to Sepilok is in sharp decline, as land-use patterns stabilize.

Sepilok is still the most accessible location to see Orang-utans in the forest in Sabah, but in view of its origins and current trends it is not necessarily the best or most rewarding – visitors will see more humans than Orang-utans.

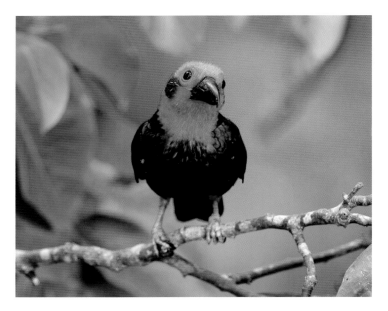

Other land animals

Sepilok is the first choice for seeking Borneo's arguably most iconic bird species, the Bornean Bristlehead (*Pityriasis gymnocephala*). Even if this species does not make a showing, there are dozens of other lowland rainforest birds, ranging from hornbills, parakeets and broadbills, to diminutive spiderhunters, sunbirds and flowerpeckers. Just before dusk Red Giant Flying Squirrels (*Petaurista petaurista*) may be seen from the Rainforest Discovery Centre, while at night the Bornean Tarsier (*Cephalopachus bancanus borneanus*) sometimes emerges on the Discovery Trail.

Plant life

On the hills behind Sandakan town, and on nearby Berhala island, are examples of original low-stature heath forest along with some fine regenerating secondary forests. Perhaps most remarkable is the 148-ha (366-acre) Sandakan Rainforest Park, also known as the Kebun Cina Amenity Forest Reserve, a relict patch of dipterocarp forest just a few kilometres from town. Despite its proximity to Sandakan town, capital of North Borneo from 1883 to 1947, and the occurrence of brush fires around the area during the droughts of 1983, 1987 and 1998, this forest survived without formal protected status until 2007, when it was finally given legal protection as a forest reserve.

A part of the interest of this site is historical as well as botanical: the very first records and descriptions of more than 100 species of wild Bornean plant are based on specimens collected here or very near here. Most of the collections were made in 1920 by Philippino collector Maximo Ramos, and in 1921 by Manila-based American botanist Adolph Elmer. The site now serves as a recreational forest for local people, as well as being unique in the Southeast Asian region for its joint biodiversity conservation and historical significance.

What has emerged after the turn of the 21st century is that Sepilok has become a unique icon for reasons

other than Orang-utans. Where else can you take a 45-minute drive from a bustling town to a well-kept example of Borneo's lowland diptercocarp forest? At Sepilok you can see, close up, centuries-old specimens of Borneo's famous ironwood trees, some of which started life long before the first Europeans set foot on Sabah. At the Rainforest Discovery Centre visitors can not only explore a Rainforest Discovery Trail, Plant Discovery Garden and Visitor Building, but also make a uniquely stable climb up into the forest canopy.

Turtles

There are several offshore islands not far from Sandakan, with Berhala being the closest. The 'turtle islands' are the most famous, with three of the islands, part of a cluster that straddles the Malaysia and Philippines marine border, designated in 1966 as a conservation area for Green Sea Turtles and Hawksbill Turtles. The significance of these three islands lies in the fact that their coral-sand beaches represent the longest established protected site in the tropical Asian region for both of these marine turtle species to lay their eggs.

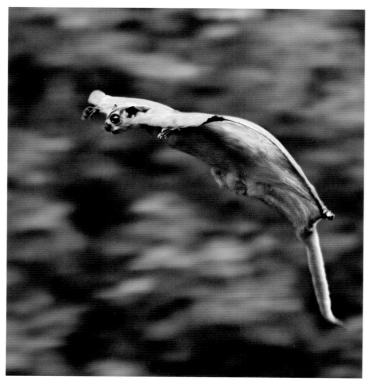

Above left: Little Spiderhunter (Arachnothera longirostra), *a very common bird of the understory in lowland forests, specializing in feeding on the nectar of wild ginger flowers.*

Left: Red Giant Flying Squirrel, *the largest gliding mammal in Malaysia, often seen at the Rainforest Discovery Centre just before dusk.*

Opposite top: Bornean Bristlehead, *a bizarre and naturally rare Bornean endemic bird that lives in family groups, sometimes seen in the forest at Sepilok.*

Opposite centre: Banded Broadbill (Eurylaimus javanicus), *a fruit-eating bird of the lowland forests.*

Opposite below: Crown of a Nibung Palm (Oncosperma spp.) with *four Pink-necked Green-pigeons* (Treron vernans), *one of five Green-pigeon species found in the coastal forests of western Sabah.*

Right: A Green Sea Turtle, feeding on algae on the seabed.

Below: A Green Sea Turtle recently hatched from its egg, heading to the sea.

Opposite: Early morning on the Menanggul River near Sukau.

Three of the islands (Selingaan, Bakkungan Kecil and Gulisaan) were legislated as Turtle Islands Park in 1977. A private conservation turtle-egg hatchery exists nearer to Sandakan, on Libaran island. Some 60 km (37 miles) to the north-west, off the mouth of the Sugut River, is the Sugut Islands Marine Conservation Area (SIMCA), consisting of three islands (Lankayan, Billean and Tegipil) and more than 46,000 ha (113,668 acres) of sea.

An unusual aspect of SIMCA is that it is established as a 'conservation area' under a section of the Sabah Wildlife Conservation Enactment, which allows any kind of land, including private land, to be managed at the direction of government for conservation purposes. This piece of legislation is unique in Malaysia, and SIMCA was the first site to be established by law as a conservation area, rather than a wildlife sanctuary, state park or forest reserve. The second unusual aspect of SIMCA is that management of the entire area has been delegated, under formal agreement and supervision, to private enterprise, whereby in return for protecting and conserving the area, the operator is permitted to use SIMCA for nature tourism. Apart from the chance to see marine turtles, these islands offer excellent opportunities for snorkelling and diving.

Access

Many tour operators offer services to Sepilok. An alternative is to hire a taxi. Public buses pass by the Sepilok junction off the Sandakan–Kota Kinabalu highway, necessitating a 2½-km (1½-mile) walk.

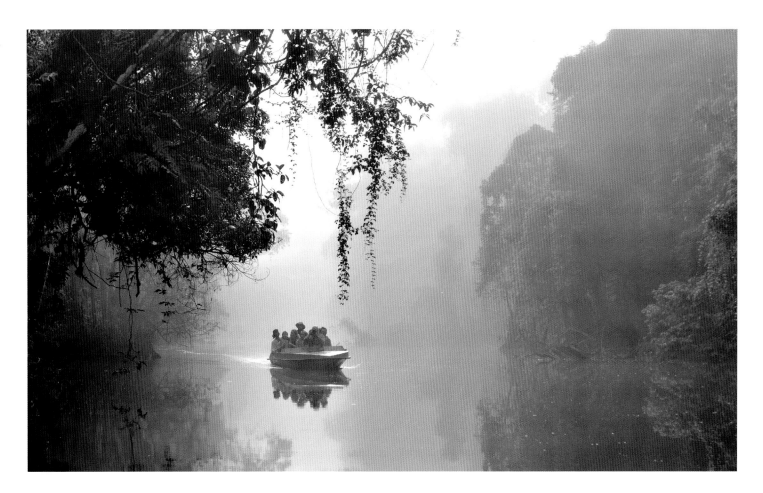

Kinabatangan Floodplain

Until the 1950s Kinabatangan floodplain was an almost undisturbed natural forest ecosystem, and the native Orang Sungai families of lower Kinabatangan planted non-irrigated 'hill' rice on the raised alluvial riverside terrace, and small quantities of a long-stemmed rice variety in natural swamps near villages. Their presence occupied well under 1 per cent of the floodplain.

It is unclear why Kinabatangan largely escaped extensive human settlement and conversion to wet-rice fields. In the 19th century the British administration of North Borneo thought that slave-seeking pirates from the southern Philippines and head-hunting raiders from Kalimantan were the main reasons for the very small numbers of human inhabitants in lower Kinabatangan. Smallpox and cholera certainly took a big toll on human communities from time to time, but the same occurred elsewhere. Perhaps the

unpredictable timing and depth of flooding, compared with that generated by the more seasonal rainfall patterns in much of Asia, made the growing of wet paddy very risky in the high but erratic rainfall zone of northern Borneo. Yet in South Kalimantan, at the southern end of Borneo, both the culture and population of the Banjar people expanded from centuries ago around conversion of the floodplain of the massive Barito River to wet paddy.

In fact, the history of human settlement in lower Kinabatangan is most closely linked not to food production, but to limestone caves, which probably provided habitation for ancient human settlers and which, starting a few centuries ago, formed the basis for the harvesting of edible birds' nests (see page 115) and their lucrative trade to China. Commercial logging in the floodplain from the 1950s to the '80s, boosted by the introduction of chainsaws in 1960, gave way to oil-palm plantation expansion starting in the 1980s and continuing up to the present.

Gomantong and several smaller limestone outcrops in lower Kinabatangan, their caves and rights over the edible nests were seized by the British in the early years of the North Borneo administration. In the case of Gomantong, this resulted in the death by shooting in 1884 of the head of Melapi village (which is now known as Sukau).

Kinabatangan represents a classic story of how real-life conservation operates, and the story will take another few decades to reach at least some degree of completion. By 1980 there was a general assumption that Kinabatangan floodplain would represent one of the major new, permanent agricultural development regions in Malaysia. There was talk of building a flood-prevention dam near Deramakot. Thus, lower Kinabatangan was omitted from the list of areas surveyed under a state-wide faunal survey conducted in 1979–1981. Misgivings over abandoning the lower Kinabatangan region to near-total conversion to agriculture built up in the subsequent years. For a start, land-suitability maps prepared in the 1970s already showed that lower Kinabatangan was a complex patchwork of soils, ranging from sites ideal for permanent cultivation, to tracts deemed unsuitable for any kind of exploitative use due to constant waterlogging and periodic floods.

In 1983 a state-wide survey showed that the greatest numbers of crocodiles in Sabah were at that time in lower Kinabatangan. From field surveys conducted during 1985–1987, it became apparent that the greatest local concentrations of Orang-utans in Malaysia, as well as of elephants and Oriental Darters (*Anhinga melanogaster*), were also in the heavily logged forests of lower Kinabatangan. It was also during this period that claims by many biologists of the time, that heavily logged forests were 'useless' for wildlife, were found to

be erroneous. However, by this time the process of issuing titles to land for the development of plantations throughout most of lower Kinabatangan was well advanced.

It seemed that the arguments for conservation were sound, but had come too late. By 1989, however, several things had changed. Prospects for nature tourism in Sabah were becoming more apparent to the government. A new State Wildlife Department had been established in 1988, and placed under the purview of a ministry where environment and tourism portfolios had been combined. In 1989 the new permanent secretary of the ministry felt that arguing for a Kinabatangan wildlife sanctuary on the basis of tourism, rather than conservation, might be attractive to the government. The idea was to preserve forest cover along the banks of the lower Kinabatangan River, thereby retaining habitat for breeding populations of all the native wildlife species, while at the same time allowing visitors to see wildlife from boats – an opportunity that was clearly unique in Malaysia.

The idea was a good one, but the initial proposal for the sanctuary attracted much opposition. Many thousands of landowners and would-be landowners were affected by the proposal. Some native Orang Sungai people were worried that their ancestral lands would be taken from them, while oil-palm plantation developers expressed concern over losing potential development land. Land speculators and brokers added to the voices against the plan for a Kinabatangan Wildlife Sanctuary. Even some conservation biologists felt that the wildlife sanctuary would be of limited value because of the degraded nature of the forest, and its long, thin shape with plenty of access for encroachers.

Eventually a compromise was reached and approved by the Sabah government in 1994. The resulting wildlife sanctuary was formed by retaining more than 20 blocks of forest, separated by rivers, plantations, roads and villages. By good fortune, tracts of forest that had been retained to protect the limestone outcrops and their swiftlet caves provided a

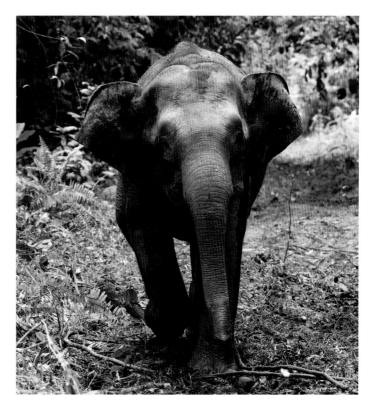

Above: A playful young Bornean elephant, or Pygmy Elephant (Elephas maximus borneensis), in the Kinabatangan Wildlife Sanctuary.

Top: A bull Bornean elephant bathes in the Kinabatangan River to keep cool and to reach its favourite food – succulent riverside grass.

Opposite: A small herd of elephants crossing Kinabatangan River, using their trunks as snorkels.

large rivers in Southeast Asia have been a focus for settlement and expansion of human societies. The ability of certain varieties of rice to grow in flooded land was one of the contributory reasons why rice expanded as the major food crop throughout Southeast Asia. Equally significantly, fish have traditionally been the major protein source for many human societies in Asia, and alluvial floodplains represent productive year-round fisheries. The moist, flat and fertile tracts of floodplain soils support high productivity of nutritious natural vegetation, and accordingly are excellent habitat for large mammals, which can achieve much higher population densities here than on the leached and less fertile slopes of hills and mountain ranges. In addition, Kinabatangan floodplain is dotted with limestone outcrops that have their own natural and human history.

Trails and trips

A key attraction of Kinabatangan floodplain is the fact that one is able to see the forests and oxbow lakes from a boat. Walking is an optional extra, and some tour operators include short walks in the non-swampy forest. A visit to the Gomantong Caves involves a short forest walk, with a climb up the limestone hill for the more adventurous. By the late 1980s a few pioneering nature-tour operators were taking small groups of visitors to Sukau and the Menanggul River to see Proboscis Monkeys (a new public road had been completed linking the village to Sandakan). Visitors were captivated by the tranquillity of the Menanggul and its dark colour, resulting from its flow from Gomantong through a peat swamp, as well as by the abundance of bird life and the Proboscis Monkeys. In the olden days, hardy Orang Sungai and natives from what is now the southern Philippines must have not only risked their lives collecting swiftlet nests from the caves, but also spent days ferrying the nests on rafts or dugout canoes down the Menanggul River to Melapi (now Sukau) to await the arrival of traders from Sulu.

stronger basis for the wildlife sanctuary proposal. Kinabatangan Wildlife Sanctuary was established over the period 1989–2004 by a bold state government, despite opposition from thousands of would-be landowners and speculators. The argument, ridiculed by many in 1989, that the sanctuary would provide a new nature-tourism destination at the expense of only some swampy lands marginal for cultivation, has proven correct. Nowhere else in Asia can you be guaranteed to see an array of native wildlife while sitting in a boat.

Significance

The Kinabatangan is Sabah's largest river, with a total catchment size of nearly a quarter of the state's land area. The lowest parts flow through the floodplain, where often-muddy waters overflow the banks during rainy periods, bringing immediate damage, but longer term fertility to the swampy, oxygen-starved soils.

Kinabatangan floodplain contains examples of a habitat type that is now extremely rare: natural vegetation on seasonally flooded alluvium. Starting some thousands of years ago, the alluvial floodplains of

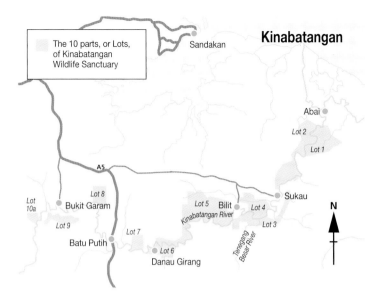

Floodplains are not a stable ecosystem. The interplay of changing water volume, speed of water flow, and attrition and redeposition of sediments, results in the river's course changing slowly but inevitably. There are more than a dozen oxbow lakes (known locally as *danau*) in the Kinabatangan floodplain, the remnants of former river bends, cut off by natural erosion and deposition of riverside silt. Some of the oxbow lakes retain thin water-channel connections to the main Kinabatangan River, making them accessible by small boats.

A few of the lakes are still quite deep, but most are in the process of slowly filling with silt and becoming covered with sedges and small trees. On the north side of the Kinabatangan, opposite the Tenegang Besar River halfway between Sukau and Bilit villages, for example, is a small oxbow lake that was a bend in the main river until, according to old residents, a great flood cut through the bend during one night in around 1952. For some reason this lake, which was almost never visited, filled up quickly, but other such lakes seem to have remained barely changed for more than 50 years. A research and training centre has been established at Danuau Girang, while visits to the lakes near Abai, Sukau, Bilit and Batu Putih are included in some nature tours.

Left: *A male and female Proboscis Monkey walk through mangrove forest on stilt roots and fallen trees.*

Opposite: *Smooth-coated Otters on the lower Kinabatangan riverbank.*

Cave swiftlets, bats and limestone caves

A genus of small birds, known as cave swiftlets, and scientifically as *Aerodramus* (formerly *Collocalia*), occurs in the region between the Andaman Islands and New Caledonia. These swiftlets do not perch on branches or wires, but instead only cling on to the surfaces of caves, rocks or buildings. A prominent feature of these species is that they echolocate in the darkness of caves – they emit fast clicking sounds, and the echoes provide them with a picture of what is in front of them as they fly.

Three swiftlet species make nests in caves in Kinabatangan floodplain, and the nests of two of them are used as the main ingredient of birds' nest soup. The ingredient is the swiftlets' own saliva, which is exuded as sticky, protein-rich, translucent strands, and fashioned in the form of a tiny stretched 'handkerchief' attached to the walls of the caves, to form a pouch-like nest in which eggs are laid. The Edible-nest Swiftlet (*Aerodramus fuciphagus*) makes its nest entirely from its own, solidified saliva, while the Black-nest Swiftlet (*A. maximus*) constructs its nest from its feathers stuck together with strands of saliva.

One clean nest of the Edible-nest Swiftlet has a retail price in Chinese medicine shops of several tens of pounds sterling. Exactly how or when this saliva was first used as an edible product prized by the Chinese is unknown, but most likely there is some connection between the nests, the caves, indigenous human inhabitants of eastern Sabah and early Chinese contacts with Borneo. In the early 1400s, the Ming government of China sent out seven naval expeditions to the Southeast Asian and Indian region, led by Cheng Ho. Although it is not certain that these expeditions reached Sabah, legends exist of contacts and intermarriage on the Kinabatangan River.

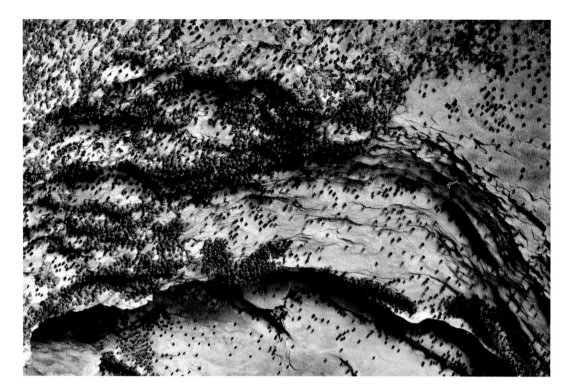

Left: Wrinkle-lipped Free-tailed Bats and White-bellied Swiftlets on the walls of Gomantong Caves.

Opposite: Wrinkle-lipped and other cave-roosting bats start to leave Gomantong Caves well before dusk, to feed on flying insects over the forest and adjacent plantations.

The largest and most famous limestone outcrop of eastern Sabah is Gomantong, 250 m (820 ft) high and the earliest still-existing nature-conservation area in Sabah. Gomantong Forest Reserve was established in 1925, to secure habitat surrounding the swiftlet nest caves, at a time when the government struggled to raise revenue, and did so in part by taxation of the sale of the edible nests. Bod Tai, Keruak, Materis and Pangi, all of them smaller limestone hills in Kinabatangan floodplain, were established as forest reserves in 1930 for the same reason. Thus, these nature-conservation areas were originally intended to secure economic interests in Sabah.

John Hunt's 1812 report (see page 101) provides a fascinating glimpse into the Sabah birds' nest trade two centuries ago. The volume of birds' nests harvested from Gomantong Caves nowadays is roughly 3½ tons per year for white nests, and about 7 tons per year for black nests. Assuming that the bulk of nests harvested in the early 1800s and now, two centuries later, come from Gomantong and pass through Sandakan, then annual production of white nests has remained remarkably similar, while production of black nests has declined, but by less than 50 per cent.

Seemingly, the retention of forest around limestone caves and the government policy of regulating harvesting of nests at Gomantong has had the desired outcome of preserving swiftlet populations in the Kinabatangan region. In Gomantong the nests are harvested according to an organized schedule that allows two harvests each year without ending up in the extinction of the birds. One harvest is done just before the bulk of the swiftlets have nearly completed making their nests and before any eggs are laid. The swiftlets then construct a replacement nest, which is used to lay eggs and rear the young. After the young are able to fly, some seven or eight months after the initial nest construction, the used nests are harvested. Methods of collecting the nests were developed hundreds of years ago and remain much the same today. They involve using long, flexible ladders and ropes, long poles and tiny lamps.

Gomantong is the roosting and breeding site of an estimated two million bats of 27 species (with the Wrinkle-lipped Free-tailed Bat, *Tadarida plicata*, in the clear majority), and one million or so swiftlets. In the late afternoon the swiftlets, which feed on the wing during the day on tiny insects, return to the caves to roost overnight. Just before dusk the bats emerge from the caves in swirling masses, to feed on nocturnal flying insects.

With such large numbers of swiftlets and bats passing in and out of the caves daily, and daily deaths of both these animal types from old age and disease, not surprisingly predators and scavengers have evolved to take advantage of the guaranteed food moving in and out of the caves. In the air, these include Bat Hawks (*Macheiramphus alcinus*), as well as other raptors and even hornbills. Positioning themselves on bushes around the cave mouths, even snakes snatch emerging bats. Most obvious of all, however, are the myriads of cockroaches, scutigerid centipedes and other specialist invertebrates that live permanently inside the caves, feeding on fallen bats and swiftlets, and their infants and eggs.

Other animals

For naturalists, lower Kinabatangan's combination of a large river, riverbank alluvial terraces, smaller tributaries and lakes, and the floodplain offers a unique opportunity to view wildlife from a boat. There is hardly a need to walk, but if you choose to do so, it will be on flat land, rather than on the endless slopes that predominate in much of Sabah.

Lower Kinabatangan is most famous for the prospect of daytime sightings of large mammals such as Proboscis Monkeys, Orang-utans and elephants, and resident waterbirds such as Oriental Darters and Storm's Storks. For birders, lower Kinabatangan probably offers the best prospect, along with Danum Valley, for a sighting of the elusive Bornean Ground Cuckoo (*Carpococcyx radiceus*), a specialist of flat forest land. A boat cruise at night offers the chance to see the Buffy Fish-owl (*Ketupa ketupu*) and Flat-headed Cats (*Prionailurus planiceps*).

For keen visitors who spend some of their time on land in the lower Kinabatangan, there are other distinctive, much smaller wildlife species of interest. These include the Plain Pygmy Squirrel (*Exilisciurus exilis*), one of the world's smallest squirrels, which periodically makes fast runs along branches and

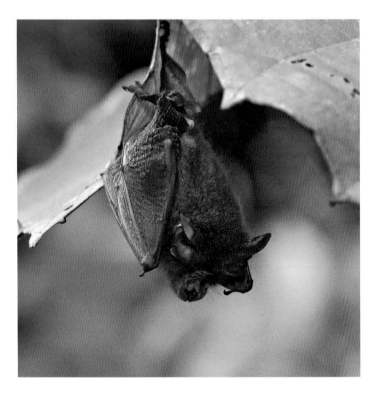

Above: One of several horseshoe bats (Rhinolophus spp.) – some species roost in caves, others in hollow trees and under large leaves.

Above right: Bat Hawk, a specialist raptor which feeds almost entirely on bats, caught on the wing as they fly out of or into their cave roosting sites.

tree-trunks in search of food. Other small creatures that can be observed where there is tree cover include 5-cm (2-in) long pill millipedes, walking on the leaf litter, and gliding lizards (*Draco* spp). In addition to the bats and swiftlets, the limestone hills support several endemic species of plant and snail.

Barring major disasters, the majority of wild species found in lower Kinabatangan can probably survive in the long term with protection and, where necessary, restoration of forest habitats. For a few species, however, the fact that the protected areas are fragmented, individually of small size and lacking old, large trees, will increasingly present problems to their long-term survival. The chief concerns relate to elephants, which are forced to travel through plantations and villages to move from one area to another; Orang-utans, which are confined to forest blocks that may not supply enough food, and which will suffer from inbreeding if they cannot move to seek mates in other blocks; and hornbills, which need holes in old, mature trees for nesting.

A major challenge now and for the coming years is to re-establish, as far as is reasonably possible, continuity of natural vegetation from the mouth of the Kinabatangan River up to the central parts of Sabah, as well as an overall increase and improvement in forest

Above: Plain Pigmy Squirrel, most often seen running quickly on the trunks and branches of trees in lowland and swamp forests.

Top left: Storm's Stork, a rare forest-dwelling bird of the lowlands, sometimes seen in oil palm plantations.

Top right: Bornean Ground Cuckoo, a very rare bird, occurring only in forests in Borneo, and almost entirely in the extreme lowlands of river valleys and floodplains.

cover. In practice, complete continuity will never be possible, especially where there are old established villages such as Sukau and where there are major public roads. For large wildlife species, more connectivity of natural habitats is better than less, but complete connectivity of closed canopy forest is not essential. In fact, we tend to assume that wild species are less tenacious or adaptable than they are in reality. Just one mature male of an animal such as an elephant or Orang-utan, crossing a river or road once in a decade, can help to spread and maintain genetic diversity in small populations.

Plant life

Due to a combination of commercial logging, along with fire escaping from plantations developed in the 1980s and '90s, attempts to grow oil palm in swamps, and excess water entering the remaining forest from drainage canals built in the plantations, much of the original Kinabatangan floodplain forest has gone or is badly degraded. Nevertheless, lower Kinabatangan is now the only large river system in Southeast Asia where there are still significant tracts of natural forest along the banks, as well as in the freshwater swamps behind the banks. Seasonally flooded forests such as this are known as *varzea* in the Amazon, but there is no local equivalent name in the Malaysian languages.

A combination of natural regeneration and active reforestation efforts since the late 1990s, by local and non-governmental groups assisted by the Sabah Forestry Department, has set the floodplain on a slow course towards a more ecologically balanced pattern of land use. One of the lessons learned in the active restoration work is that floods are likely to kill the majority of seedlings planted on flood-prone lands, even those of specialist floodplain tree species. Tall seedlings and cuttings of certain tree species can be used for active restoration work, but this is laborious and costly work. For the most flood-prone sites, just allowing a natural vegetation-regeneration process to

take place may represent the best decision.

As is the case with most kinds of research into tropical rainforest ecosystems, each new observation and conclusion tends to raise as many new questions as answers. Up to the 1980s flood-prone lands in Kinabatangan bore quite a diversity of tree species, with only the very wettest sites supporting stands of one species. The question arises, how did the original forest develop on flood-prone land in the face of flooding events, but with unpredictable timing and severity? Some people believe that there are more or worse floods in Kinabatangan now than in the past, but this seems unlikely. Old records reveal that there were indeed periodic massive floods before the era of logging and plantations. What seems to have changed – although there are inadequate records to be sure – is that flood waters tend to rise more quickly than in the past, and that their timing is less clustered around the northern monsoon season than it was.

The redevelopment of a diverse forest on the Kinabatangan would probably take at least a century, even with human assistance in replanting. Possibly, random periods of several contiguous years without a major flood would provide the best 'window of opportunity', when the most flood-sensitive species could be re-established through active planting, and by dispersion of seeds by fruit bats, birds and wind.

Oil palm grown on the floodplain requires drainage to keep the plantation land from waterlogging and to channel away waters during floods. This deliberate redirection of floodwater out of plantations and on to the remaining forest areas probably tends to support a process whereby flood-tolerant tree species continue to thrive, and these hardy species may tend to suppress the re-establishment of a diverse array of trees and strangling figs.

Owners of land in Kinabatangan floodplain who wish to aid long-term conservation of wildlife species that require native tree cover can make one or more of several possible contributions. One is to abandon the most waterlogged and flood-prone areas to nature, and even block some of the drainage canals. The other is to

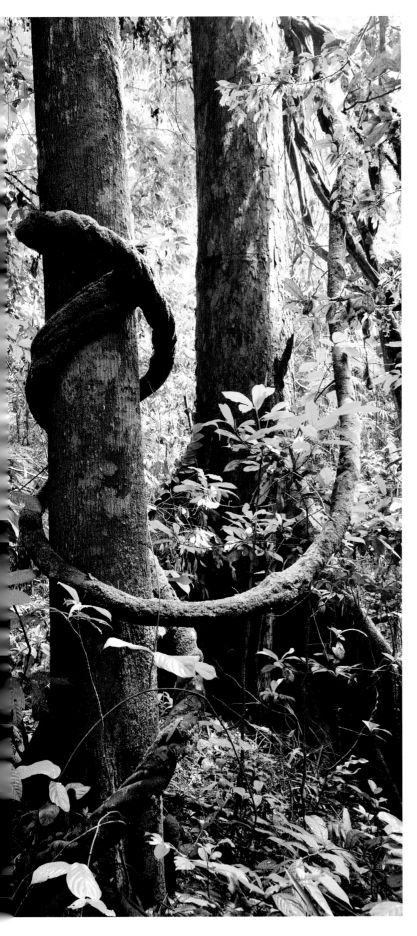

replant parts of their land with native floodplain tree species. It is possible that, in the long term, they might not regret such action, at times when palm-oil prices are low and wood prices are high, and they have the opportunity to cut some of the trees and sell the wood. Another option – perhaps at the next replanting of over-mature oil palms – is to allocate relatively small areas of flood-free land, carefully chosen in the context of the overall Kinabatangan floodplain landscape, to restore a diverse tree cover. Oil-palm plantation owners who are members of the Roundtable on Sustainable Palm Oil leave old palms along the banks of small rivers when they replant with young palms at 25-year intervals. It is anticipated that this practice will promote the natural regeneration of wild plants along the rivers.

Access

Access to the riverside and floodplain forests is via one of the Kinabatangan riverside villages, usually either Batu Putih (on the Sandakan–Lahad Datu highway, next to the bridge over the Kinabatangan River), or Bilit or Sukau. All three villages can be reached by road, within two hours' drive from Sandakan. Another option is to go to Abai village, at the mouth of the Kinabatangan River, which has no road access and is instead accessible by boat from Sandakan via the mangrove forests. Gomantong can be reached via a junction off the Sukau–Sandakan road. There are several tour operators to each of these access points, as well as homestay accommodation in all the villages.

Left: Extreme lowland dipterocarp forest, a natural habitat once widespread but now confined to small patches inside protected areas. This view shows two characteristic features of dipterocarp forests: buttresses on the tree-trunk behind and old woody lianas.

Kinabatangan Floodplain

The approach by land to Kinabatangan floodplain has little to attract attention. The last hour on the road before arriving at one of the Kinabatangan riverside villages is one never-ending landscape of oil-palm plantations. Oil palm has received unduly bad press in recent years. Developing nations change much more rapidly than long-established ones. It just happens that oil palm is the most profitable form of land use in the lowlands of the equatorial tropics in our current period in history. It yields far more edible oil per hectare per year than any other crop. So, what we see is oil palm. In fact, palm trees are not particularly unattractive. The feeling that it would be better for wildlife to still have tropical rainforest is what tends to make us critical.

Arrival in a riverside village seems sudden. You notice houses, a few people, small gardens and parked cars, then realize that you are near the bank of the Kinabatangan River. The wooden riverside platform and the boat into which you are about to step bob almost imperceptibly. Somehow, the quiet, silty power of the constantly slow-flowing water is mesmerizing. You are drawn to watch it and the movement of its flow. The only immediate distractions are debris going with the flow, small boats, distant voices of people and whatever you can see on the opposite bank.

Stepping into the small boat is the beginning of a small but potent adventure. Wear a peaked hat and perhaps a small towel to protect your head if it is sunny and hot. Wear a lightweight raincoat if it is cloudy and threatening to rain. A lifejacket is an essential precaution. A small knapsack or waterproof bag is the only other basic item needed, together with camera, binoculars, valuables and drinking water.

The constant growl of the boat's outboard engine obscures other sounds. You must rely on sight. Scan the forests along the riverbanks, and the sky above, and also the boatman, who is likely to spot wildlife quicker than visitors. Look out for Estuarine Crocodiles (*Crocodylus porosus*), either in the water or more likely visible resting on a mud bank. A quick, fast-flying flash of blue and orange is most likely a Stork-billed Kingfisher. Large black-and-white birds will probably be Oriental Pied Hornbills, the riverine specialist among Sabah's eight hornbill species. A large, dark bird with a long, thin neck will be an Oriental Darter, champion among all the freshwater fish-eating birds in diving underwater to pierce its prey with its sharp beak. The darter is commonly first spotted perched on a riverside tree or snag, with wings outstretched to dry.

Three monkey species live in the riverine forests: the Proboscis Monkey, Long-tailed Macaque and Silvered Leaf-monkey. From a distance the Proboscis Monkey can be identified by its distinct combination of reddish coat and whitish tail and legs, and heavy movements. The large nose becomes obvious at close quarters. Some groups consist of a single, large dominant male with a harem of females and offspring, while others comprise all-male 'bachelor' groups. Why Proboscis Monkeys are almost entirely confined to forests near open water remains a mystery. In similar numbers to the Proboscis Monkey are the Long-tailed Macaques. They are smaller and more slender than the Proboscis Monkey, greyish-brown in colour, and feed on a mix of plant and animal matter.

The rarest monkey species is the Silvered Leaf-monkey. In lower Kinabatangan about half of these monkeys are reddish in colour, rather than the more normal grey, and at a glance may be confused with the Red Leaf-monkey or even the Bornean Orang-utan. The lucky visitor may spot an Orang-utan, most likely feeding on the fruits of a riverside Tangkol (*Ficus racemosa*) tree.

If wild elephants are in the vicinity, the boatman will probably know where to find them. The problem will be that all other tour boats locally will also know about them, and there will be a rush to see them. Whatever anyone else says or does, do not go on to land to obtain a better view. Apart from stressing the elephants, accidents can happen when noisy people mix with stressed large mammals in tall grass on soft, muddy soils.

Watch the sun go down and the riverside vegetation becoming darker. Enjoy the change in feeling that the approach of dark brings. It is quieter, cooler, damper, more peaceful. The flow of the river remains the dominant presence, although we can barely see it.

Opposite: *Stork-billed Kingfisher.* **Right:** *Orang-utan feeding on riverside figs* (Ficus racemosa). **Below:** *Estuarine Crocodile.*

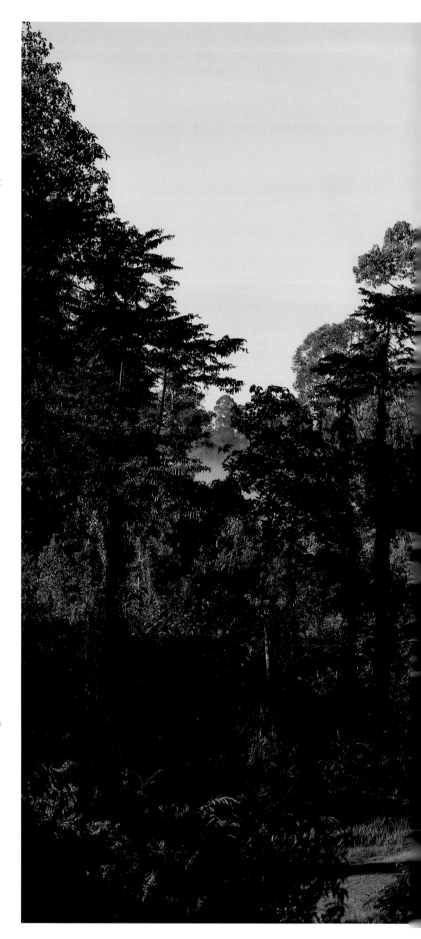

Tabin Wildlife Reserve

The story of Tabin provides a historical context that normally remains undescribed for rainforest protected areas. The old name for the Dent Peninsula, representing the entire coastline between what are now the towns of Sandakan and Lahad Datu in eastern Sabah, was Unsang. Alexander Dalrymple of the East India Company noted in his 1771 book, *A Plan for Extending the Commerce of this Kingdom: And of the East-India-Company*, that 'the east part of Unsang abounds with wild elephants'.

In the early 19th century, when the Spanish had long consolidated their colonization of what is now the central and northern Philippines, and the Dutch and British were apportioning their power in what are now the western parts of Indonesia and Malaysia, an indigenous system of trade was flourishing in the region between Mindanao (the southern Philippines) and the Straits of Makassar. The eastern half of what is now Sabah provided a range of resources into this system, largely free from interference from the European colonial powers. These resources included camphor (from *Dryobalanops* trees abundant in the forests of Borneo), rattan canes, beeswax, rhino horns, tortoiseshell (from Hawksbill Turtles that nested on sandy island beaches), swiftlet nests (from caves) and dried sea cucumbers (from shallow seas), the latter two ingredients in Chinese soups.

The majority of published texts from before the 20th century come from entirely European sources, but research presented in the publications of James Warren on Sulu, Iranun and Balangingi provides fascinating glimpses of that era, including statements made by indigenous people. The statement of a man named Mr Ayer in 1851 is a starting point to understanding the situation at Unsang before the

advent of British influence over what is now Sabah. In 1845 Ayer was a crew member of a boat sailing from the town of Biwa on the island of Sumbawa, Indonesia, to collect a cargo of dried sea cucumbers and beeswax. (Lacking native wax-producing bees, the Spanish traded in wax obtained from wild bees in Borneo and the southern Philippines in order to manufacture high-quality candles for churches in their colonies in the Americas. This Manila-Acapulco galleon trade started in 1565 and was ended in 1815 during the Mexican War of Independence, but by then the beeswax trade had other buyers.)

A major centre of trade for eastern Sabah by the early 19th century was the sultanate of Sulu, based on Jolo island, 200 km (124 miles) from Unsang. As in the case of most trading empires of the past two millennia, the use of slave labour was an integral part of the Sulu sultanate's system. Major procurers of slaves included the Iranun (also known as Illanun) people, who originated in Mindanao in the southern Philippines, but who had slave-raiding bases at Tempasuk on the west coast of Sabah, and the Tungku River on the south side of the Dent Peninsula.

A few kilometres inland up the Tungku River, which has its source at the Tabin Wildlife Reserve boundary, is the location of a small indigenous minority group known as the Bagahak, which up to the present day retains some elements of the economy formerly practised by Sabah east-coast riverine natives, including planting of non-irrigated rice, hunting of wild animals for meat and burial in hardwood coffins with traditional buffalo-head motifs. The Iranun slave raiders probably chose Tungku as a base because it was next to the sea, yet with an existing community that could supply foods and forest products, only one or two days' travel using wind or slave oarsmen to Jolo.

An Iranun slave-trading fleet of 20 boats led by Raja Muda captured Ayer's boat in 1845, some 1,500 km (932 miles) south of Tungku, then cruised for another year, capturing a further 30 or more boats, mainly in the Celebes Sea. Ayer was taken via Sibat (now called Sahabat, and central to a large oil-palm plantation managed by the Federal Land Development Authority, immediately east of Tabin Wildlife Reserve), to Raja Muda's house at Makawau (now spelled Makuao), just west of Tungku. He was then sold as an oarsman to another slave raider from Jolo, and thence to another trader from Sambas in Indonesian Borneo; in 1851 he was finally manumitted by a Mr Meldrum of Labuan, who sent him to work at Menggatal, just north of present-day Kota Kinabalu. A flotilla of British boats destroyed Tungku in 1852, but after refuging in nearby forest, the survivors rebuilt the settlement. Following the signing of an agreement between British interests and the Sultan of Sulu in 1878, the British steam gunboat HMS *Kestrel* visited Tungku in 1879, finally destroying the slave-raiding forts and vessels.

Within the years after 1881, when Queen Victoria granted a charter allowing the British North Borneo Company to operate in what is now Sabah, it became apparent that the anticipated riches of gold did not exist. Alternative forms of economic activity and sources of income generation had to be found in order to support the company's operations. During the 1880s the company issued leases to over 230,000 ha (568,342 acres) of land to various British, Dutch and German interests, with the possibility of planting tobacco on rich alluvial soils being the main attraction.

Not many of the leased areas were in fact planted with tobacco, although one of those early tobacco plantations survived until 1960 on the lower Segama River. Of particular interest to the story of Tabin, however, is that a lease was issued for 4,000 ha (9,884 acres) of land straddling both sides of the lower Segama River at Litang, this land eventually being acquired by the Guthrie Corporation, one of the pioneering rubber and oil-palm planting companies in Malaysia. In around 1950, partly planted with rubber, the land was acquired by River Estates Ltd. In 1961 the company started planting oil palm, naming the plantation Tomanggong. The extent of oil palm at Tomanggong was gradually increased by further local land acquisition after Sabah's independence through Malaysia in 1963.

Following the introduction of bulldozers into British North Borneo in 1950, and the potential that this allowed for cutting and hauling huge logs from previously inaccessible forests far from the sea and roads, the administration legislated much of the central and eastern regions of Sabah as forest reserves. The intention was to allow long-term government control over what were at that time unclaimed and unexploited natural forests for the purpose of timber production.

The area now comprising Tabin Wildlife Reserve was initially secured as Silabukan Forest Reserve (140,640 ha/347,529 acres in 1957) and Lumerau Forest Reserve (75,112 ha/185,605 acres in 1959). The logging part of the River Estates business expanded in 1957 with the first commercial logging in Lumerau. Chainsaws and bulldozer tractors were introduced here in 1961. Narrow-gauge railways were built to bring logs from the area now occupied by the northern part of Tabin, and the last of these was closed in 1981. The southern fringes of Tabin were logged by the Kennedy Bay Timber company in the 1960s. The bulk of Tabin was still old-growth rainforest by 1970.

In the meantime, in the early 1950s some ethnic Tidung people had moved from their community at the mouth of the Labuk River, north of Sandakan, to a part of the lower Segama River named Teluk Bayur, and founded a village there named Kampung Tidung. Attracted by the income-generating job opportunities offered in forestry work, some moved to Dagat near the lower Tabin River, where the River Estates logging camp and sawmill were situated. This is the origin of the small village of Dagat, now the only native community on the boundary of Tabin.

The tallest peak in Tabin is Mount Hatton, named after Frank Hatton, who was appointed by the Chartered Company to seek natural resources of value. Hatton never reached this hill, but was killed in 1883 at the age of 21 in a shooting incident that occurred on the Segama River.

Geological investigations were made periodically in the Tabin area by Dutch and British petroleum interests, commencing in 1913 and continuing to the 1950s; they were summarised in a 1951 report, *Geology of the Colony of North Borneo*, by Max Reinhard and Eduard Wenk. One feature of interest to the geologists was mud volcanoes, which consist of outpourings of salty, kaolin-rich, greyish mud, expelled by methane gas, and were believed in the early 20th century to have been linked to the presence of petroleum. Two large mud volcanoes (about 180 m/590 ft in diameter) and several small ones occur in Tabin, one being readily accessible from the Tabin headquarters. A 4-km (2½-mile) long, 100-m (328-ft) high limestone outcrop on the south side of the lower Tabin River contains about 35 small caves, probably formed by an underground river before geological uplift.

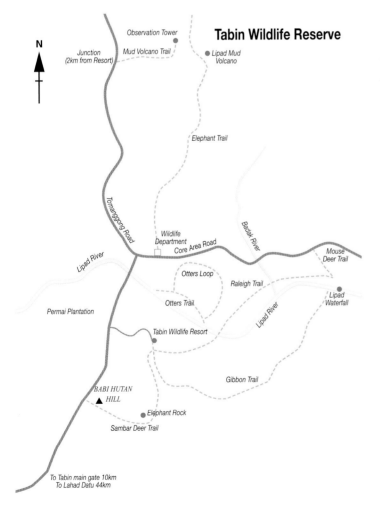

Tabin Wildlife Reserve

Significance

Tabin Wildlife Reserve (120,915 ha/298,787 acres; Tabin for short, established in 1984) is located in the middle of the Dent Peninsula of eastern Sabah. It is largely surrounded by oil-palm plantations, but it is contiguous with mangrove and nipa forest to the north, and thus represents the only remaining large tract of forest stretching from the coast to the hills in eastern Borneo. All but about 8,500 ha (21,003 acres) of Tabin's forests, mostly in the hilly centre known as Mount Hatton Protection Forest Reserve (highest peak 570 m/1,870 ft), were logged commercially between 1958 and 1989, but have since been left to regenerate.

The fact that most of Tabin's forests have been logged, and that logging continued to be allowed for five years after the date of the reserve's establishment based on logging licences already issued, reflects a significant change in perception in the global conservation community over recent decades. Until the late 20th century there was a prevailing view that only old-growth, undisturbed tropical rainforests should be eligible for inclusion in 'protected areas', in bizarre contrast to the fact that 'protected areas' in Europe represented largely man-made landscapes and habitats. The logic of this view, if held rigorously, meant that only small patches of old-growth forest would remain in the longer term, while all forests that had been disturbed by logging (in other words, most forests in Borneo) would remain available for eventual conversion to plantations and other non-forest land use.

Fortunately, some far-sighted individuals recognized in the early 1980s the risks associated with the prevailing conservationist view, and argued successfully that large tracts of damaged rainforest are as important as small tracts of undisturbed forest. Damaged rainforests regenerate naturally with time, and provide a mosaic of forest structure that can sustain almost all lowland animal and plant species, and actually benefit a few species, notably large mammals. When in 1983 the government of Sabah decided to allocate about half of the state as permanent forest reserve, Tabin was proposed as a conservation area for large mammals, as large-scale conversion of forests to plantations was underway in eastern Sabah.

Trails and trips

The majority of travel in Tabin for short-stay visitors is by vehicle on rough gravel roads. Beyond the headquarters area next to the Lipad River there are two roads, one of 10 km (6 miles) heading east into the reserve, the other going northwards to Tomanggong oil-palm estate. From the latter, the Lipad mud volcano can be reached via a 800-m (½-mile) walk on a muddy trail. There is also a short walking trail to a waterfall on the Lipad River. Generally, walking into the forest is not encouraged due to a small risk of unexpectedly encountering elephants.

Animal life

Tabin supports a typical Bornean lowland forest fauna, with 82 recorded mammal species, about 260 birds, 46 frogs, 42 freshwater fish, 24 termites, 150 ants and more than 240 butterflies. Due in part to the good visibility afforded by regenerating logged forest, Tabin is a prime location for birdwatching. Oriental Pied Hornbills, Rhinoceros Hornbills (*Buceros rhinoceros*), Black Hornbills (*Anthracoceros malayanus*), Bushy-crested Hornbills (*Anorrhinus galeritus*) and White-crowned Hornbills (*Aceros comatus*) are often seen from the western perimeter road of Tabin, while Helmeted Hornbills (*Rhinoplax vigil*) and Wreathed Hornbills (*Rhyticeros undulatus*) may be heard or seen from the eastern end of the road inside the reserve.

Left: A family group of Bushy-crested Hornbills.

Above: The iconic Rhinoceros Hornbill, often seen at Tabin on the forest edge.

Opposite: White-crowned Hornbill, a species of the low, dense forest, and most active just before dusk.

Above: Leopard Cat, the most common wild cat at Tabin, often seen after dark as it hunts for rats in oil-palm plantations.

Above right: Bearded Pig, a species which has adapted to the rainforest and oil-palm plantation interface.

Right: Southern Pig-tailed Macaque, another mammal which has adapted to the forest and plantation landscape.

Opposite top: A Water Monitor, Malaysia's largest lizard.

Opposite below: Sumatran Rhinoceros, Malaysia's rarest species.

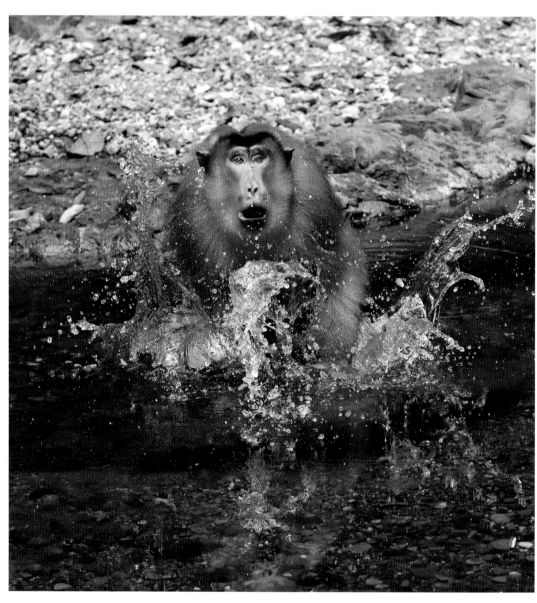

As the main access road forms a transect between forest and oil-palm plantation, species that thrive at forest edges can often be seen. These include Water Monitors (*Varanus salvator*) and pig-tailed macaques during the daytime, and Bearded Pigs, civets and Leopard Cats (*Prionailurus bengalensis*) at night. Tabin has an estimated 300 elephants, some of which visit the roadside periodically. The original main aim of Tabin was to provide a sanctuary for the last known breeding population of the Sumatran Rhinoceros in Borneo. Now that the species is on the verge of extinction, international collaboration, captive breeding and advanced reproductive technology are seen as the only possible ways to prevent its extinction.

*Right: Wild bee (*Apis dorsata*) nests in a Mengaris (*Koompassia excelsa*) tree.*

Plant life

The plant life seen around the Tabin headquarters by most visitors consists of regenerating logged forest, which is dominated by 'pioneer' tree species that started life during the logging era of the early 1980s. Common trees visible along the roadside include Laran (*Neolamarkia cadamba*), Sesendok (*Endospermum diadenum*), Binuang (*Octomeles sumatrana*), bayur (*Pterospermum* spp.), Magas (*Duabanga moluccana*) and Maitap (*Neonauclea gigantea*).

A survey conducted in 1982 by the Sabah Forestry Department in the central part of Tabin in old-growth forest recorded 616 tree and woody bush species, and 72 woody liana species. The original old-growth forest of Tabin was dominated by about 40 tree species of the family Dipterocarpaceae, most notably Urat Mata Beludu (*Parashorea tomentella*), Melapi Kuning (*Shorea symingtonii*), Seraya Majau (*S. johorensis*) and Keruing Putih (*Dipterocarpus caudiferus*). Other large tree species of special interest in Tabin include Belian, or Borneo Ironwood (*Eusideroxylon zwageri*), Merbau (*Intsia palembanica*), once widespread in the eastern lowlands of Sabah but now very rare, and Red Camphorwood (*Dryobalanops beccarrii*) on sandy soils inland from the mangroves. About 130 species of ground herb have been collected from Tabin's forests. Several plant species characteristic of mangroves occur on the fringes of the mud volcanoes.

Access

Tabin is accessible by road from Lahad Datu town. Initially there are about 22 km (14 miles) of sealed road (the highway to Tungku and the Federal Land Development Authority oil-palm plantation), followed by about 28 km (17 miles) of gravel road, mainly through oil-palm plantations, to the Tabin headquarters site. The headquarters is next to the Lipad River, which flows out of Tabin to the Segama River. A more time-consuming option, by boat, is to visit Dagat village on the north side of Tabin, which has no road access.

Maliau Basin

Maliau Basin was provisionally designated in 1982 as a conservation area within the Sabah Foundation logging concession. In 1988 a multi-institution expedition was organized and conducted in Maliau Basin, arranged by Sabah Foundation and WWF-Malaysia, for which a large group of researchers was flown by a Royal Malaysian Air Force helicopter into the centre of the basin. During a breather on a hike on the last day of the expedition, on the slopes south of Rafflesia Camp, a shard of celadon ceramic was found by luck in the course of a random dig into the soil with a *parang* (jungle knife). This site must be one of the remotest in Sabah, yet evidently someone had passed by, probably more than 100 years before, and for some reason had left part of a broken pot there. The expedition report advocated formal protection for Maliau Basin.

Unknown to the expedition organizers, the government had granted a coal-prospecting licence to an Australian mining company, which had already gained evidence that commercial coal deposits lay within the basin. Remarkably, the government of Sabah then commissioned a detailed independent environmental impact assessment of Maliau Basin, which concluded that even the most environmentally friendly mining techniques would be incompatible with conservation, because the main feature of the basin was its unique wilderness value. This left the government with a stark choice. The conservation option was chosen, and in 1997 Maliau Basin was 'upgraded' to Protection Forest Reserve status, while in 1999 further protection was afforded when the basin was made a cultural heritage site under the Cultural Heritage (Conservation) Enactment.

From time to time the idea of mining the coal is revived, most famously by a federal minister who, referring to Maliau Basin in 2000, asked if Sabahans wanted 'monkeys or gold'. Further expeditions and scientific research from the late 1990s have added to knowledge of the flora and fauna.

Significance

Maliau Basin is a giant, roughly saucer-shaped depression enclosed by a mountainous rim, about 25 km (155 miles) wide, formed by the collapse in the centre of the basin of thick layers of sedimentary rocks. This massive structure is covered by a variety of undisturbed natural forest types. Altitude ranges from 300 m (984 ft) in the south-east, where the Maliau River drains the basin into the Kuamut River, to 1,600 m (5,249 ft) at the northern rim. Special features include the Maliau Falls (a series of seven waterfalls), a gorge, the north rim escarpment, layers of coal between mudstone and sandstone, high-altitude heath forest and Lake Linumunsut. The lake is actually outside the basin, accessible only from the north, and formed by a blocked stream on the northern side of the basin. Maliau Basin is thus a remarkable geological feature of Borneo, with few visitors, yet it is accessible by road.

Trails and treks

There are no roads inside the basin, only designated walking trails and established campsites. The main Belian Camp, which has been developed as a magnificent research and visitor centre, is located outside the basin, near the confluence of the Maliau and Kuamut Rivers. The starting point for walks into the basin is Agathis Camp, from where you walk for much of the day over 7½ km (4½ miles) to Camel Trophy Camp. From the latter camp several trails exist to four additional camps, through various forest types.

Next pages: Malian Falls are spectacular seven-tiered waterfalls in the heart of Maliau Basin, with old-growth, hill dipterocarp forest lining the steep sandstone and mudstone valley walls.

Right: The rugged northern rim of Maliau Basin, showing the sharply contrasting scarp and dip slopes, and the frequent clouds which make this a high rainfall area.

Opposite top: All nine Bornean species of barbet have been recorded in Maliau Basin; this is a Golden-naped Barbet (Megalaima pulcherrima).

Opposite below: Nepenthes veitchii, one of eight species of pitcher plant in Maliau Basin, epiphytic on small trees on the white-sand plateau at the southern part of the Basin.

Maliau Basin

N

Maliau Falls
Lobah Camp
Takod Akod Fall ● ● Giluk Falls
Belian Camp
Nepenthes Camp ☐
Ginseng Camp
MB Studies Centre
Water Catchment
☐ Agathis Camp

To Keningau
Water Catchment
Security Gate
To Tawau

Animal life

Entering Maliau Basin by road from the south, there is a chance to see Tembadau (*Bos javanicus*), a species of wild cattle, grazing on the roadside at dusk or in the early morning. Interesting mammals of Maliau Basin include two squirrel species endemic to the hill forests of Borneo: the naturally very rare Tufted Ground Squirrel (*Rheithrosciurus macrotis*), mysteriously reputed to be partly carnivorous, and the Red-bellied Sculptor Squirrel (*Glyphotes simus*), whose lower incisor teeth have a concave front surface that splays outwards in a V shape, used to scrape food off the lower surfaces of large leaves.

Being at predominantly high altitude, with rugged terrain and rather poor soils, Maliau Basin is not a prime area for large mammals. Rather, its significance for animal life lies in the great diversity of smaller animals that it supports, and in the variety of

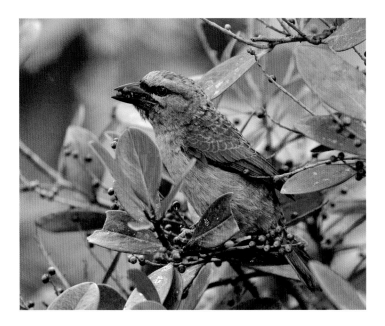

The Agathis–Camel Trophy route allows you to ascend the southern, relatively low rim of the basin through dipterocarp and lower montane forests into a large tract of unusual upland heath forest above 900 m (2,953 ft) in elevation. Camel Trophy Camp is the base for exploring the heath forest. A new species of *Rafflesia* was discovered on the slopes of Trus Madi and in Maliau Basin in the 1980s, differing from others in being a uniform warm orange colour, resembling the glowing embers of a fire. It was named *Rafflesia tengku-adlini*, in honour of the great Malaysian conservationist and adventurer Tengku D. Z. Adlin.

During dry spells the Maliau River is a clear dark reddish colour, a feature arising from humic acids produced by and washed from the very slowly decaying leaf litter beneath the heath forests and highest montane forests. After heavy rain the river may rise in depth by more than 2 m (6½ ft). The water becomes a dense chocolate-brown colour, due to rapid natural erosion of soil particles from the prevailing steep slopes.

undisturbed wild forests. Bird life here includes Bulwer's Pheasant (*Lophura bulweri*), all eight of Sabah's hornbill species, all nine Bornean barbet species and more than 20 Bornean endemic species from a variety of families.

Plant life

At a general level, three main soil types can be distinguished within and around Maliau Basin, each with characteristic associated vegetation: yellow clay soils rich in dipterocarps and palms; white sand soils that bear low, dense heath forest with epiphytes, including pitcher plants; and yellow sandy soils that have few dipterocarps or palms, but more oaks, myrtles and conifers.

The vegetation along the access road into Maliau Basin includes a wild banana species endemic to Borneo, *Musa borneensis*. Entering the basin from Agathis Camp to Camel Trophy Camp, en route you can see an unusual combination of typical lowland and hill dipterocarp forest, together with a big coniferous tree more commonly associated with sandy higher elevations, *Agathis borneensis*, with its characteristic grey-red, pockmarked bark and pearls of whitish resin, as well as several species of large dipterocarp tree.

Access

Maliau Basin is accessible via road from the Kalabakan–Sapulut highway. Visitors may start the road journey from Kota Kinabalu via Keningau passing by Sapulut, or from Tawau. Either way, the journey takes about six hours.

Semporna and Offshore Islands

Situated on the coast, with numerous offshore islands stretching between what is now Malaysia and the Philippines, Semporna was historically linked to the seafaring Bajau and Suluk communities. These communities relied on resources from the sea for food and trade, while the rich volcanic soils around Semporna would have been favourable to cultivation.

Located on the Sabah mainland near Semporna town is Bukit Tengkorak, which means 'Skull Hill'. The hill is a remnant of one of many volcanic crater rims that dot the Semporna landscape. People were making clay pots at Bukit Tengkorak several thousands of years ago, bringing wet clay up from the base of the hill to its top, most likely choosing the site to catch and funnel sea breezes through boulders to fire the clay. Most remarkably, however, flecks of obsidian, a naturally

formed glass, found at Bukit Tengkorak have been shown to probably originate from the island of New Britain, 3,500 km (2,175 miles) away at the eastern end of the island of New Guinea. Dating of charcoal at the site suggests that the obsidian has been at Bukit Tengkorak for at least 3,000 years. However, the origin and fate of the people who lived around Bukit Tengkorak, apparently for a period of about 2,000 years, is unknown.

Very few of Sabah's existing nature-conservation areas were established before 1940. In those days before roads, bulldozers and chainsaws, ideas of nature conservation tended to focus on accessible areas with special features, such as islands with rare birds, rather than on protecting large areas of dipterocarp forest. Among these islands with rare birds were two that are accessed via Semporna: Sipadan and Boheydulang, both legislated in 1933 under the Land Ordinance as bird sanctuaries.

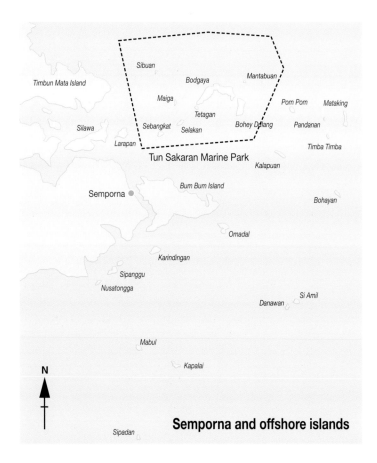

Semporna and offshore islands

Significance

Semporna is a hub for the western fringes of the Coral Triangle, a roughly triangular area of the tropical marine waters of Indonesia, Malaysia, Papua New Guinea, the Philippines, the Solomon Islands and Timor-Leste. It is a region of global significance for marine conservation. Semporna represents the Malaysian, and easiest, international route into the Coral Triangle; it includes a variety of options for divers and snorkellers.

Semporna is most significant and best known not for the town on the Sabah mainland, but for the adjacent shallow seas and offshore islands, some of which (Sebangkat, Selakan, Sibuan, Maiga, Mantabuan, Bodgaya and Boheydulong) are incorporated into the Tun Sakaran Marine Park. These islands represent at least three forms of geological origins. The last two are an extension of an old volcanic chain stretching

Opposite: Aerial view of Bodgaya island, part of the rim of an extinct volcano and home to several extremely rare plant species.

between Tawau Hills and Sulu in the southern Philippines, with the spectacular Bodgaya and Boheydulang islands being remnants of the rim of a massive extinct volcano.

These large islands support several rare wild plant species with affinities to the natural flora of the Philippines rather than Borneo. Two species, *Dracaena multiflora* and *Euphorbia lacei*, as well as the biologically ancient cycad *Cycas rumphii*, all of which grow as scrub thickets on the hilltops, look like plants from a desert rather than from a rainforest region. A 1998 botanical expedition found at least eight plant species not known from elsewhere in Borneo. Other islands surrounding the rim are raised limestone platforms, or clumps and cays of coral sand.

There is an increasing array of opportunities for diving, snorkelling and other marine activities from the various islands off Semporna, eastwards towards the border with the Philippines and southwards towards the border with Indonesia. Other islands further from Semporna town that have facilities operated by tour companies are Mabul, Kapalai, Pom Pom and Mataking. Semporna has for years been the gateway to the third geological type of island, and Malaysia's sole oceanic island, Sipadan, is iconic for its steep drop-off and fabulous diving experience.

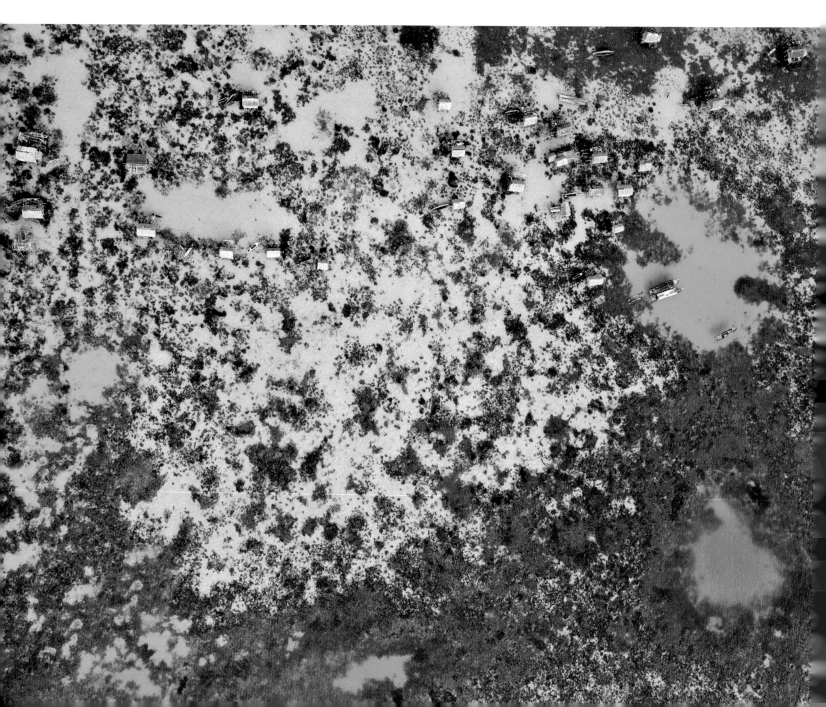

Marine life

There are at least 500 species of reef-building coral in the western ecoregion of the Coral Triangle, and about 3,000 fish species in the Coral Triangle overall, with perhaps 1,000 fish species in the Semporna region. Visitors to the marine waters off Semporna are able to see only a small portion of this richness, yet what they do see while diving or snorkelling is nonetheless as rich as any diving experience globally in terms of species diversity.

The health of the coral reefs off Semporna is variable but generally rather poor, due to various forms of damaging fishing activities over recent decades. With a combination of management of the Tun Sakaran Marine Park, stabilization of tourism, better law enforcement on marine resources and alternative livelihoods for local residents, it is hoped that the quality and abundance of marine life will increase with time. This will leave increasing temperatures, linked to global climate change, as the main challenge for sustaining marine life at Semporna.

Access

Semporna town is about one hour by road from Tawau airport. Tawau can be reached by daily flights from Kuala Lumpur or Kota Kinabalu. There are numerous tour operators offering a variety of options for visits to the offshore islands.

Above: Corals amongst the Semporna Islands.

Opposite: Houses of the Bajau Laut (Sea Gypsy) community on the coral reef of Bodgaya island.

Danum Valley and Ulu Segama Malua

As was the case in the rest of eastern Sabah, the upper (Ulu) Segama River catchment was almost entirely covered in ancient tropical rainforest until the commencement of commercial logging in the mid-20th century. The Dusun Segama people lived in small, scattered, hill-rice growing and hunting communities, which until the 19th century extended to a tributary of the upper Segama, the Danum River. In 1961 a North Borneo Forest Department officer wrote: 'A proposal was made in 1933 to reserve a considerable area in the upper Segama and Tingkayu drainages in order to protect the rhinoceros, but this proposal had to be abandoned due to opposition by timber interests.'

The initial proposal for a Danum Valley conservation area dates from 1970, when officers of the Forest Department recommended that this part of Ulu Segama be established as a 'game reserve'. Geological, soil and forest surveys done in the late 1960s to collect information for a Sabah 'Land Capability Classification', as a basis for changing Sabah's economy from logging of virgin forests to agriculture and industry, had noted the presence of 'game' (large mammal species preferred by hunters) along the Danum River. The observation was pure luck, and there is no special reason why the Danum River would have accommodated more or fewer large animals than any other river in eastern Sabah at that time. Fortunately, however, the idea stuck and provided the germ of the idea for today's Danum Valley.

A classical view that nature-conservation areas should be distinct areas with unusual features, not disturbed by resource extraction, persisted in Sabah right up to 1980. As a consequence, Sabah nearly lost

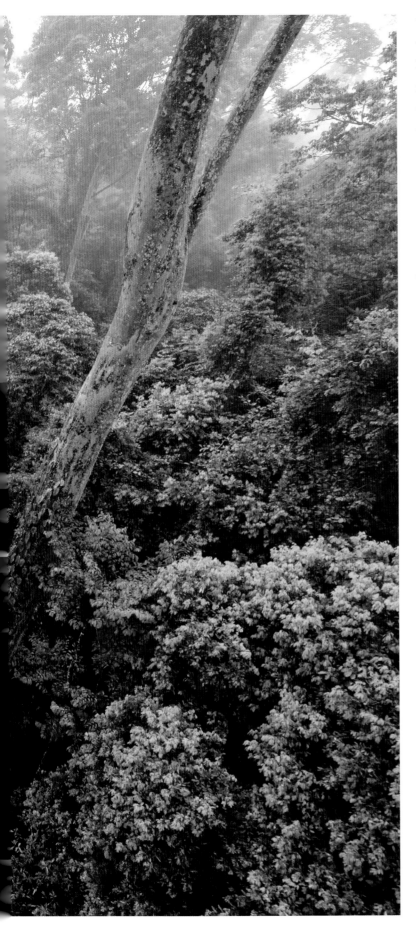

what is arguably its most compelling wildlife feature: the east-coast lowland dipterocarp forests with iconic large mammals. The classical view was given an implicit stamp of approval in the Land Capability Classification document when it was published in 1976, in which for the entire state of Sabah, only one small area (Danum Valley, initially about 15,000 ha/37,065 acres) of forest land was proposed for conservation, seemingly as an afterthought to the main text.

However, by 1976 the great majority of lowland dipterocarp forest had been logged or was already licensed for commercial logging. This historical background indicates why Sabah has no large conservation area of primary lowland dipterocarp forest in the wildlife-rich eastern lowlands of Sabah. In that year the Sabah Parks authority and WWF-Malaysia formally proposed a bigger 'Danum Valley' as a national park, basing the 43,000-ha (106,255-acre) proposed area on the extent of all remaining forest in Ulu Segama that had at that time not been logged. The logging licence holder for that area (a joint venture between Sabah Foundation and the Weyerhaeuser company) objected. The concept was reformatted and agreed in 1982 as a conservation area within the Sabah Foundation forest concession area. Danum Valley eventually became a protection forest, managed by a legislated committee, in 1995.

In the late 1990s the remainder of the forest land legislated as Ulu Segama Forest Reserve suffered a new threat, when the government of the day decided to clear the bulk of the remaining regenerating logged forests and replace them with *Acacia* plantations, to supply a proposed pulp and paper mill to be built further south, near Tawau. When the non-Sabah partners of this ill-fated project withdrew a few years later, another proposal surfaced, to plant oil palm instead of *Acacia* in the northern part of Ulu Segama. Sabah Forestry Department and non-governmental organizations resisted the idea, and in 2006 the government of Sabah decided to retain the entire Ulu Segama Forest Reserve,

Left: *The canopy walkway at Borneo Rainforest Lodge.*

and to restore the most degraded areas. Malua Forest Reserve, to the north of Danum Valley, with its rivers flowing northwards into the Kinabatangan, also heavily logged, was added to the plan, and hence the name Ulu Segama Malua was introduced.

Significance

Danum Valley is the most accessible and largest remaining example of undisturbed lowland and hill dipterocarp forest in Sabah, set in a much larger tract of regenerating logged forests, known as Ulu Segama Malua. Danum Valley and the surrounding logged forests are also the location of the most comprehensive tropical rainforest research programme in Asia. In visitor reviews, Danum Valley consistently receives among the highest ratings of any rainforest with visitor accommodation globally.

Treks and trails

Development of a field-studies centre was initiated in 1985 on the eastern edge of Danum Valley, and after three decades of support sustained by Sabah Foundation, the Royal Society and other local and international institutions, Danum Valley Field Centre is now judged to be one of the finest tropical forest

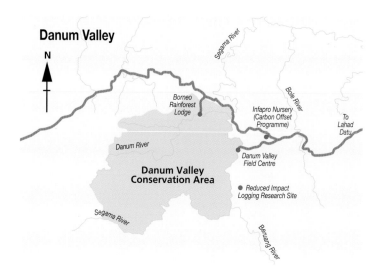

research sites and programmes in the world. Due to its beautiful and relaxing setting, quiet accommodation, and the frequent presence of enthusiastic researchers and students, Danum Valley Field Centre quickly became a magnet for adventurous tourists. In order to separate the research and education element of Danum Valley from tourism, the idea of a special visitor resort was mooted in the early 1990s. Borneo Rainforest Lodge was opened at a separate site, on the north side of Danum Valley, in 1996.

There are well-marked trails, short and long, in the vicinity of both Borneo Rainforest Lodge and Danum Valley Field Centre. Visitors can expect to see a diversity of lowland bird species, and have a fair chance of seeing a wild Orang-utan, as well as a variety of smaller mammals, especially in the primary forest around Borneo Rainforest Lodge and at Danum Valley Field Centre. A drive along the road at night-time in the logged forests provides the chance to see additional animals, including civets, deer, flying squirrels and other nocturnal mammals. Wild elephants are sometimes seen on cool, wet afternoons and mornings on the road between Silam and Danum Valley.

An interesting side visit from the road between Lahad Datu town and Danum Valley can be taken to Mount Silam, where a 33-m (108-ft) tower (Menara Kayangan, or Tower of Heaven) has been built near the top of the 884-m (2,900-ft) peak at the end of a narrow road. This small mountain is composed of ultramafic rock, which has its own unique flora. The prevailing temperature at the tower is noticeably cooler than in the surrounding lowlands, and outstanding views can be obtained of the sea and islands south of Lahad Datu.

Animal life

The great significance of logged forest for most wild organisms apart from a few very specialized species –

a heresy among many conservationists until recent years – became apparent in Sabah through the 1980s. It became especially clear in a state-wide survey of Orang-utans conducted by WWF-Malaysia with Sabah Forestry Department in 1986–1987, which (after the 1984 legislation of Sabah's permanent forest estate) showed that the species was most abundant in the logged forests of the east-coast lowlands. The 1976 Land Capability Classification maps are revealing. The areas shown to have the most fertile soils had the highest densities of Orang-utans (and elephants) up to the 1980s, while areas shown as 'best suited to forestry or conservation' had few or no Orang-utans. It appears that there is a correlation between high population densities of large vertebrate animal species and fertile soils. In contrast, rare plant species, and plant biodiversity in general, are not linked to soil fertility.

Now, together, the regenerating logged forests of Ulu Segama Malua (about 240,000 ha/593,052 acres) and the old-growth forests of Danum Valley Conservation Area (about 43,000 ha/106,255 acres) represent the single most important habitat in Malaysia for Orang-utans and elephants, as well as for a great variety of other wildlife including Red Leaf-monkeys (*Presbytis rubicunda*), and the rarely seen Bornean endemic Bay Cat (*Pardofelis badia*).

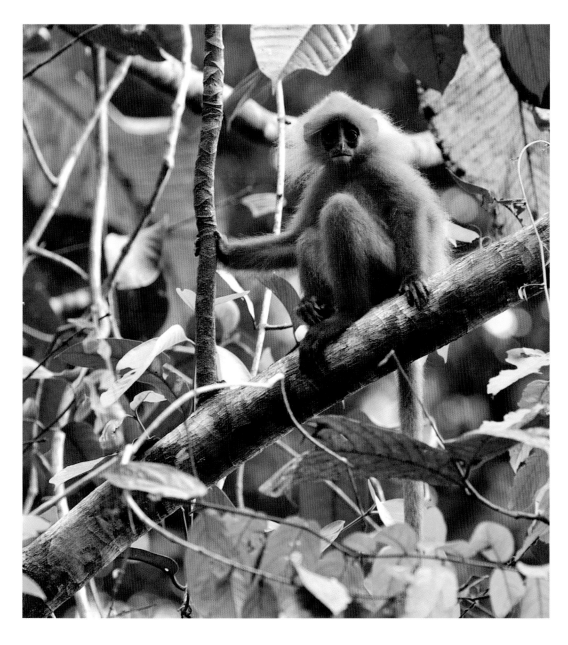

Left: The Red Leaf-monkey is a sparsely distributed and shy species, and the best chance to see it is at Danum Valley.

Plant life

The forests in and around Danum Valley are located on one of the geologically most diverse spots in Malaysia, with a mix of Triassic, Cretaceous and Tertiary rocks. As a consequence, there is a variety of forest types and a great diversity of plant life. Apart from the virgin forests within Danum Valley and on Mount Silam, most of the forests of Ulu Segama Malua have been greatly modified by commercial logging.

Parts of Ulu Segama have been very much degraded not only by past commercial logging, but also by fire during the 1983 El Niño drought, which wiped out much of the original tree cover, as well as some tree species locally. A major programme to restore the most damaged areas began in 2008, with the aims of restoring a functioning dipterocarp forest ecosystem, and the quality of habitat for rare wildlife, especially the Orang-utan. Funds for the restoration work are

sourced from the government of Sabah, several Malaysian and overseas corporations and foundations, and non-governmental organizations.

In 1992 a programme was initiated and funded by Sabah Foundation and New England Power Company of USA to explore the possibility of reducing collateral damage caused during logging operations, to the extent that more young trees would be maintained and grow to contribute to carbon-dioxide capture. Some of the early practical experiments in 'reduced impact logging' in tropical evergreen rainforests were thus conducted in Ulu Segama. Various methods were tried with the aim of reducing the adverse impacts of logging, including:

- Identifying and marking trees that had to be retained as future crop trees, with a fine imposed on the contractor for allowing them to be felled or damaged.
- Cutting lianas before felling commercial trees (on the theory that falling large trees draped with lianas tend to pull down other, adjacent trees).
- Training chainsaw operators to cut trees so that they would fall in a direction that would cause the least collateral damage.
- Prohibiting any logging activities near streams and rivers.
- Building simple drains at an angle across abandoned log-hauling trails and roads to help divert rainwater into undisturbed leaf litter rather than into streams.
- Prohibiting bulldozer operators from driving on to steep slopes and from scraping soil with the steel blade mounted at the front.
- Prohibiting felling of trees on steep slopes.
- Stopping logging operations during wet weather.

The Infapro programme, also started in in 1992, aims to actively restore logged forest with the intention of boosting carbon-dioxide capture during the forest-regeneration process, covering an area of 25,000 ha (61,776 acres). One of the lessons of this programme, not initially envisaged, is that most forests will regenerate unaided. Attention needs to be focused on cutting weedy climbing plants that suppress native tree growth, and planting of tree seedlings is needed only on the most degraded sites, which turn out to be difficult and expensive to restore.

In Malua Forest Reserve is the Sabah Biodiversity Experiment, where 500 ha (1,235 acres) of logged forest have been replanted experimentally with various combinations of dipterocarp tree seedlings in order to see if different replanting treatments yield long-term differences in forest biodiversity. The Malua Biobank, which began in 2008, seeks to help rehabilitate and preserve 34,000 ha (84,015 acres) of heavily logged forest through activities partly financed by sale of 'biodiversity conservation certificates'. In 2011 work started on the measuring, mapping and identification of more than 250,000 trees and saplings in a 50-ha (123-acre) plot near the Danum Valley Field Centre. This massive undertaking is part of a global network of more than 30 similar research plots in 20 countries that is being coordinated by the Smithsonian Tropical Research Institute, to monitor quantitatively how tropical rainforest composition changes in the coming era of global climate change.

Access

Ulu Segama Malua and Danum Valley can be reached within 2–3 hours by road from Lahad Datu town. Permission, accommodation and transportation have to be arranged in advance, both for Borneo Rainforest Lodge and Danum Valley Field Centre.

Right: Danum Valley at Borneo Rainforest Lodge, the only place in Sabah where pristine lowland dipterocarp forest can be seen from a motorable road.

Opposite: Many parts of Ulu Segama were logged in the 1980s, and are regenerating naturally, with natural seedlings growing to form closed-canopy rainforest three decades later.

Danum Valley

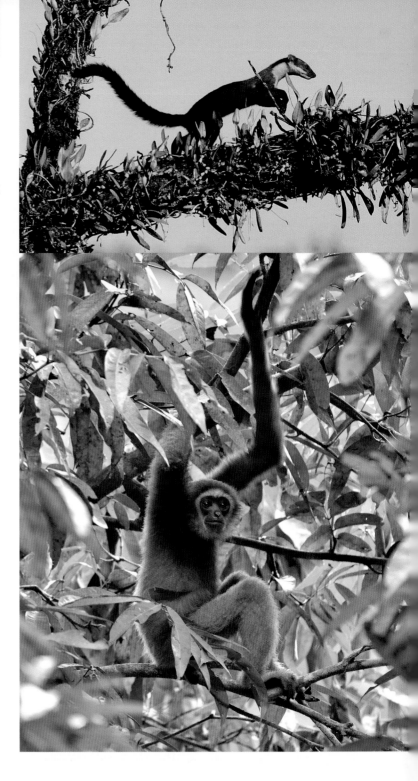

Whether you are staying at Borneo Rainforest Lodge or Danum Valley Field Centre, Danum Valley is the perfect place to experience and enjoy lowland tropical rainforest with minimal discomfort. The last hour of driving to reach Danum Valley is through uninhabited forest. The place is remote, the forest here is ancient and the ambience is entirely natural. Yet accommodation and logistics are well organized. Three hearty meals per day and a comfortable bed are available. Make the most of it. Be guided, both in terms of what to do, when and where, and on forest walks, by the local guides, who know the trails and specific animal habits better than anyone.

There are a few general things to bear in mind that will help to minimize missed opportunities, and the risk of even minor irritations. The two best times of day to enjoy nature at Danum Valley are from dawn (before 5.30 a.m.) to mid-morning, and again in the late afternoon until just after dusk. These are the coolest times to see things without the need for artificial light, and the best times to see and hear diurnal wildlife. Try to catch those times for the walking parts of your visit. The middle part of the day is best reserved for lazing on a shady veranda or under a big tree, or perhaps for a dip in the river.

During the daytime enjoy the grandeur of the overall structure and complexity of the forest. Equally, look closely at the individual plants that make up the forest. Remember that most of the animals are not mammals, and that the animal life is mostly very small and quiet (mainly invertebrates), or medium-sized and noisy (notably birds). Seek and enjoy these creatures. Sightings of big mammals like primates and elephants are really just a bonus.

Promise yourself not to be bothered by snakes, mosquitos or leeches. You will almost certainly not even notice either of the former, but may encounter the latter during walks on trails under forest cover. Ignore the usual advice. If a leech starts to bite, calmly and firmly grip its head, pressing very close to your skin or trousers, and using the tips of your thumb and one finger, pull it off with a sideways swipe, using your thumbnail to dislodge the mouthparts. If there is bleeding, staunch it with tiny fragments of tissue and nothing else.

Most rainforest animal species have evolved to communicate by sound or odour. This is not surprising, as visibility is poor in the tall, dense, complex vegetation. Humans rely so much on sight in order to experience things, and to communicate, that we bring the tendency to want to see everything, everywhere. Our sense of smell is much poorer than that of invertebrates and other mammals. So, in addition to seeking wildlife at Danum Valley by looking for it, why not take advantage of our rather good sense of hearing? The quietest time at Danum Valley tends to be just before dawn, and the first distinctive sound to be heard at this time of day is likely to be the quiet, plaintive song of the male Bornean Gibbon (*Hylobates muelleri*). As dawn breaks, a multi-species chorus gradually begins, usually involving series of plaintive descending notes of the *Malacopteron* babblers, plus some cicadas, joined a little later by barbets, trogons and flycatchers. The female and male gibbons may enter with their duets a little later, the shrill, loud bubbling call of the female carrying for distances of up to a kilometre.

Later still, at intervals throughout the day until late afternoon, calls to listen out for include those of the Helmeted Hornbill (a series of *poops* initially spaced, and gradually quickening to maniacal laughter), Rhinoceros Hornbill (*geronks* as a pair of birds prepares to fly), Great Argus Pheasant (a series of distant, resonant *ku-wows*) and Cream-coloured Giant Squirrel (short, sharp bursts of sound like distant machine-gun fire).

As daylight fades there is a very perceptible change in the quality of forest sounds, as well as a drop in temperature. The Jade-green Cicada (*Dundubia vaginata*) becomes noisy as the light intensity drops drastically, and has a constant high-pitched, rattling sound, interspersed every three or four seconds as if by a quick gasp. Most distinctive of all the cicadas, not only in size (20 cm/8-in wingspan) is the Emperor, or 'six-o-clock', Cicada (*Megapomponia imperatoria*), with the most startling vocalization, a series of loud, trumpeting sounds blasted out just before dusk, which many newcomers guess to be those of a large hornbill.

The majority of mammal species are active only or mainly at night. The only significant exceptions are monkeys, apes, squirrels, martens and mongooses. Wildlife seeking at night is best done during a drive along the road with a spotlight, or perhaps a guided walk on a forest trail with a headlamp.

This page from top: *Diard's Trogon (*Harpactes diardii*), Malaysian Blue Flycatcher (*Cyornis turcosus*) and Black-headed Pitta (*Pitta ussheri*), all characteristic of closed-canopy lowland dipterocarp forests, and the latter endemic to eastern Sabah.*

Opposite from top: *Yellow-throated Marten (*Martes falvigula*), one of a few Malaysian carnivores normally active during daylight hours; Bornean Gibbon.*

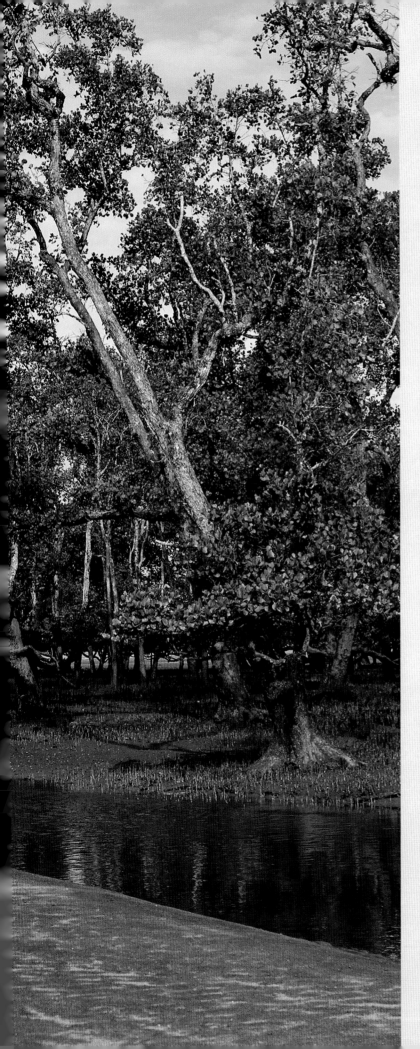

3
Sarawak

The largest of all the Malaysian states, Sarawak is situated in the north-west of Borneo, bordering Sabah to the north-east and Kalimantan to the south, and embracing the independent nation of Brunei Darussalam. Sarawak covers 124,450 sq km (48,050 sq miles) and the capital is Kuching. The coastal region is low and flat, with large extents of swamps and other wet habitats, and most large cities and towns have been built there for ease of access to the sea and to settlements upriver. Further inland, hill regions comprise the majority of readily inhabited land. A broad mountainous zone extends all along the border with Kalimantan in the south and south-east. Sarawak still contains large tracts of tropical lowland and highland rainforest with a huge variety of plant and animal species. Examples of key ecosystems are contained in protected areas such as Gunung Mulu (lowland and montane forest, and cave-riddled limestone), Bako (coastal and heath forest), Niah (caves), Similajau (coastal strand forest), Batang Ai (hill forest) and Maludam (mangroves and peat-swamp forest).

Left: Receding tide at the entrance to Bako National Park in the morning. Note the high-water mark on the trunks of the trees.

Bako, Buntal and Santubong

In the 1980s one of Santubong's commercial hotels used the tag-line 'one of Asia's best-kept Secrets' for this area. Since then, as more research has been conducted into wildlife in the area, including crocodiles, dolphins, migrant birds on the coastal flats and Proboscis Monkeys, and a suite of pristine forests has been gazetted as a protected area from Bako to Santubong and Kuching Wetlands National Park, a growing number of people have visited the area. In fact, over 30,000 people visited Bako in 2013, and quite a few of them also visited Santubong or the Buntal Bay area. This region is now increasingly becoming a good weekend getaway for visitors, including those who want to experience wildlife watching from boats, trek up a mountain or spend time on a beach.

The avid historian might be interested to know that in 1855, the British naturalist and explorer Alfred Russel Wallace collected specimens at a site in Santubong and later published a seminal paper titled

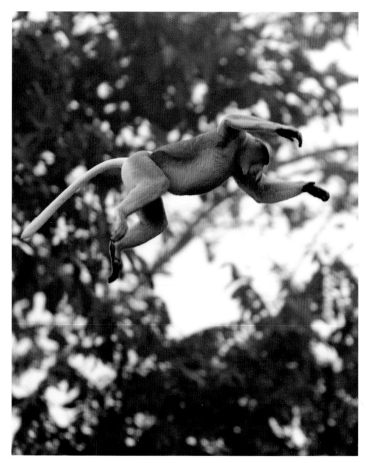

On the Law Which Has Regulated the Introduction of New Species, commonly known as 'Sarawak Law'. This paper was written at almost the same time as Charles Darwin's *On the Origin of Species*.

Bako National Park

Significance

Created in 1957, Bako National Park was the first national park in Malaysia. It is also one of Sarawak's smaller parks, at 2,747 ha (6,788 acres), but it is rich in plant and animal diversity. The park contains numerous habitats, ranging from beach forest and mangroves to lowland dipterocarp forests. Terrestrial and arboreal animals are readily seen in the park, because they have been protected from hunting and are habituated to humans. Proboscis Monkeys, Silvered Leaf-monkeys, Long-tailed Macaques, Bearded Pigs, Asian Fairy-bluebirds (*Irena puella*), minivets, White-bellied Sea-eagles, otters and even colugos can be seen around the park headquarters.

Trails and treks

There are 17 colour-coded trails in the park, ranging from short ones of less than 1 km (½ mile) in length (Sapi Trail) to the Lintang Trail (a 5.3-km/3.3-mile loop), and overnight trails at Teluk Kruin (a 7–8-hour trek). Each of these trails has its own attractions. For example, large, tall dipterocarp trees can be seen on the Ulu Serait and Bukit Keruing Trails, and Ulu Assam takes you to the mangroves.

For those interested in a variety of habitats, the Tajor Trail is attractive, taking you past mangroves and sections of heath or pole forest (locally known as kerangas forest), before arriving at a plateau with scrub-like vegetation. It is here on the plateau that

pitcher plants, ant-plants and liverworts can be seen. These plants are extremely interesting as they are adapted to life in the relatively dry environment on the plateau. The rest of the journey is on the plateau and ends at waterfalls and a small freshwater pool.

Bako does not have any canopy walks. However, there are quite a few high cliff faces for those who like spectacular views of beaches, the sea and the sunset dropping behind Santubong National Park. Visitors are always encouraged to inform the park headquarters before going on long treks and also into Teluk Delima, because this part of the park floods during high tides.

Proboscis Monkey

These strange, large-nosed monkeys are one of the major attractions of the park. They can be seen close to the park headquarters around Teluk Paku, Teluk Assam and Teluk Delima, and the best times for this are the early morning and late afternoon. Their presence is often betrayed by loud, grunting honks and the sound of crashing branches among the trees. They tend to be spotted in a group comprising a male and several females with their offspring. In the park, groups or harems of more than six animals are often seen, although larger harems have frequently been reported elsewhere.

Male Proboscis Monkeys are larger than females, ranging between 15 and 25 kg (33–55 lb) in weight. They have large, bulbous noses and big bellies, whereas the females are petite (around half the size of the males at about 10 kg/22 lb in weight), with smaller, stub-like noses. Even the mature females do not develop the large noses of the males. New-born individuals are quite striking and can be seen clinging to their mothers. They tend to have blackish-coloured fur and have blue faces. After the fourth month the youngsters' fur changes to the brownish, bomber-jacket look of the older adults, while the blueish tinge to the face remains for about a year.

park headquarters. It grows to more than 50 kg (110 lb) in weight, and has a large beard of long, wiry hairs on its snout. The young are striped light and dark brown. They lose their stripes when they get older, and the adults' fur colour ranges from slightly pink to blackish; some individuals have whitish tips to their grey body fur. In the forest you can see evidence of the pigs' foraging, with the ground often being gouged out after they have searched for roots, fungi and invertebrates in the soil, as well as for small vertebrates. Around the park they can often be seen near the canteen.

Birds

Some easily seen birds at Bako National Park include the Asian Fairy-bluebird, Common Iora (*Aegithina tiphia*), White-collared Kingfisher (*Todiramphus chloris*), Mangrove Whistler (*Pachycephala grisola*), minivets and Olive-winged Bulbul (*Pycnonotus plumosus*).

Silvered Leaf-monkey

This beautiful leaf-monkey can often be seen in front of the canteen or near the jetty in the morning or evening. Adults are grey in colour and appear to sport spiked haircuts; newborns are orange. The monkeys are often seen feeding on the flowers and leaves of the hibiscus along the beach front at Teluk Assam. They can also be seen running across the grassy patch in front of the canteen – they do not raid the canteen as do their noisy and aggressive counterparts, the Long-tailed Macaques. This is one of the few places in Sarawak where these graceful and unassuming leaf-monkeys can be seen without being spooked, as they have been habituated to tourists.

Above: *Far Eastern and Eurasian Curlews (*Numenius madagascariensis and N. arquata*). A scope is needed to see them up close.*

Top left: *Silvered Leaf-monkeys can often be seen among the beach forest trees, such as barringtonia and the Sea Hibiscus.*

Bearded Pig

The only species of wild pig that can be found in Borneo, the Bearded Pig can be easily seen around the

Opposite: *A Proboscis Monkey harem.*

Plant life

The park has at least seven vegetation types, and as it is itself limited in area these are in small pockets. Their full list comprises beach forest, cliff vegetation, kerangas forest, mangrove forest, mixed dipterocarp forest, scrub-like or grassland vegetation, and peat-swamp forest.

The mangrove and peat-swamp forests are not extensive, and in the last 20 years the mangroves around Bako have seen some interesting changes. The mangroves at Teluk Assam appear to be dying or are gradually becoming defoliated. Several reasons for these losses have been theorized, ranging from over-eating of the plants by Proboscis Monkeys, to a change in the flow of the tides due to the construction of the causeway along the Sarawak River. However, no studies have yet been made to ascertain the cause of the slow defoliation of the trees. Meanwhile from Kampung Bako to the park, mangroves can be seen on either side of the river and also at Teluk Delima. The mangroves here seem to be extending into the sea, and this has increased the chances of visitors seeing Proboscis Monkeys close to the riverbanks, and also when walking into the mangroves at Teluk Delima.

The beach forest in the park is a thin strip of casuarina, Sea Hibiscus (*Hibiscus tiliaceus*) and barringtonia trees. The beach here is not composed of pristine golden sands, but has a layer of silt or mud. The attractions at the beach are actually the birds frequenting the casuarina and barringtonia trees. Pairs of minivets, Asian Fairy-bluebirds, kingfishers, sea-eagles, Common Ioras and other birds are easily seen in the early morning and late afternoon.

Access

The park is less than 40 km (25 miles) from Kuching City. From Kuching, visitors travel on a tar-sealed road to Kampung Bako, after which boats are used to get them to the park. The boat ride takes you from the village to the open sea, then to Teluk Assam, the entry point into the park. With favourable tides the whole journey usually takes more than an hour (45 minutes by road and at least 25 minutes by boat). In instances where visitors get to the boat terminal at low tide, they may have to wait for several hours until the tide is high enough to allow boats to access the park. If you are travelling without a travel agency, you can charter a boat at the national parks boat-ticketing counter next to the jetty. Upon arrival at the park following the boat ride, you have to register your arrival at the park-arrival booth.

Bako National Park is one of the most frequented parks in Sarawak, with more than 20,000 visitors annually. Potential overnight visitors are advised to book their stays well beforehand – perhaps up to two weeks in advance. This is especially the case during the months of April to September, as the park has limited rooms, beds and bunks. The park intends to keep tourist numbers within its carrying capacity, especially along the trails – hence the limit in the numbers of overnighters. The accommodation and facilities are basic, and air-conditioned rooms, heated showers and laundry services are not yet available. For the more adventurous, a campsite exists but visitors have to bring their own tents. Park guides can be hired at the boat terminal, and local tour operators and travel agencies also provide guides into the park.

Buntal Bay

Significance

Apart from nature, Buntal Bay is renowned for fresh seafood, a few rustic Malay fishing villages with home stays, comfortable hotels and easy access to an international airport. The bay is semi-circular and is bordered by Gunung Santubong National Park to the west and Bako National Park to the east.

Although the Buntal Bay mudflats are a globally significant migrant waterbird site – in fact Malaysia's most important site – they were largely unvisited by non-birders until the late 1980s and early '90s. Buntal started getting more non-nature visitors when it became more accessible after the completion of the Santubong bridge, which reduced the travel time and

costs for tourists and Kuchingnites to both Buntal Bay and Santubong beaches.

Before the construction of the bridge, journeys to Buntal and Santubong would involve taking a ferry or other boat from Kuching and could take up to two hours. The bridge shortened the travel time to less than an hour. Within ten years several hotels, rustic rainforest lodges, homestays and local seafood restaurants mushroomed, and a travel industry partly based on nature (including birding, Proboscis Monkeys, crocodiles and dolphin watching) came into being. Other major attractions of the Buntal-Santubong area include the reknowned Cultural Village and its three-day Rainforest World Music Festival of music workshops during the day, cultural displays, food stalls and concerts in the evening.

Birds

Bako-Buntal Bay is considered an Important Bird Area (IBA) for 32 species of wintering wader, with an estimated 15,000 birds counted. The Chinese Egret, which is a rare migratory bird to Malaysian shores, is regularly seen in large numbers in Bako-Buntal Bay. The wetland also supports other threatened and near threatened species such as Spotted Greenshank (listed as Endangered on the IUCN Red List), the Asian Dowitcher (*Limnodromus semipalmatus*, listed as Near Threatened) and the Far Eastern Curlew (listed as Vulnerable). Bako-Buntal Bay was officially recognized and included in the East Asian Australasian Flyway Site Network in 2013, and is the first area included in the partnership in Malaysia.

Other animals

Animals that are reported in the area do not appear to be habituated to humans, and tend to be shy and slink away when they are approached. They are also not numerous and this, coupled with their evasive behaviour involving moving into the trees (primates) or diving into the river (crocodiles), makes them hard to see. Nevertheless, six Estuarine Crocodiles about 2–3 m (6½–10 ft) in length were observed during a daytime, 40-km (25-mile) survey of crocodiles in January 2014. According to the crocodile specialist, the number of crocodiles he saw during the survey is probably the highest he has seen outside Australia and Papua New Guinea. During the same survey migrant waterbirds were also seen, but not dolphins or Proboscis Monkeys.

Dolphins have been reported in this area since the 1950s. Three species have been spotted in the waters of the bay: the Indo-Pacific Humpback Dolphin (*Sousa chinensis*), Indo-Pacific Finless Porpoise (*Neophocaena phocaenoides*) and Irrawaddy Dolphin (*Orcaella brevirostris*).

For all the wildlife-watching activities, high-powered binoculars are a bonus if you want to observe the animals close-up.

Access

There are several ways to enjoy a boat ride in the area looking at crocodiles, dolphins, migrant birds and Proboscis Monkeys. Boat rides can be arranged in Kuching via the larger travel agencies or hotels, or through a local contact at one of the resorts or at Buntal Village. For the latter, you have to drive or catch a ride from Kuching to Buntal or Santubong Village, and meet their boatmen after prearranging the trip. These customized trips can be quite expensive, with a two-hour journey costing up to RM 400.

Not all the boat operators are experienced, and you should check with the major hotels in Santubong or Kuching before booking them. Inexperienced boat operators can actually harm some of the wildlife – for example, the propellers of their boats may nick the dolphins. Also note that the rivers are tidal and that some boat operators working out of Buntal cannot take visitors during low tide, when their boats are stuck on the banks of the river. The Sarawak Alamanc has great tide tables and visitors should make sure of their times before embarking on a trip to Buntal.

Right: A Long-tailed Macaque (sometimes called the Crab-eating Macaque) forages at the mangroves. The monkeys are very common, especially around the canteen.

Opposite: A colugo gliding between trees.

Santubong National Park

Significance

The main attraction of the 1,410-ha (3,484-acre) Santubong National Park is the 810-m (2,657-ft) mountain, with its pristine forests and its trails. Some iconic fauna found in the park includes Rhinoceros Hornbills, Proboscis Monkeys, colugos, Silvered Leaf-monkeys, Bearcats, or Binturongs (*Arctictis binturong*), and Reticulated Pythons (*Python reticulatus*). On the coast bordering the park Irrawaddy Dolphins and Indo-Pacific Finless Porpoises can be seen. The turtle beaches of Talang and Satang are also within an hour's boat ride (depending on the speed of the boat) from Santubong. Because the peninsula has numerous hotels as well as rustic ecoresorts and homestays, arrangements for boat rides can be made quite easily.

Trails and treks

Some of the useful activities at Santubong include adventure climbing, kayaking and walking on the trails in the park. Adventure climbing takes you from the base of the mountain to almost submontane forests. Rope ladders are located on strategic sections to help you access the peak.

There are two trails in the park. The first is called the Santubong Jungle Trek and is less than five minutes from Damai Beach. The trail is about 2 km (1¼ miles) long and begins at Green Paradise Cafe. This relatively gentle trail takes you along the base of the mountain and is less steep than the Mount Santubong Summit Trek. The summit trail commences from Bukit Puteri, along Santubong Road. It is a shorter trail, but visitors often take three to four hours to reach the summit.

Those reaching the summit can enjoy panoramic views of the city, and of Bako National Park to the east and Kuching Wetlands National Park to the west.

Animal and plant life

Observant visitors can view many attractions at various locations along the trails.

A variety of animals may be seen at the foot of the mountain: butterflies including birdwings such as Rajah Brooke's Birdwing, and *Nymphalis* species, File-eared Tree Frogs (*Polypedates otilophus*), leaf frogs, Water Monitors, Long-tailed Macaques and Wagler's Pit Vipers (*Tropidolaemus wagleri*).

In the middle section of the trail (from the waterfall to Viewpoint 3), it may be possible to see skinks, geckos, bronzeback tree snakes (*Dendrelaphis* spp.), Prevost's Squirrels (*Callosciurus prevostii*), giant pill millipedes, flat-backed millipedes and Rhinoceros Hornbills.

During the last leg of the climb (from Viewpoint 4 to the summit), it is possible to see plants such as lianas, gnarled, stunted trees, orchids and tropical pitcher plants (Veitch's Pitcher Plant), and dragonflies and rock gardens.

Access

The park is only about 35 km (22 miles) from Kuching City and there is road access from the city to the park. It is possible to get to the trails from the city within 45 minutes.

Batang Ai National Park

Constituted in 1991, Batang Ai National Park is the eighth-oldest national park in Sarawak. It has, arguably, three major attractions: the Orang-utans, the rivers and the Iban communities living in the area.

The first impression of Batang Ai is of steep hills, vast expanses of water and swift-flowing rivers with intermittent currents, and regrowth of trees from ex-plots of hill padi or rubber planted by the local Iban communities. The forested areas in the park can be divided into mixed dipterocarp forests, kerangas forests, old secondary forests (more than 30 years old), and young secondary forests (less than ten years old). The park is dissected by several major rivers, among them the Bebiyong, Beretik, Delok, Jengin, Lubang Baya, Mujan and Ulu Lalang. The common characteristics of these rivers are that they are clear and fast flowing, and are intermixed with small rapids. In fact, the waters are considered so clean that locals and field biologists still drink directly from them, upriver of any longhouse communities.

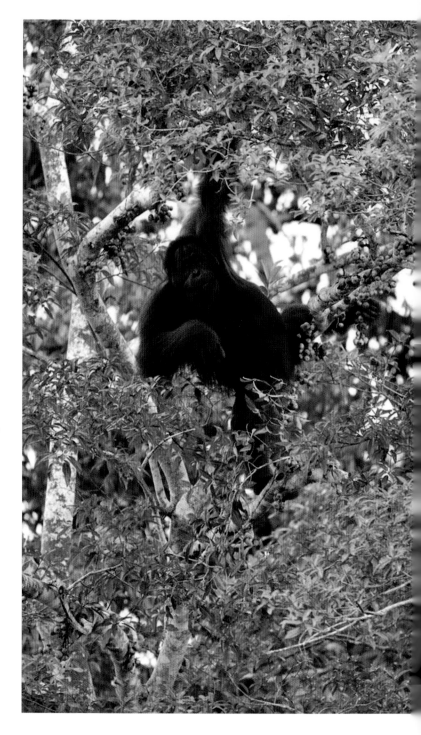

Significance

This 24,040-ha (59,404-acre) park was created for various ecological reasons, the most prominent being the protection of the iconic Orang-utan and the dipterocarp forests in the water catchment above the Batang Ai dam. It is contiguous with Lanjak-Entimau Wildlife Sanctuary (168,758 ha/417,010 acres) and also with Betung Kerihun National Park, West Kalimantan (800,000 ha/1,976,843 acres). This combined patch of protected areas makes it one of the largest protected areas in Borneo, surpassed only by Kayan-Mentarang National Park (1,360,500 ha/3,361,868 acres) in the north (East Kalimantan).

The Batang Ai area is considered to be the traditional heartland of the Iban people. According to oral history the Iban originated from the Kapuas River in Kalimantan and settled in the Batang Ai region about 500 years ago. They are generous, friendly and very welcoming to visitors. Historically, however, they were among the fiercest of warriors, had a tradition of headhunting and rebelled against the might of the colonial Brooke Administration in the 19th century. In older wood-based longhouses, rare, century-old smoked skulls can still sometimes be seen. The Ibans' traditional belief systems of Hinduism, Animism and Augury have largely been replaced by Christianity.

When Batang Ai National Park was created, the inhabitants of seven longhouses were given rights and privileges because parts of the park included their Native Customary Rights (NCR) lands. Some of the approved activities in these NCR lands are subsistence farming, fishing at designated rivers, hunting certain non-protected wildlife and collecting non-Timber Forest Products for the inhabitants' own consumption. The longhouses are located at Tapang Jarau Entambah, Nanga Beretik, Tibu, Nanga Jengin, Pala Taong Delok, Nanga Sumpa and Nanga Jambu. A few years after the constitution of the park, the inhabitants of an eighth longhouse were given similar rights and privileges – the Delok park headquarters had to be built on their lands because they were in a strategic position overlooking two rivers accessing the park, that is the Lubang Baya and Batang Ai Rivers.

All eight longhouses are located along the four major rivers within the park – the Batang Ai, Jengin, Lubang Baya and Delok. While some of the inhabitants have moved into a resettlement scheme downriver of the hydroelectric dam, the rest can still be found in their original surroundings upriver. Apart from these eight, there are communities that claim ancestral rights to other places in proposed extension areas to Batang Ai National Park.

Iban longhouses are, in essence, linked homes. Each family lives in its own separate apartment or compartments, and all the apartments are under a single long roof. The traditional Iban longhouses tended to be wooden structures built on stilts above hardened earth floors. Domestic animals such as pigs, chickens and dogs would use the area beneath the houses. A longhouse also usually had a verandah, or *tanju*, where families would mingle, and an outdoor platform made from bamboo used for drying clothes, forest produce and cash crops such as peppers. The communities were mostly self-sustaining, living off the land and rivers. They consumed jungle produce and fish, and tended small hill rice and vegetable plots to provide their food, supplemented with protein from domestic livestock.

Due to government efforts to modernize these villages by providing septic tanks for better sewage disposal, healthcare, electricity and access to schools, the traditional wooden-poled and bamboo-platformed longhouses have slowly and partially been replaced. There is even satellite-based Wi-Fi at some of the villages. Nevertheless, the modernization has not had much effect on the welcoming culture of the Iban, and visitors to the area may be awed by their hospitality.

Trails and treks

The trails in the park range from easy to strenuous with steep slopes. Among the gentler trails are those at Padalai and Bebiyong. Outside the park is the world-famous Red Ape Trail close to the Delok River. This gentle two-hour trail is where most visitors get a glimpse of Orang-utans or their nests. Information on the trails is shown in the table overleaf, and details can be found at www.sarawakforestry.com/htm/snp-np-batangai.html.

Opposite: A male Orang-utan among the figs.

LOCATION OF TRAIL	NAME OF TRAIL	ATTRACTIONS	NOTES	LENGTH (KM)	GRADE	TIME
Batang Ai National Park	Padalai			1.8	Easy	1 hr 30 mins
	Bebiyong			4	Easy	2 hrs 30 mins
	Bilitong			4.6	Moderate	4 hrs
	Enggam			8.2	Strenuous	6 hrs
	Sium			7.6	Strenuous	5 hrs 30 mins
Proposed extension to Batang Ai National Park	Red Ape Trail	Orang-utans and their nests	Certain to see the nests. Perhaps a 30% chance of seeing Orang-utans	not available	Moderate	2 hrs
Smuggler's Trail	Water catchment area around the dam	Orang-utans and their nests		not available	Moderate	not available

Orang-utans

The islands of Borneo and Sumatra are the only places where Orang-utans are found. Those in Sarawak are considered the rarest of all Orang-utan subspecies worldwide, with a population in the low thousands. The concerns over the animal's rarity and its reported demise were voiced in the 1950s, and resulted in the first scientific Orang-utan surveys being conducted in 1960–1961. Since then at least five Orang-utan surveys have been carried out in Batang Ai and Lanjak-Entimau. Some of these were of actual Orang-utan sightings, while others were of all nests and yet others only of fresh nests.

Due to the rarity of sightings of Orang-utans, nests are used as an indicator of Orang-utan presence and, indeed, via a mathematical algorithm, can be used to generate total numbers of Orang-utans in an area being surveyed. The current estimated number of Orang-utans in Batang Ai National Park and its proposed extensions is 474 animals, based on surveys completed in mid-2000 and 2013.

There appears to be a population gradient for Orang-utans in Batang Ai, with the highest densities being found in the south and south-west corner of the park and areas surrounding it.

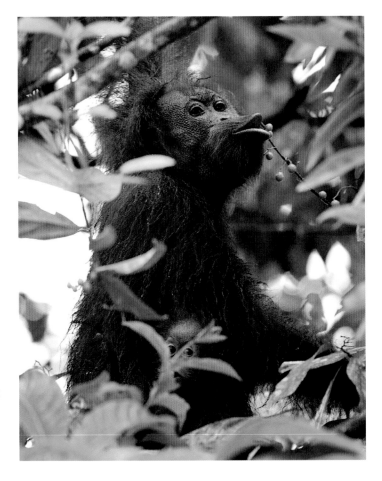

Above: A mother and young Orang-utan feeding on fruits. They can sometimes be seen at various locations in the park.

Opposite: An adult male Orang-utan staring at a survey team.

The Orang-utans here are the largest arboreal animal in Sarawak, with adult males weighing up to 75 kg (165 lb). Adult females are smaller and on average weigh about 40 kg (88 lb). Males can be up to 1.5 m (5 ft) in height, with an average arm span of about 2.25 m (7½ ft). Some adults, such as dominant males, have large cheek flanges on either side of the face. They also have longish red beards and a huge sac of skin on the throat that hangs down onto the chest. With these sacs, the males can produce loud calls – often called 'long calls'. Studies in Batang Ai have shown the males calling several times a day, with most long calls being heard in the morning and late afternoon. Recent research into the long calls in the wilds in Sumatra on a different species of Orang-utan (*Pongo abelii*) indicates that the dominant males use them as a means both of informing females where they are and of repelling competing subadult males. Females tend to stay closer to the adult males to avoid being harassed by the competing subadult males.

The Orang-utans in Batang Ai are clearly breeding – young have been seen by tourists as well as by biologists and photographers. In the wild the Orang-utans behave very differently from those in captive situations. They tend to avoid humans and can only be seen clearly with long-range telephoto lenses or powerful binoculars. Tourists who have seen, photographed or videoed the Orang-utans in Batang Ai are a fortunate lot, as not many visitors to the forests here have seen them. When Orang-utan sightings have been reported, they tend to be of a solitary animal, a mother with her young or in very rare cases a group of individuals in a single large fruiting tree.

Not only do Orang-utans avoid humans; they also appear to discourage humans from coming too close. Among some of the reported behaviours designed to ward off curious tourists are: breaking of branches; collecting their own faeces and throwing them in the direction of the tourists; quietly eyeing the tourists while probably hoping that they will overlook them; and moving to a site further away from any tourists, if the latter stare at them for an extended period.

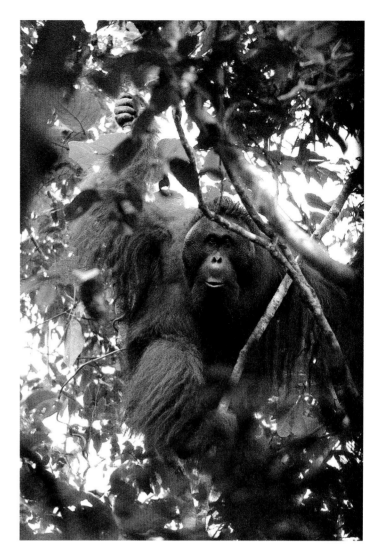

Orang-utan nests can be found throughout most of the park, but the chances of seeing the nests and a live Orang-utan are highest in the south-east part of the park. Both day and night nests can be seen from various trails in the park and in its proposed extensions. The sizes of the nests can be estimated from the sizes of the field assistants in the photographs. Orang-utans in Batang Ai make nests on numerous species and sizes of tree, ranging from lowly young trees 7 m (23 ft) in height, up to majestic 30-m (100-ft) tall trees with a diameter of more than 50 cm (20 in). Among some of the trees in which Orang-utans construct nests are Kumpang (Myristaceae), Pudun (*Nephelium* spp.), Perawan (*Shorea* spp.), Ubah (*Eugenia* spp. and *Syzygium* spp.) and Empili (*Lithocarpus* spp.). Even Rubber Trees (*Hevea brasiliensis*) are sometimes used.

The Orang-utans in this area have been seen feeding on *Ficus* fruits, and anecdotally, the Ibans have reported seeing more Orang-utans around their longhouses during the months when durians and other fleshy fruits are ripening.

Other animals

Apart from the iconic Orang-utans, at least 35 other mammal and 121 bird species are found in the park. A breakdown of the list of animals seen or camera trapped in the park includes five species of hornbill, Bulwer's Pheasant, Crested and Crestless Firebacks (*Lophura ignita* and *L. erythrophthalma*), several nightjar species, at least 15 bulbul species, 17 babbler species, Bearded Pigs, several civet species, several deer species, flying foxes, Sunda Clouded Leopards (*Neofelis diardi*), martens, otters, porcupines, Slow Lorises (*Nycticebus menagensis*), Sun Bears (*Helarctos malayanus*), 13 snake species including Reticulated Pythons and Bornean Short-tailed Pythons (*Python breitensteini*), tarsiers, Water Monitors and weasels. There are also at least 52 frog species and 80 fish species in the park.

Not all of these animals are easily observable as hunting in the park is still quite extensive, which makes the animals wary. Of those that can be most easily heard or seen, four are highlighted here: the Bornean Gibbon, Great Argus Pheasant, Rajah Brooke's Birdwing and some squirrels.

The Bornean Gibbon can often be heard throughout the park, mostly at dawn and dusk, although its whooping calls can sometimes be heard even at midday. It is much easier to hear than to see these gibbons, and if you hear them in a valley the echo of their calls makes them appear to be all around you.

The beautiful calls of Great Argus Pheasants can be heard throughout the park and, in fact, throughout the day. This is the largest ground-dwelling bird in Borneo and the males are much larger than the females, with long tail feathers that have traditionally been used for

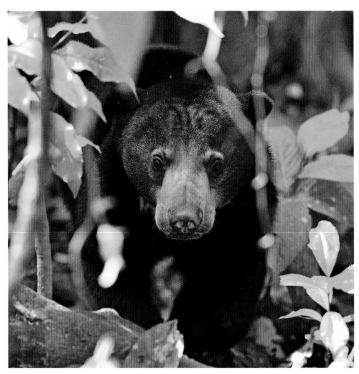

decorating ceremonial costumes, especially headgear. The presence of these large, ground-dwelling birds is often betrayed by bald patches on the ground, called their dancing grounds. These can be seen along ridges and will have been cleared of most vegetation and debris. The males use them to carry out elaborate courtship displays in order to attract females. The grounds are used almost daily.

Rajah Brooke's Birdwing is a lovely butterfly that can often be seen along the riverbanks throughout the park. It was named after the first Rajah of Sarawak by Alfred Russel Wallace (see page 152). The males are bright green, the females dull green or brown with white flashes on their wingtips. While the males tend to be found near the ground, the females are generally more secretive and stay up in the canopy.

Various species of squirrel are also easily seen close to the trails. These include Prevost's and Plantain Squirrels, as well as pygmy squirrels.

Plant life

The park has a rich plant diversity, with over 1,000 tree species and almost 200 herbs, shrubs and climbers recorded. The local communities use more than 140 kinds of medicinal plant, and eat at least 114 species of wild fruit and at least 36 varieties of jungle vegetable. Other forest products used by the locals include wood, resin, bark, rattan, bamboo and weaving materials.

Access

There are various ways to get to the park, with the most common being a road journey of 4–5 hours from Kuching City to the Batang Ai hydroelectric dam (275 km/170 miles), followed by a 90–120-minute boat ride (depending on the size of the boat engine and the water levels along the rivers) to the ranger station at Nanga Lubang Baya. On the way you pass the Delok park headquarters.

Left: A male Argus Pheasant at one of the dancing grounds. Note that the centre of the dancing ground is cleared of vegetation.

Opposite top: A Bornean Gibbon close up. They can often be heard but not seen, usually early in the morning and in the late afternoon.

Opposite below: Sun Bears are the only bears in the park. Their presence is betrayed by scratchings on trees.

Smuggler's Trail

The name of this trail implies that it is used by smugglers to travel between Indonesia and Sarawak. However, once you are on the trail it becomes evident that the name of the trail is just a quirky gimmick. No movements of humans can be seen – in fact the area appears to be quite undisturbed by human activity, apart from the occasional appearance of an electrical pylon cable at the start of the trail. This 5.6-km (3.5-mile), undulating loop trail takes you from the edge of the dam near the Batang Ai Longhouse Resort close to the international boundary with Indonesia.

The start of the trail is about 30 minutes by boat from the jetty at the hydroelectric dam, or about ten minutes from the resort. The trail has an unassuming entrance, hidden among the Resam Ferns (*Dicranopteris* spp.). It takes you into secondary vegetation, some of which intermingles with rubber trees. Among the trees that can be seen at the start of the trail are Buan (*Dillenia suffruticosa*), Ubah (*Syzygium* spp.), Jambu Aka (*Bellucia pentamera*) and Enteli (*Prunus* spp.). These are shortish trees, and the beginning of the trail appears to be former farmland. However, once you get past the start of the trail, the thrill begins as the canopy starts to close, and the leaf litter on the trail appears largely undisturbed.

Some visitors to this trail have reported that they have seen, mist netted and heard more than 50 species of animal (birds, mammals and reptiles). The list of plants is also very interesting, and more than 30 have been identified as of 'general and medicinal' use to the local Iban communities in the area. Plants to be seen include Bungkang (*Syzygium polyanthum*), Engkerabai (*Psychotria* spp.), Kelindang (*Artocarpus anisophyllus*, or *Parartocarpus venenosus*), Kacip Fatimah (*Labisia pumila*) and Tongkat Ali (*Eurycoma longifolia*).

Some of the most iconic animals in Sarawak can be seen here, including Orang-utans and hornbills. The density of Orang-utan nests can be surprisingly high, and it is interesting to take the time to count the numbers of fresh and old nests. Close to 30 old and new nests were seen by a visiting group in 2014. New nests indicate that Orang-utans have been in the area recently. In the period between late 2013 and the first three months of 2014, about half a dozen Orang-utans were seen using the area. These animals may or may not be resident when you proceed along the trail, but there is always a chance of seeing them if you are quiet and do not smoke on the trail.

A group of White-crowned Hornbills, with their distinctive calls, and Oriental Pied and Rhinoceros Hornbills, can be seen or heard if you pay close attention. These birds are visible on the ridges as well as close to the streams.

Birders should not forget to bring their binoculars, because quite a few small to medium-sized birds can be seen here. A shortlist of the most commonly seen ones includes the Ashy Tailorbird (*Orthotomus ruficeps*), Asian Fairy-bluebird, Banded Kingfisher (*Lacedo pulchella*), Black-bellied Malkoha (*Phaenicophaeus diardi*), Black-and-yellow Broadbill (*Eurylaimus ochromalus*), Bronzed Drongo (*Dicrurus aeneus*), Brown-throated Sunbird, Chestnut-bellied Malkoha (*Phaenicophaeus sumatranus*), Green Iora (*Aegithina viridissima*), leafbirds, Raffles's Malkoha, Rufous-backed Kingfisher (*Ceyx rufidorsa*) and Rufous-tailed Tailorbird (*Orthotomus sericeus*). Pheasants seen and heard in the area include the Great Argus and Crested Fireback.

The trail itself is quite undulating and in some of its latter parts you have to scramble across big rocks. At the ridges the forest is almost immaculate – the thick forest litter provides the impression that you are walking on a sponge. The trail also takes you across some shallow streams, and it is here that you can see fish such as the native 'Tiger Barb' (*Puntius tetrazona*). Close to the streams you can also see the scratchings or wallows made by Bearded Pigs; the guide can provide information about how recent the wallows are.

Access is by boat, so you should make arrangements with the boatman for pick-up to be five to six hours after the initial drop-off. The area can get dark early and is sometimes misty in the morning. Go to the site on a sunny day to fully enjoy counting nests and searching for Orang-utans (if they are there at the time) – do not rush through the trail.

*Opposite, clockwise from top right: Black-and-yellow Broadbill displaying; and perching in the rain; Bornean Whistling Thrush (*Myophonus borneensis*); one of the many Ubah trees in the park: the species has a very strong, hardy wood and its fruit provide sustenance to many wild animals.*

Lambir Hills National Park

In the mid-1990s Lambir Hills National Park had the highest number of visitors among the national parks in Sarawak, with close to 60,000 people frequenting the park in 1993. This was double the number of visitors to the next most-frequented park in Sarawak. Surveys done in the mid-1990s indicated that the Latak Waterfall proved to be the major attraction to the visitors, and the majority came to the park to have a picnic and a swim. Most did not proceed to the trails, which would have enabled them to see even more beautiful waterfalls (some with clear waters appearing almost green in colour), the amazing tall trees, the famed floral biodiversity (although a few world-renowned universities did come to see this), numerous bird species and even signs of Sunda Clouded Leopards and Sun Bears.

Those keen on walking quietly in the forest should proceed to the park on a weekday. At this time they can have the park almost to themselves, and can wonder at nature's creation – the tall trees, the really high floral and faunal diversity (including 237 bird species) and the amazing waterfalls.

Significance

Lambir Hills National Park's tallest peak is about 450 m (1,476 ft) above sea level. At 6,952 ha (17,178 acres) it is not one of the largest parks in Sarawak. However, it was and still is marginally contiguous with the larger forests surrounding it. Thus it is no wonder that even large mammals such as Sunda Clouded Leopards and Sun Bears are found here. Lambir Hills is also the water catchment to Miri town, so there is an added impetus to protect the park. Visitors looking at the park from the main access road will note in wonder the tall trees nestled in the hills.

Unfortunately, Lambir Hills is increasingly becoming isolated due to the advance of development and industrial agriculture around its edges. There are also peer-reviewed reports of some hunting of wildlife within its borders. Even so, Lambir Hills National Park was considered so biodiverse that a 52-ha (128-acre) plot within the park was selected as part of a permanent network of long-term ecological research plots worldwide. A survey of the flora in the plot yielded more than 1,100 tree species, and the site was deemed the richest in tree species of all forest types in Malaysia. The park received rave reviews for its biodiversity and the BBC filmed this in 2002. The canopy was included in the filming, and the crane used for lifting researchers into it is still used by researchers to date.

Trails and treks

There are 13 trails in the park, all of which are interconnected and branch off the Main Trail. All are quite short, and a return journey to and from the park headquarters and the respective destinations ranges from about 30 minutes to seven hours. The list of trails as indicated by the management authority comprises: Main Trail, Latak Waterfall, Pantu, Inove, Bukit Pantu, Lepoh Ridan, Pantu Waterfall, Oil Well, Bakam, Pancur Waterfall, Tengkorong Waterfall, Dinding Waterfall and Summit Trail.

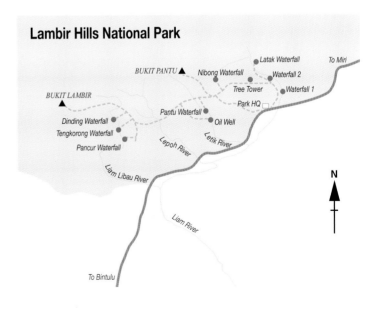

Lambir Hills National Park

Opposite: Eugeissona minor, *one of the many palm species to be seen in the park.*

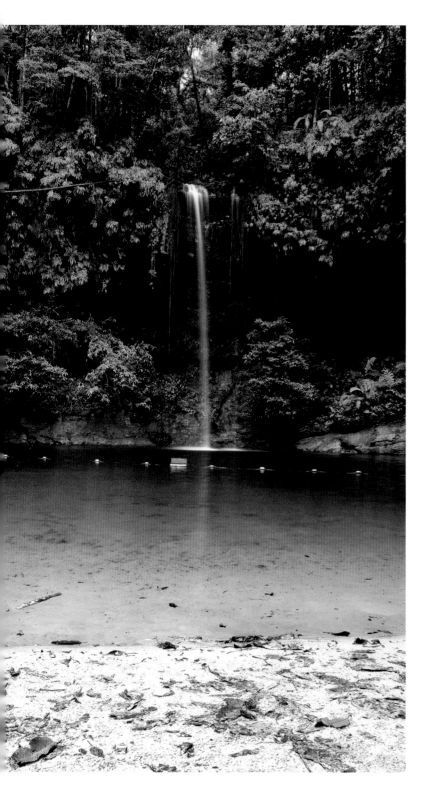

Above: Latak Waterfall during the drier season. Be aware that the volume of water spilling through the gap can double or triple after heavy rains.

Opposite: A Licuala species seen on the side of the trail. This leaf pattern is often used as an icon to depict wild plants.

There are two different approaches to using the trails. The first is via the Main Trail located close to the park headquarters, which is itself linked to other trails taking visitors to remote sites in the park such as the Pantu and Nibong Waterfalls. The other main access into the park lies to the west of the Main Trail and has its entry-point trail along the Miri-Bintulu Road. This second access joins up with the trails commencing at the Main Trail as they access the single trail taking visitors to the summit of Lambir Hills. The second access presents a quicker way to get to Tengkorong and Dinding Waterfalls. It is advisable to obtain a permit at the park headquarters before using it. Trekkers are not encouraged to camp, but make daily forays into the forests starting out from the accommodation at the park headquarters.

The trails at Lambir are varied in their demands of the fitness of trekkers. The shorter trails (Main Trail, Latak Waterfall, Inove and Pantu) tend to be somewhat gentler than the other trails, and are not physically demanding of trekkers. The other trails are much longer and quite undulating. The trail to the summit is strenuous because certain sections are steep. Ladders and ropes are in place to help trekkers, but the trails do get a bit slippery after rains. The Summit Trail is also not for those with a fear of heights, as parts of the trail near the summit are narrow with steep sides.

The summit is reportedly prone to lightning strikes, and these were thought to be the cause of some of the fires seen at the peak in the mid-1990s. Lightning strikes are quite common in tall forests and have caused the deaths of some tall trees, including the Kapur used as the tree tower in Lambir.

The most popular waterfall with the largest pool is Latak. It is also the closest to the park headquarters, and the trail to it is the most gentle of all the trails in the park. At 25 m (82 ft) high, Latak is the tallest waterfall in the park. It is the most developed in terms of visitor amenities, and has picnic benches and shelters close to the pool. The water in the pool is cool and the current is quite strong, especially after heavy rains; you not permitted to leap into the pool from the

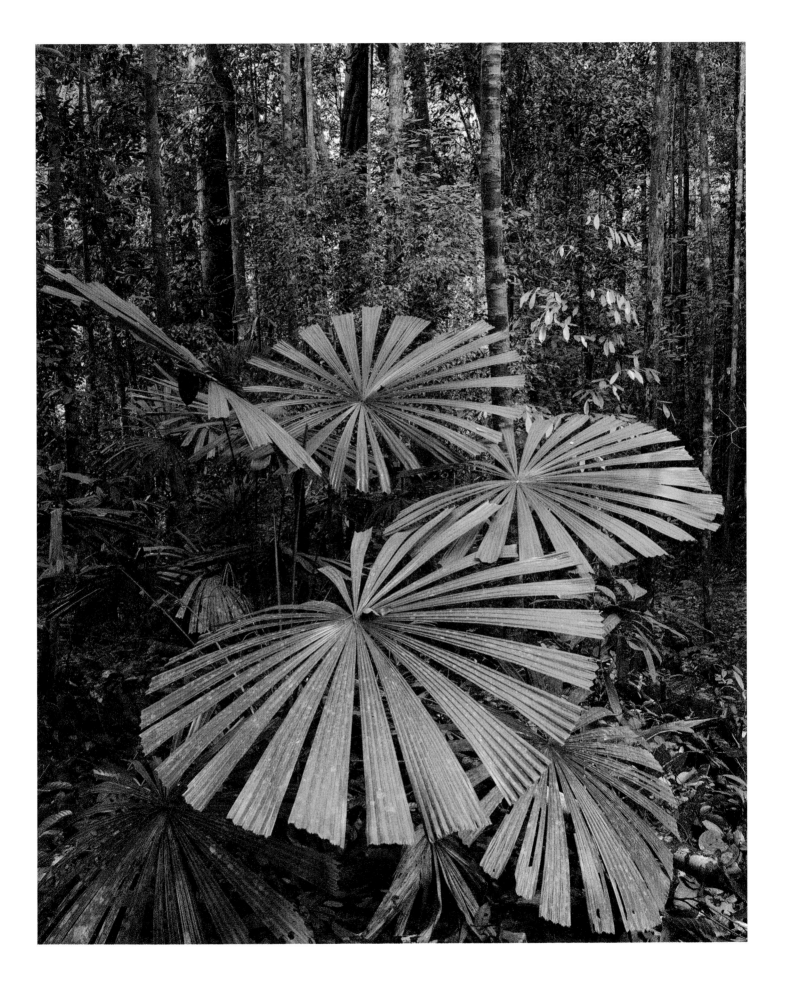

25-m (82-ft) high edge. There are two smaller waterfalls that you have to pass through before arriving at the main waterfall. The trail has interesting tall trees and some of them, such as Selunsur (*Tristania* spp.), appear as though they are shedding bark. Apart from these tall trees there are large *Licuala* fan palms (this is the type of palm used as a logo for the park).

Tengkorong and Dinding Waterfalls are faster to get to than Latak Waterfall, via the second access along Miri-Bintulu Road. Along the way you walk close to the 52-ha (128-acre) research plot, where all the trees have been identified, labelled and measured. Visitors are reminded that this is a long-term research plot and that they should not harm any of the plants here. A return trip to both Tengkorong and Dinding Waterfalls takes about four hours. The waterfalls have a beautiful greenish-blue hue, and they are quite secluded because not many visitors make this trek. Some people have actually seen species of large wildlife on this trail, including *kijang*, or muntjacs, and primates such as Long-tailed Macaques.

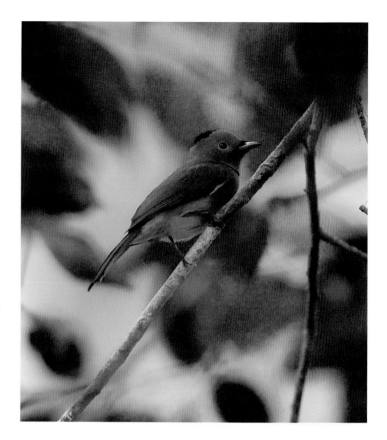

Birds

Trogons and Asian Paradise Flycatchers (*Terpsiphone paradisi*) are among the most striking birds seen in the park. They can be observed early in the morning or late in the afternoon on the main trail, as well as on the trails to Tengkorong and Dinding Waterfalls. Other birds seen on the trails include the Banded Broadbill, Garnet Pitta (*Pitta granatina*), Short-tailed Babbler (*Malacocincla malaccensis*) and Raffles's Malkoha (*Phaenicophaeus chlorophaeus*).

Those interested in smaller canopy birds may find the Streaked Bulbul (*Ixos malaccensis*), Blue-eared Barbet (*Megalaima australis*), Scarlet Minivet (*Pericrocotus flammeus*) and Greater Racket-tailed Drongo (*Dicrurus paradiseus*) flying among the upper reaches of the tall trees. Larger birds such as hornbills and raptors are also resident in the park. At least six

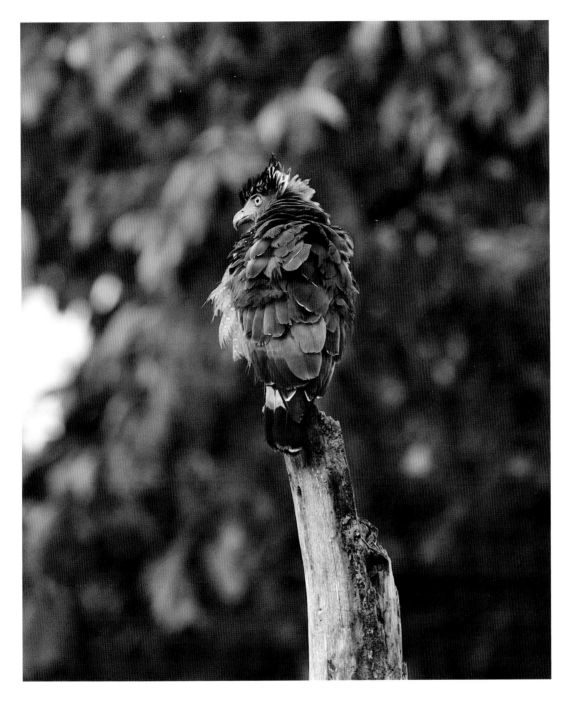

Left: A Crested Serpent-eagle on a perch. The animal is fluffed up which initially makes it diffcult to identify.

Opposite top: A Black-naped Monarch (Hypothymis azurea) seen perching next to one of the trails.

Opposite below: A Blue-headed Pitta (Pitta baudii), which is endemic to Borneo, foraging among the leaf litter. Pittas are difficult to see unless you are very lucky.

hornbill species have been observed here, and the most frequently seen is the Bushy-crested Hornbill. Wrinkled Hornbills (*Aceros corrugatus*) are sometimes seen in gregarious flocks of five to eight individuals. Rhinoceros Hornbills may be seen flying at canopy level on the Miri-Bintulu Road.

Raptors can be observed hovering on thermals around the park. The most common of these are the Brahminy Kite, Crested Serpent-eagle (*Spilornis cheela*) and White-bellied Sea-eagle. Giant Flying Foxes

(*Pteropus vampyrus*) have also been noted on a seasonal basis feeding on the Benuang on the hills.

Mammals

Mammals seen in the park include Banded Palm Civets (*Hemigalus derbyanus*), Malay Civets (*Viverra tangalunga*), Small-toothed Palm Civets (*Arctogalidia trivirgata*), Sunda Slow Lorises and Western Tarsiers

(*Tarsius bancanus*). Primates include Long-tailed Macaques, Southern Pig-tailed Macaques and two species of leaf-monkey. Gibbons are sometimes heard in the mornings and late afternoons. Small mammals such as Plantain and Prevost's Squirrels can often be seen among the trees close to the Latak Waterfall trail.

Insects

Insect lovers will enjoy this park. At night a cacophony of music emanates from cicadas, forest geckos and frogs. The cicadas produce a wood-sawing sound that lasts for several minutes in each session. The sound often starts in the late afternoon and continues until the next day. Cicadas are smallish insects of about 8 cm (3 in) in length, ranging in colour from green to dark brown. There are at least 33 species in Lambir, which is more than 40 per cent of all cicada species found in Sarawak. Cicada mud-tubes may be seen on the ground. The nymphs spend several years underground before emerging and joining the adults in their orchestra of music. The park is also well known for its many species of stick insect, which can be easily seen in the evenings, especially on the trees near the wooden bridge at the start of the Main Trail.

Plant life

Among the tall trees found in the park are Tapang (*Koompassia excelsia*), figs, Benuang (*Octomeles sumatrana*), Selunsur and several species of dipterocarp, including the Illipe tree, locally known as Engkabang (*Shorea* spp.). The fruits of some of these trees are very important to wildlife. Fig fruits are a major source of calcium for hornbills and other birds, and during the fruiting season flocks of birds can be seen aggregating in these trees. Some fig trees can be found on trails to the waterfalls. Illipe nuts are also a food source for Bearded Pigs, which can often be seen feeding below fruiting trees. The seeds drop off the tree and locals liken them to helicopters due to the way they twirl when they fall.

An interesting phenomenon is the mass flowering and fruiting of dipterocarp trees, known as masting. This has been observed and recorded in Lambir in 1992, 1996, 1998 and other years. During the masting period most of the forest is coloured with flowering dipterocarps, and the seeds can be seen a few weeks after this. After gently falling off the mother tree (on their wings), the seeds germinate and thereafter form a uniform carpet of young plants at about the same time. Studies have shown that the onset of this mass flowering is triggered by a pronounced dry period following a prolonged wet season. Dipterocarps flower only after they have achieved maturity, and studies indicate that it may take close to 60 years before these majestic plants mature.

Pinanaga mirabilis is a palm commonly seen along the waterfall trails. Another common plant is *Eugeissona minor*, which has huge, tall stilt roots. Those interested in what a commercial, commonly harvested dipterocarp looks like should search for the Kapur tree (*Dryobalanops kappa*). The bark of this tree tends to be lightly coloured. The dried leaves have thick venation, and trekkers trampling on them on the trails will notice crunching sounds underfoot.

Access

Lambir is about 32 km (20 miles) from Miri City. There are several ways to get to the park. Visitors can drive, hire a vehicle or use public transport to the park. The road from Miri takes you right to the park entrance, which can actually be seen from the Miri–Bintulu trunk road. The public bus also stops in front of the park. The journey time is about 30–40 minutes.

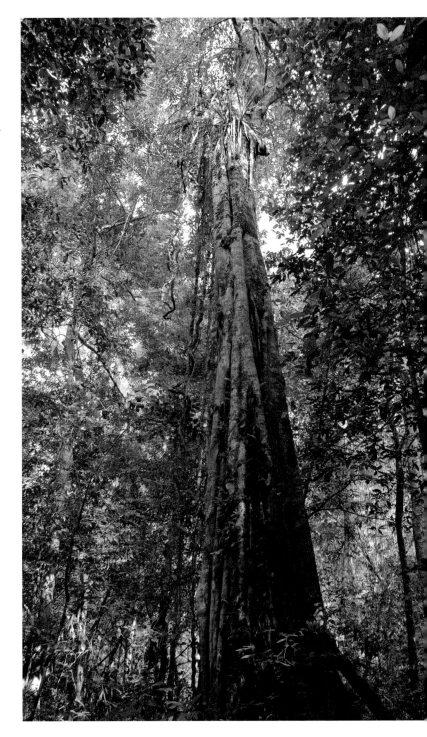

Above: One of the many fig trees in the park, providing food for many of the animals foraging there.

Opposite left: The Western Tarsier is usually seen at night and is about the size of a human palm.

Opposite right: Rhinoceros beetles are among the large insects that can be seen in the forest.

Main Trail to Latak Waterfall

The administration area of Lambir Hills National Park is the point where you begin walking into the Main Trail. Here you can see several brown timber-and-concrete buildings. To get to the trail you have to pass the registration booth. After the booth you immediately see a multicoloured picket fence, a sign indicating 'Main Trail' and a 30-m (98-ft) bridge that will take you across a small stream and into the trail.

At the start of the bridge you may notice a very large palm to the left. It is known locally as Bidang (*Borassodendron borneense*) and is endemic to Borneo. Its fan-shaped leaves are glossy green and their undersides are silvery-white. The stalks of the palm are razor sharp and can make an excellent cutting tool. An interesting fact to note is that even though this palm looks very large indeed, it has not reached maturity and has yet to begin fruiting.

As you cross the bridge you realize that the roar of vehicles on the main Miri–Bintulu road can still be heard. It is only after a little walk past the bridge that the cacophony of cicada calls and the wall of trees crowd out the traffic noises to your right as you walk along the trail. Immediately into the trail, you can see that the canopy is closed and the trees almost hide the sky. If you are an avid birder you may spot birds such as Black-headed Bulbuls (*Pycnonotus atriceps*), Raffles's Malkohas and Green Ioras among the trees past the bridge. (If you return to the bridge in the evening, you will see stick and leaf insects and also planthoppers, Flatidae, feeding on the leaves next to the bridge.)

The trail is well marked and is also terraced with earthen steps. Past the bridge there is a little hill, and here you cannot miss a big strangling fig on the left of the trail with roots growing around its host tree. At night you can hear many different types of amphibian calling, such as the Crested Toad (*Bufo divergens*), File-eared Tree Frog and Tree Hole Frog (*Metaphrynella sundana*). On a good night you will be able to see all manner of animals, including the aforementioned amphibians, lizards, spiders and insects.

Futher along on your left there is a tree with a hollow. This collects rainwater, and if you are lucky you may surprise a frog or two here – Brown Tree Frogs (*Rhacophorus harrissoni*) have been seen laying their eggs in the hollow. There is also

an old liana with a girth of about 20 cm (8 in) on the trail, and visitors have to walk through it. After the hill you can see digging marks left by Bearded Pigs rooting on the sides of the trail and along the stream. It is at this juncture that the trail follows the Latak stream – be aware that this stream floods during heavy rains. Along this flat area you can see clumps of wild banana (*Musa* spp.) and rattans (*Calamus* spp.). Beware of the climbing whips at the ends of the rattan fronds; these are armed with hooks that overhang the trail and may catch your face, hair, clothes and even bags.

Within five minutes of the walk you will see a suspension bridge (10 m/32 ft long). It is quite high and gives you a good view of this section of the stream valley, as well as the exposed sandstone bed of the stream. As you walk along the bridge you may hear Cream-coloured Giant Squirrels going about their day, as well as Banded Broadbills, Garnet Pittas and Short-tailed Babblers.

After the bridge the trail continues and follows the route of the stream. Pretty soon you can see the first waterfall, with colourful sandstone below the falls – the colour ranges from ivory to a dark chestnut. This particular waterfall is only 2 m (6½ ft) high and about 4 m (13 ft) wide. The stream of water is divided due to a protuberance in the rock that causes the water to fall in two curtains. The water falls into a very shallow pool and spreads out onto the flat expanse of sandstone that makes up the stream bottom. There are no loose stones or sand here, and the sandstone slopes gently down, carrying the water from the fall downstream. It is a good place in which to cool your feet.

As you continue walking along the stream bank, you will see Selunsur trees with peeling chestnut bark revealing an orange colour beneath. Palms that you will see here include *Pinanga mirabilis*, *Licuala* fan palms and a clumping palm supported by 2-m (6½-ft) high stilt roots (*Eugeissoma minor*). Further along there is a large Illipe tree on the side of the trail. Mammals and birds can sometimes be seen here, including the Plantain Squirrel, Greater Racket-tailed Drongo and Asian Paradise Flycatcher. Beyond the Illipe tree is the second waterfall, which is below the third bridge in a valley. It is higher than the first one, but is not as wide. If you want

to visit it you have to go off the path and follow the stream before the third bridge.

The final destination for most visitors on the Main Trail is the third waterfall. To get there you have to cross the Latak stream twice, using small wooden bridges. This waterfall is the tallest in the park, at about 25 m (82 ft) high. During heavy rains it swells to more than 5 m (16 ft) wide, while at times of drought it may shrink to less than 2–3 m (6½–10 ft) in width. The pool here is large and deep, and the water has a beautiful green hue, perfect for those who can swim. There is a sandy beach and the facilities here include gazebos, changing rooms, toilets and a barbecue pit.

Above: *Black-and-red Broadbill* (Cymbirhynchus macrorhynchos).

Right: *Short-tailed Babbler.*

Loagan Bunut National Park

Loagan Bunut National Park is located in the Tinjar floodplain in north-eastern Sarawak and covers an area of 10,736 ha (26,529 acres). The park was gazetted in 1990.

The park contains Sarawak's largest natural freshwater lake, the water level of which fluctuates several times a year. During the wetter season water from the Teru River flows into the lake, expanding its perimeter and depth, with the water level reaching 3 m (10 ft) deep in certain areas. During the drier season

the water flows out of the lake back into the Teru River, and in its extreme the lake bed can actually be seen. There have been records of the lake bed drying to a hard crust, and when this happens you can walk from one end of the lake to the other across the lake bed.

Significance

Loagan Bunut National Park is well known for its rich biodiversity and unique aquatic ecosystem. It is a very good spot for keen birdwatchers – there are at least 187 bird species, including rarities, in the park, which is about 34 per cent of the total number of birds known to occur in Sarawak, or 30.2 per cent of all Bornean bird species. The park also harbours 36 bat species, including endemics and globally threatened species, as well as leaf-monkeys, crocodiles and a large population of flying foxes.

The Berawan people from Long Teru were given rights and privileges when the park was created. The core activities of the Berawan in the 1990s were farming, hunting for subsistence and fishing. It is only with the onset of plantation agriculture, such as oil-palm cultivation, that the Berawan ventured into large-scale, commercial monocultures.

The fishing style of the Berawan is very interesting – they work from a floating house or platform, and use a huge net to catch fish during the receding and advancing tides that accompany the rise and fall of the water level. Selambau appears to be most used when the waters drain to and from the Tinjar River. Fresh fish are often caught and sold at Lapok Town (the nearest town) or to visitors in the park.

The Berawan people have a custom of burying those who can afford it in burial platforms, or *klirieng*, which are supported by Belian tree columns. Some of the columns are in the lake and are submerged at the high-water mark. The intricate carvings that were created on the Belian columns and sometimes on the *klirieng* itself can be made out if these structures are viewed close-up.

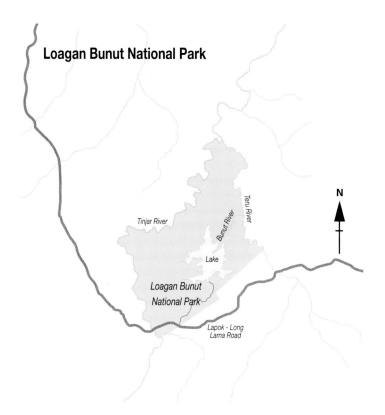

Opposite: One of the many Oriental Darters in the park. They can often be seen foraging in the waters and this one has a fish in its beak.

It should be noted that the Estuarine Crocodile has been observed in the lake, as this reptile is also found along the Tinjar River. Sleeping dogs have been reported missing by the Berawan who reside in the floating boat houses, and also from the Selambau. No humans have been attacked.

Trails and trips

There are three short trails in the park. Although they are slightly undulating, most visitors are able to enjoy them and observe panoramic views of the lake, as well as common yet interesting flora and fauna. The Hydrology Trail is a 2-km (1¼-mile) walk – it was cleared when there was hydrological work to study the fluctuations of the water levels in the lake, as well as the extent of flooding in the peat swamp. Visitors are able to walk into the peat swamp and see how the

Right: A juvenile Wallace's Hawk-eagle hunting bats in the evening.

Below: An adult Wallace's Hawk-eagle perched on a fig tree.

Opposite: A rare Storm's Stork perched on a dead tree overlooking the lake.

plants, with their stilt roots, survive in the flooded environment. The trail also takes you along some parts of the cleared areas in the park, and it is here that quite a few bird species can be seen.

The Tapang and Belian Trails are much shorter, at 260 m (855 ft) and 720 m (2,360 ft) in length, respectively. They take you into the dipterocarp forests, where taller trees can be seen.

You can hire a boat to explore the lake, especially when the water levels are favourable. This can be done at the park headquarters, where you may be referred to the local Berawan. The best times to explore are early morning and late afternoon. Not only is it coolest at these times, but you may get to see waterbirds fishing in the lake. The boat driver may take you into the forest, especially when the peat swamp is flooded. Wooden boats are the norm for such forays into the lake. Note that the Berawan have a local taboo for visitors who intend to explore the park by boat. Traditionally, they will not take any person who is dressed in red into the lake. This tradition may have waned lately, but those wanting to respect local cultures should do as their guide suggests when it comes to this taboo.

Birds

This park is an exciting place for birders, particularly because Storm's Stork has been recorded here. This species is listed as Endangered on the IUCN Red List of Threatened Species, and is one of the rarest birds in the world. There are estimated to be less than 1,000 individuals worldwide, hence the bird is very high on birdwatchers' lists. It has been seen along the Sungai Pelalang, a small tributary of the Sungai Bunut.

Another four bird species found here are listed as Vulnerable: Wallace's Hawk-eagle (*Nisaetus nanus*), Crestless Fireback, Large Green-pigeon (*Treron capellei*) and Hook-billed Bulbul. Forty-six other species are listed as lower risk but Near Threatened. In the cleared areas accessible from the Hydrology Trail, you may see

the Bornean Bristlehead, Hook-billed Bulbul (*Setornis criniger*) and Grey-breasted Babbler. The Hook-billed Bulbul is a peat-swamp endemic, while the Bornean Bristlehead and Yellow-rumped Flowerpecker (*Prionochilus xanthopygius*) are endemic to Borneo. Large birds that can be seen in the park include the Brahminy Kite, White-bellied Sea-eagle and Osprey (*Pandion haliaetus*).

The Oriental Darter is an icon for the park, and its image is engraved on the welcome sign that greets visitors to the park. This species can be found in creeks and small tributaries, notably along the Sungai Babi and Paron Cove. Spotting the bird in the field requires some skill, as it usually remains submerged in water. Only the neck sticks out of the water; it resembles a snake, hence its vernacular name, snakebird, as it is known by the local people. It is able to dive and search for food underwater, but because its feathers lack the layer of coating that would make them waterproof, it

needs to dry them in order to fly. On sunny days after rain or in the early morning, the Oriental Darter can be easily spotted perched on a stump or branch with its wings spread out to dry. In the early 1980s the darters were a common sight, forming big rookeries on large trees fringing the lake. However, the species is now listed as Near Threatened on the IUCN Red List.

The Purple Heron is the most commonly encountered heron species around the lake. This large bird is often solitary and creeps through the shallow sections of water close to the bank. It frequently cocks its head low to strike at fish and other food in the water.

During the migratory season, when the lake begins to dry up, hundreds of egrets converge onto the lake to feed. The most abundant egret species in the park are the Little Egret and Cattle Egret (*Bubulcus ibis*). The other egret species that have been recorded here are the Great Egret (*Casmerodius albus*) and Intermediate Egret.

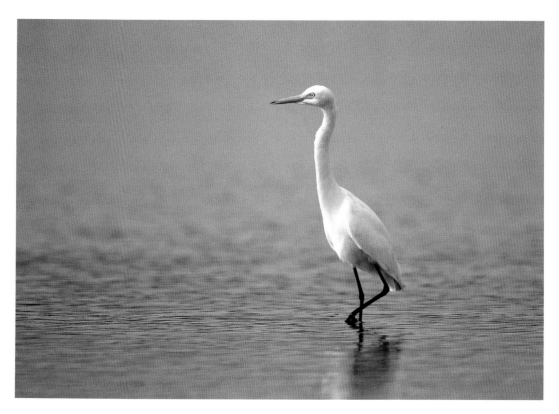

Left: An Intermediate Egret, one of whose identifying characteristics is a yellow bill with black tip. Often seen around Loagan Bunut.

Opposite: The Bornean Bristlehead is endemic to Borneo – a very loud bird if you happen upon it.

Below: The Oriental Darter is sometimes called a snakebird by the local communities because of the shape of its neck.

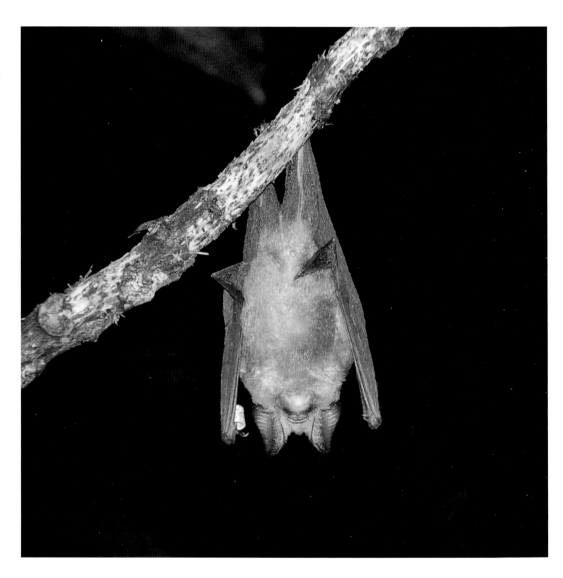

Mammals

Thirty-six species of bat, consisting of five megachiropteras and 31 microchiropteras, have been recorded in the park to date. This represents a high proportion (39.1 per cent) of the total number of bat species that occur in Borneo. Under the IUCN Red List of Threatened Species, Ridley's Roundleaf Bat (*Hipposideros ridleyi*), Gilded Tube-nosed Bat (*Murina rozendaali*) and Bare-backed Rousette (*Rousettus spinalatus*) are listed as Vulnerable, and two others, the Small Woolly Bat (*Kerivoula intermedia*) and Least Woolly Bat (*Kerivoula minuta*), are listed as lower risk but Near Threatened. Two species, the Dayak Roundleaf Bat and Gilded Tube-nosed Bat, are endemic to Borneo.

Among the larger wildlife that can sometimes be seen in the park are Bornean Banded and White-fronted Leaf-monkeys (*Presbytis chrysomelas cruciger* and *P. frontata*), and Giant Flying Foxes, as well as Estuarine Crocodiles.

The largest population of flying foxes in Sarawak is found in this park. More than 25,000 animals have been seen leaving the roost, with over 40 minutes between the first observed departing flying fox and the last one at dusk. The best place to see these animals is on the main road to the park headquarters, and also behind the park buildings. They are often hunted by the locals and trigger-happy hunters. However, they are protected in Sarawak, and such incidences should be reported to either the Sarawak Forestry Corporation or Forest Department Sarawak.

Plant life

There are two main forest types in the park, namely peat-swamp and lowland mixed dipterocarp forests. Four vegetative or phasic communities have been recognized in the peat-swamp forest, and there is a gradual transition of the different communities from the periphery to the core of the peat swamp. The mixed swamp forest (MSF) occurs on alluvial soils on the periphery of the park nearer to the rivers. Away from the rivers, the MSF is gradually replaced by Alan Batu forest, followed by Alan Bunga forest and eventually Padang Alan in the centre of the peat swamp. These three Alan habitats are dominated by the Light Red Meranti (*Shorea albida*), which is listed as Endangered on the IUCN Red List, with canopies that gradually become lower further away from the river.

The lowland mixed dipterocarp forest in the park was logged before the final designation of the area as a national park. As a result, most of this habitat is completely disturbed with significant loss of its composition and structure. The remaining stand comprises timber species of low economic value and grades, or economically valuable trees that were too small to be harvested commercially. Nevertheless there is still quite a diverse array of trees.

As their names suggest, Tapang (*Koompassia excelsia*) and Belian trees are the main attractions on the trails of the same name (see page 181). An interesting fact about Tapang, a smooth-barked tree, is that it is considered to be one of the world's tallest trees (the third, in fact). While its bark appears pale and soft, it is actually a hardwood and is used for making blowpipes (hunting implements of various indigenous Sarawakians, such as the Iban, Penan and Kayan).

Sometimes beehives can be found on these trees. The wild honey and the honeycombs are often collected and are considered to be a delicacy among the rural communities. It is an ardous task collecting the honey as the hives may be located some 30 m (100 ft) above the ground. Honey collectors often hammer wooden stakes into the tree-trunks as steps for climbing up to the branches to access the wild honey. Given that the living tree can bestow such benefits, some communities actually have a taboo against the felling of these trees. Craftsmen belonging to the communities only use trees that have fallen due to storm damage or natural causes.

Belian is a medium-sized tree, and is increasingly becoming rarer throughout the state. The wood from it is extremely durable and is considered to be perhaps the hardest of all hardwoods in Malaysia. It is also popularly known as ironwood, and due to its resistance to weathering and termite damage it has been harvested in an unsustainable manner, to the extent that very little is now being produced in Sarawak. The timber was used for pepper poles, house construction (Belian shingles), plank-walks, jetties and other structures. The extent of its durability can be seen in Sarawak's pepper farms, located around the park. Some pepper poles have been reused for more than 30 years, and the only signs of their age are the slight green fungus stains on the covered parts of the poles. Belian shingles can be seen in older rustic longhouses in the interior of Sarawak, as well as in older Malay and Melanau houses in villages and towns such as Mukah.

Access

Loagan Bunut National Park is situated in the Miri Division in north-western Sarawak and is accessible by road. The nearest town to the national park is Lapok, and the estimated distance from Miri town to Loagan Bunut is about 130 km (80 miles). From Miri there are several ways to get to the park, ranging from public transport to private taxis and rental vehicles. However, a four-wheel-drive vehicle is recommended as the road is not completely tar sealed from Miri to the park, and can be quite slippery during the wet season.

Gunung Mulu National Park

Officially created in 1974, Gunung Mulu National Park is the second oldest park in Sarawak. At present, after the first of several proposed extensions, it is the largest national park in Sarawak, with an extended area of 81,116 ha (200,442 acres). Mulu is also contiguous with Gunung Buda National Park (11,307 ha/27,940 acres), and the combined Mulu and Buda National Parks (92,423 ha/228,382 acres) rank as the second largest protected area in Sarawak after the Batang Ai National Park/Lanjak-Entimau Wildlife Sanctuary landscape.

Significance

Containing one of the most amazing cave systems on Earth, Mulu is full of superlatives. Its Deer Cave has the largest cave passage in the world, the Sarawak Chamber is the world's largest underground chamber and incredible spectacles of bat emergences can be seen at the caves. The forested and mountain landscapes were first explored in 1858 by the diplomat and explorer Spenser St John. He was unable to reach the summit of Mulu, and it was not until 1932 that an Oxford University Expedition led by Edward Shackleton, son of Sir Ernest Shackleton, achieved this feat. By 1961, after exploring the caves, G. E. Wilford of the Malaysian Geological Survey indicated that Mulu still had many unexplored caves, and that its secrets would be exposed via better expeditions. Since the earliest expeditions there have been another 21 scientific-based expeditions into Mulu.

In 1977–1978, the Royal Geographical Society with the Sarawak Government led a 15-month-long expedition into the park. Results from this and subsequent expeditions (year ending 2013) revealed the uniqueness and spectacular biodiversity of the park. Notable discoveries include more than 2,000 flowering plant species of at least 3,500 plant species; and at least 20,000 animal species, of which the majority are insects. As for larger wildlife, there are more than 60 mammal species, 262 bird species, 23 lizard species and 75 frog and toad species. Because of its uniqueness, the park was recommended as a World Heritage Site and listed in 2000. It is one of two natural World Heritage Sites in Malaysia.

There are many natural attractions to enjoy at Mulu. They are too numerous to list in full, so only some of the obviously popular and 'wilder' ones are described here.

Several indigenous communities live in and around the park, such as the Berawans and the Penans. Of the two, the Penans are probably more famous as they were (and some still are) hunter-gathers living in the Baram hinterland. The Penans achieved fame worldwide from the mid- to late 1980s onwards due to advocacy groups highlighting their fight against logging and the construction of dams. There are two Penan communities living close to Mulu, and some individuals work at the park as guides and porters. The Penans are expert hunters and Mulu is part of their hunting range; it has been reported that the rarity of

Above: Dring's Slender Litter Frog (Leptolalax dringi).

Previous pages: Deer Cave has a huge entrance as can be seen by the size of the humans in the centre of the image.

larger animals in the park is due to their quiet harvesting and consumption of wildlife.

The Berawans have longhouses that are several hours' away by boat from Mulu itself, with the most famous longhouse being at Long Terawan. Berawans also work in the park, and some operate travel agencies ferrying tourists from Marudi. Several Berawans serve as guides at the park.

Ibans can also be seen around Mulu. Although their original heartland is in the Batang Ai area, due to their *berjalai*, or wanderings, they have established communities at Limbang (northern Sarawak). Some Ibans work in Mulu, and they originally used the Headhunter's Trail to go home during the festive season (the trail is named after the historical headhunting route used by tribal headhunters along the Tutoh and Mendalam Rivers).

Trips, trails and treks

Wildlife at the canopies can be viewed using the Mulu Canopy Skywalk. This ½-km (1,640-ft) long walkway close to the tree canopy allows you to see birds and insects living in the canopy. The walkway is not for those with a fear of heights, as it is 15–25 m (49–82 ft) above the forest floor.

The show caves were first identified as a tourist attraction in the early 1980s. Work on the lighting and trails within the caves and the protective 'see-through' barriers started in the mid-1980s. According to local belief, the constant failure of electrical items and other such devices was due to the spirits inhabiting these caves. Thus, a miring ceremony, consisting of local appeasements and prayers to the spirits, had to be performed. The first miring ceremony was initiated by the first cave-development officer stationed in Mulu. As of now there are four show caves, namely Clearwater, Deer, Lang and Wind Caves.

The Wind Cave and Clearwater Cave are close to each other, and visitors often investigate these sites one after the other. You can walk or take a boat to the

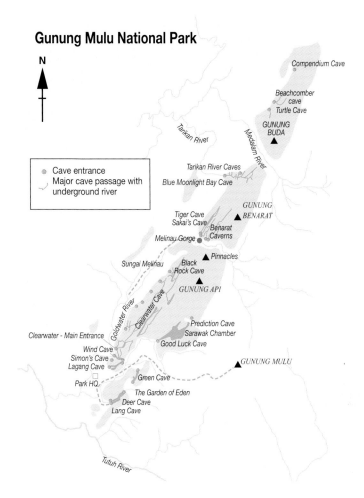

Gunung Mulu National Park

N

- Cave entrance
- Major cave passage with underground river

Compendium Cave
Beachcomber cave
Turtle Cave
GUNUNG BUDA
Tarikan River
Medalam River
Tarikan River Caves
Blue Moonlight Bay Cave
GUNUNG BENARAT
Tiger Cave
Sakai's Cave
Benarat Caverns
Melinau Gorge
Pinnacles
Sungai Melinau
Black Rock Cave
Clearwater Cave
GUNUNG API
Goldwater River
Prediction Cave
Sarawak Chamber
Good Luck Cave
Clearwater - Main Entrance
Wind Cave
Simon's Cave
Lagang Cave
GUNUNG MULU
Park HQ
Green Cave
The Garden of Eden
Deer Cave
Lang Cave
Tutuh River

entrances of the caves. The Wind Cave is so named because you experience a cool rush of air the moment you enter the cave. The route is lighted, and the attractions include the King's Room and the amazing stalactites and stalagmites found here. This cave is considered by many to be one of the most beautiful caves in Mulu.

The Clearwater Cave system is extremely long, and up to 197 km (122 miles) of explored passage have been charted; it is the ninth longest cave in the world. Most visitors only get to see the entrance, and it sits about 30 m (98 ft) above the Melinau River. Apart from its long passage and beautiful stalagmites, the cave is home to the rare one-leaf plant (*Monophyllaea* spp.). Those who love big fish should also take a peek at the wonderful Semah (*Tor duoronensis*), gliding in and around the jetty or platform. Most of these fish have become habituated to humans and gravitate towards visitors. Swimming is permitted here.

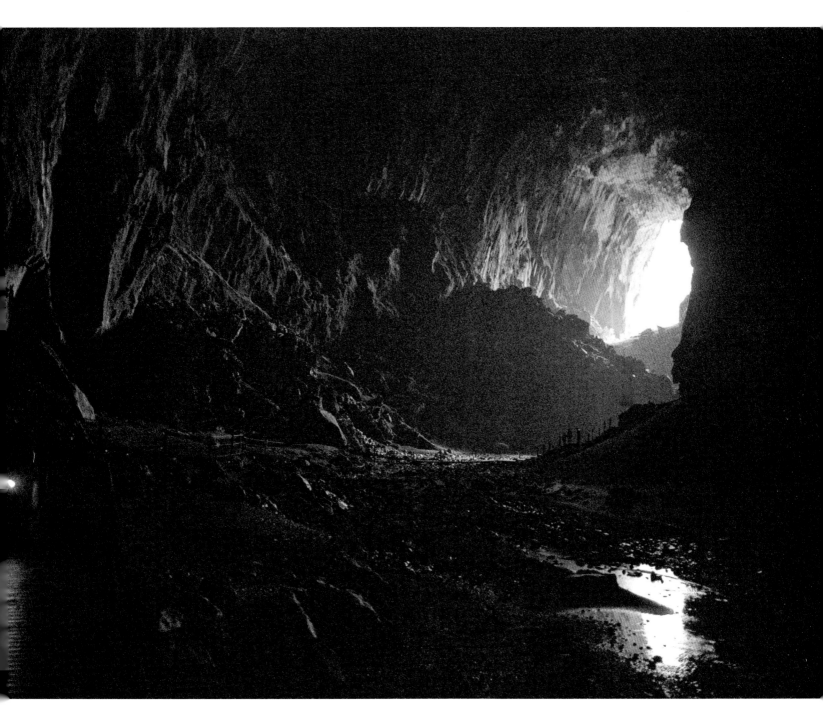

A trail (the Rainforest Discovery Walk) links the park headquarters to the Deer and Lang Caves. The trail traverses lowland dipterocarp forests, and observant visitors may note myriads of interesting plants and animals. It takes about an hour to walk from the headquarters to the entrances of the caves.

The entrance to the Deer Cave is huge (it is much used in photographs highlighting nature tourism in Sarawak). It is 120 m (394 ft) high, 175 m (574 ft) wide and about 2 km (1.2 miles) long. Visitors tend to proceed to the Garden of Eden at the back end of the cave. Beyond this are the Eden River and walking trails, which end at rockpools that are great for a dip.

The Lang Cave is a short walk away from the Deer Cave. The cave is fairly small and delicate, and has beautiful stalactites, stalagmites and helictites.

Above: The iconic entrance to Deer Cave.

Opposite: A massive stalagmite in Lang Cave.

Visitors interested in getting themselves a bit dirty can opt for some adventure caving – there are various levels in Mulu, rated at the introductory, intermediate and advance levels. Those intending to engage in adventure caving have to show that they are able to do so, either by physically proving their fitness to the guides in one of the introductory or intermediate caves, or by showing that they have current membership of an internationally recognized speleological society or caving group. Adventure caving is done at Racer Cave, Lagangs Cave, the Clearwater-Wind Cave connection and Sarawak Chamber. The latter two caves are listed for the advanced caver. All visitors are provided with a caving helmet, headlamp and ropes (where needed). Sturdy shoes are requisites, and you are reminded that you will get wet in some of the caves.

The sharp limestone outcrops called the Pinnacles are another icon of Mulu National Park and are among the most recognizable images depicting the park. Photographs of the Pinnacles often under-represent their true size and magnificence. Visitors also often underestimate the fitness levels required to trek up to the Pinnacles, as this site is about 1,200 m (3,937 ft) above sea level. It is at least a three-day journey to view the Pinnacles from the park headquarters, and you have to stay overnight at a midway point called Camp 5. To get to Camp 5 you have to take a boat for up to three hours, then walk along the lowland dipterocarp forest for another 3–4 hours. The walk to Camp 5 is relatively gentle, and during it Belian, several species of fig, bamboos and the Giant Voodoo Lily (*Amorphophallus hewittii*) can be seen.

From Camp 5 you can head into Limbang via the Headhunter's Trail. To do so the Melinau River has to be crossed using a suspension bridge. Although the journey is quite gentle, guides should be used for this onwards journey.

The trek to the summit of Mulu can take between four and five days for a return journey. Much depends on the fitness of the individual. The fittest porters have been known to make the return journey in two days.

The summit is about 2,376 m (7,795 ft) above sea level, and the trek starts at the park headquarters. Lowland riverine and dipterocarp forests can be seen on the first day's walk, hill dipterocarp forest on the second day and montane forest from the third day.

Bats

After visiting the caves mentioned above, you can stay to witness the emergence of millions of bats (on most days) from the entrance to the Deer Cave. A bat observatory is located at a strategic location; from here this wonderous spectacle, which may last for up to 45 minutes, can be watched. The bats sometimes come up in a swirling band, and they appear almost as a single moving and twisting, longish ribbon or cloud. Winged predators such as Bat Hawks and hornbills can be seen loitering at the entrance, and swoop in to take bats on the wing.

The bats that are taken are mostly Wrinkled-Lipped Free-tailed Bats. They feed on insects and are great as a biological pest control, especially on farms and plantations. While the free-tailed bats create a spectacular emergence scene, the Deer Cave may also have the world record for the number of bat species in a single cave. Eleven other species have been seen here: the Common Nectar Bat (*Eonycteris spelaea*), Small Asian Sheath-tailed Bat (*Emballonura alecto*), Bornean Horseshoe Bat (*Rhinolophus borneensis*), Large-eared Horseshoe Bat (*R. philippinensis*), Cantor's Roundleaf Bat (*Hipposideros galeritus*), Fawn Roundleaf Bat (*H. cervinus*), Dayak Roundleaf Bat (*H. dyacorum*), Diadem Roundleaf Bat, Malayan Tailless Roundleaf Bat (*Coelops robinsoni*), Little Bent-winged Bat (*Miniopterus australis*) and Greater Naked Bat (*Cheiromeles torquatus*).

With each passing year Mulu has been found to be home to an increased number of bat species. There were five new discoveries between 2011 and 2013, and the list of new species includes Temminck's Tailless Fruit Bat (*Megaerops ecaudatus*), Intermediate

Horseshoe Bat (*Rhinolophus affinis*), Greater Dawn Bat (*Eonycteris major*), Great Woolly Horsehoe Bat (*Rhinolophus luctus*) and Hardwicke's Woolly Bat (*Kerivoula hardwickii*). There are now 47 bat species recorded for the park, which is close to half of all the bat species recorded in Borneo.

Other wildlife

Among the various birds that may be seen along the Mulu Canopy Skywalk are Scarlet-rumped Trogons (*Harpactes duvaucelii*), Red-crowned Barbets (*Megalaima rafflesii*), Greater Green Leafbirds (*Chloropsis sonnerati*) and Mountain Imperial-pigeons (*Ducula badia*).

The common fauna and flora seen on the Rainforest Discovery Walk trail includes pygmy squirrels rushing up and down the boles of trees, babblers and bulbuls

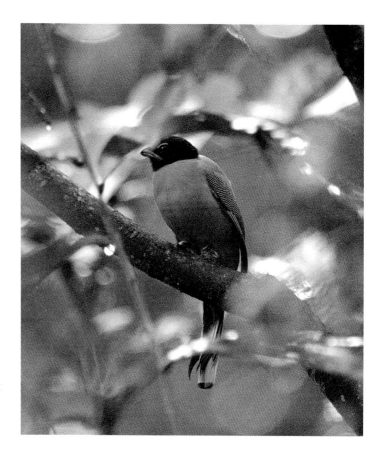

Above: *A male Scarlet-rumped Trogon.*

Left: *A leafbird hovering before perching on a tree.*

flying among the lower canopy, nuthatches picking insects off tree bark, and climbing plants such as rattan and assam. A spectacular strangling fig can also be seen here. Quite a few of the trees and other plants are labelled.

The greenery at the Garden of Eden, at the back of the Deer Cave, comprising ferns, shrubs and stunted trees, is quite refreshing to the eyes after the plunging darkness of the Deer Cave. There is the constant sound of clicking, chattering and chirping in the cave. These sounds are made by the millions of Wrinkle-lipped Free-tailed Bats and other bat species roosting on the ceilings and walls of the cave. The chirping noises emanate from Mossy-nest Swiftlets (*Collocalia salangana*).

The iconic trees that should not be missed in the hill dipterocarp forests on the way up to the summit of

Mulu are Kapur Bukit (*Dryobalanops beccarii*), huge hollow figs and Engakabangs. Several species of locally endemic pitcher plant and orchid can be seen in the montane forests.

Access

Mulu National Park is approximately 100 km (62 miles) east of Miri City. There is an airport close to the park and visitors can fly from Kuching, Miri or Kota Kinabalu to Mulu. There are alternative routes – one is an interesting boat ride from Miri to Marudi, then Long Terawan and finally Mulu. It takes close to a day of boat travel and arrangements have to be made with local boatmen. The second alternative is a walk from Limbang to the park via the Headhunter's Trail.

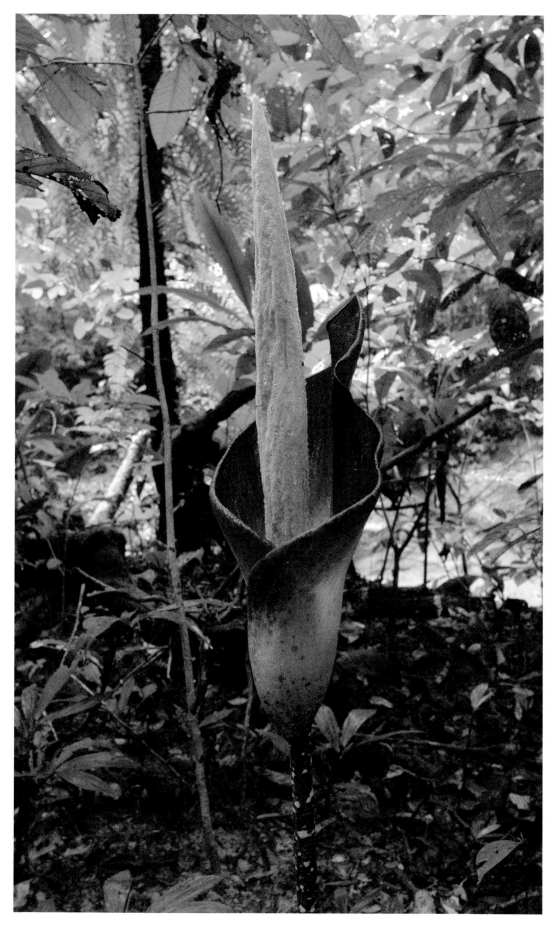

Left: The Giant Voodoo Lily has one of the largest flowers in the world. It has a very pungent aroma.

Opposite left: A Mountain Imperial-pigeon on a Kruing tree.

Opposite right: Little Cuckoo-dove *(Macropygia ruficeps) on a* Macaraga tree.

Sedilu and Maludam National Parks

The two parks are separated by the Batang Lupar River and the Ulu Sebuyau National Park. They are within about 10 km (6¼ miles) of each other, with Sedilu being to the west of Maludam National Park. The parks protect one of the least-known forests in Sarawak.

Sedilu National Park

Significance

Sedilu National Park is located in predominantly peat-swamp forest formed on alluvial flat plains. Islands of small hills exist in the flat plains, among them Melingkong, Sadong, Sadong Besar, Serabu and Ngili Hills. The highest point in the park is Sadong Besar Hill, which rises to about 300 m (985 ft) above sea level. The swamp is drained by the Belanga, Sebangan, Tebelu and Sebuyau Rivers.

Sedilu National Park is much smaller than Maludam, at 6,311 ha (15,594 acres), but it was created because it harbours Orang-utans and a resident population of flying foxes that is one of the largest in Sarawak, with counts of more than 15,000 animals during the breeding season. The park is contiguous to Simunjan and this town is historically linked to Alfred Russel Wallace, the naturalist who wrote the seminal manuscript commonly known as 'Sarawak Law' (see page 152). The forest traversed by Alfred Russel Wallace still exists, as do the famed rail tracks at the Simunjan Coal Mines.

At present there are no trails for walking into the park. Boat trips to the park are extremely pleasurable and arrangements for them can be made with the shop owners at at the small seaside village of Sebangan (see page 200). The river route passes by mangrove and Nipah Palm (*Nypa fruticans*) forests near to the sea, then alluvial forests with trees overhanging clear black waters. In the open sections of the alluvial forests you can see vast expanses of waterlogged grasslands littered with *Pandanus* species blocking sections of the rivers. The 1–2 hour road journey from Sebangan takes you along a tarred bund on the banks of the Sadong River and along plantation roads (since the early 2000s, oil-palm plantations have increasingly become the norm here). Attractions here include several species of egret, bitterns, herons and other birds.

The hills have different vegetation. In the lower portions of the hills where the communities have their farms, Rubber Trees and countless fruit trees can be seen, including durians. Higher into the hills there are old-regrowth mixed dipterocarp forests, and these have been retained by the communities for subsistence use in the building of their boats and houses.

False Gharial

The elusive False Gharial (*Tomistoma schlegelii*) is a crocodilian that is considered a rarity, and not much is known about its distribution in Malaysia. Among the

Sedilu and Maludam National Park

Opposite: A False Gharial basking on a log on the banks of a river in the early morning.

sites where this species has been seen are the Engsengei, Kroh, Runjing and Engkelili Rivers. In northern Sarawak it has been seen in the Tubau and Tinjar Rivers. All the reported distributions are along rivers flowing out of peat-swamp forests. It has been speculated that due to the species' limited distribution and affinity to peat swamps, losses of these swamps could result in a major reduction in its distribution.

The False Gharial can be distinguished from the Estuarine Crocodile by its a sharper, thinner snout; the snout of the crocodile appears broader and shorter. Field studies of the animals are limited and there has only been one recorded case of a captive-breeding incident in Malaysia, at Zoo Negara.

From field and captive observations it has become apparent that this is a fish-feeding animal that has not been noted as a 'man-eater'. While it can be seen basking on logs on riverbanks, such observations are uncommon. It can also be observed during evening and night cruises along the Sebangan River.

Flying foxes

During the evenings and early mornings visitors can watch in awe as more than 15,000 flying foxes fly overhead to forage or return home. As already noted, Sedilu is home to one of the largest flying fox populations in Sarawak, and indeed in Malaysia. This gigantic bat (the Giant Flying Fox) has had a scientifically reported resident maternity root in the area since the 1990s. Historically, however, it has appeared in panoramic sketches of the area by travellers such as Hornaday in the late 1870s.

Above: Flying foxes in mid-morning. They can often be seen hovering above the roost when disturbed.

Right: Red Giant Flying Squirrel, one of several species of squirrel in the park.

Opposite top: Red Giant Flying Squirrel gliding among large trees, though it is a rare sight.

Opposite below: Brown Wood-owl (Strix leptogrammica) sometimes seen near permanent field camps. It is reported to feed on rodents and other small mammals.

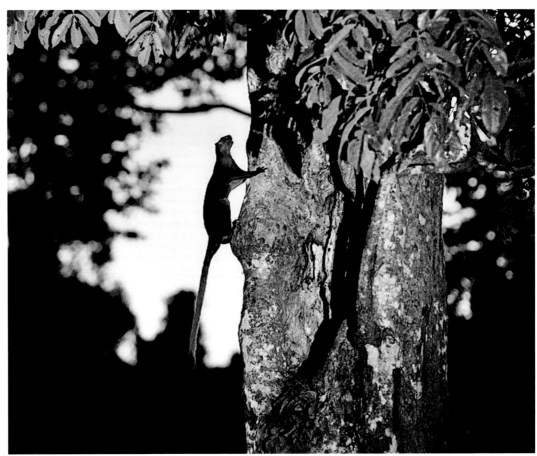

This is the largest bat in Sarawak. The biggest individuals weigh more than 1 kg (2¼ lb), and have a wingspan of over 1 m (3¼ ft). They have manes ranging in colour from grey to straw, deep red and almost black. The young cling on to the mothers for several weeks. Older pups are subsequently parked in trees by their mothers when they forage in the evenings. Flying foxes hang upside down in trees ranging in size from 10 m (33 ft) to more than 20 m (66 ft) tall. Up to 200 animals can be seen roosting in large trees. Due to the frequent roosting of the bats in some trees, batches of them are defoliated and appear as patches of 'balding' trees from the air.

In the course of the day the flying foxes fan their large wings to cool down. Birds of prey are often seen harassing them and preying on them; White-bellied Sea-eagles have been noted successfully killing these bats and eating them on a perch.

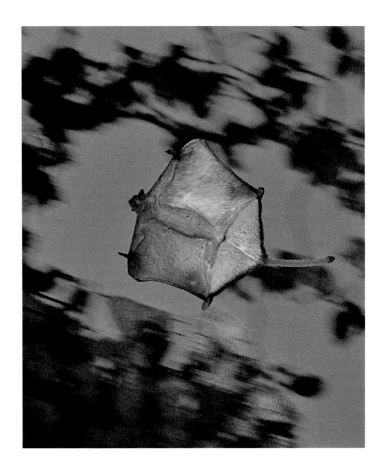

Other wildlife

There are several interesting plant species in Sedilu, ranging from the commercially attractive Ramin (*Gonystylus bancanus*), to the under-appreciated Benuang and Ubah. Smaller plants such as the *Pandanus* species have an aromatic smell, which is obvious when you get close up to them. The waterlogged grasses provide homes for a considerable amount of wildlife, from numerous species of fish, frogs and False Gharials, to owls that spend much of the night perched on branches overlooking these areas for prey.

Access

There are two ways to get to the park. For going by boat you can drive or catch a private van from Kuching to Pendam. The journey takes more than an hour, depending on the traffic (45 km/28 miles). There is a wharf at Pendam where you can pay for a fare to

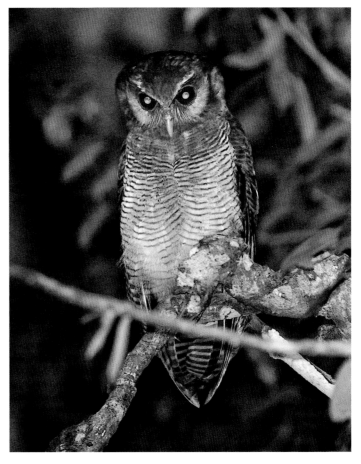

Sebangan town, and this journey takes about 20 minutes (depending on the size of the outboard motor). From Sebangan a boat or van can be taken to the park. The boat journey takes up to 2–3 hours, and is much more pleasant than a journey by road. Different habitats can be seen at water level, and the waterlogged grasslands and clear black waters of the peat swamp can be appreciated. The road journey from Sebangan takes 1–2 hours (see page 196).

Maludam National Park

Significance

Maludam National Park is home to the little-known Critically Endangered Red-banded Leaf-monkey (*Presbytis melalophos cruciger*), Asia's rarest primate. It also has Sarawak's most extensive protected peat swamp, at 43,147 ha (106,618 acres). While it is home to the Red-banded Leaf-monkey, the Orang-utan, Asia's largest ape, is strangely never reported from this site. Exhaustive surveys in the 2000s by various government agencies and NGOs also indicated a strange absence of Orang-utans here, although they are found across the river at Ulu Sebuyau.

Apart from the Red-banded Leaf-monkey, other notable iconic faunal species seen here are the Lesser Adjutant (*Leptoptilos javanicus*), Buffy Fish-owl (*Ketupa ketupu*) and Flat-headed Cat (*Prionailurus planiceps*). The previously common commercial timber species Ramin is also found here. It is now becoming rare throughout the state.

Lesser Adjutant

The Lesser Adjutant is potentially Sarawak's largest stork. With its bald head, longish thick beak and sometimes red face and orange neck (during the breeding season), this bird is hard to miss at the mudflats of Maludam. In the 1970s there were reports of a large colony of the birds at the mudflats. However, surveys in the mid-2000s showed that the numbers had decreased to less than 20 birds.

Buffy Fish-owl

The Buffy Fish-owl is one of the largest owls in Sarawak, reaching a length of up to 45 cm (18 in). The birds are elusive but sometimes appear close to field researchers' base camps. They also sometimes get caught in bat researchers' mist nets. The owls reportedly feed on fish and frogs, but have also been recorded feeding on insects and rats. They employ a variety of calls, which range from drumming notes to ringing.

Flat-headed Cat

This elusive small cat (about the size of a domestic cat) can be seen on the banks of the Maludam River in the

evenings. Visitors using lights while they drift down the river may sometimes see it sitting on a bank. The animal has a straw-coloured head, and has been observed swimming in the river and even diving. Not much is known about it, but its distribution has generally been close to riverine systems, although a single roadkill of the species has been reported from a major highway in Peninsular Malaysia.

Plant life

Although Maludam is a peat swamp, the physical appearance of the swamp is markedly different from that of swamps seen in Sedilu. There is an absence of waterlogged grasses and the river is much narrower. The river dries up during the dry season and access may be blocked by the thick *Pandanus* as well as the logs that lie across the smaller rivers. As the forest in the park dries up, and due to the fact that it is sitting on a peat dome, there is fear that a major fire could cause immeasurable harm to the area and its wildlife. For this reason, visitors should make the journey only in the wetter months and be prepared to get wet. They should also be aware that the park has had a past history of logging, and that the remnant vegetation is therefore shorter and scragglier than that in pristine unlogged areas. Legal logging ceased in the late 1990s.

Ramin is a hardwood that is a favourite for homes because it is not just easily workable, but also considered beautiful due to the fact that it is lightly coloured. The finish of the timber looks like that of softwoods such as pine. Ramin is only found in peat swamps, and in scattered stands in some parks such as Bako, Sedilu and Maludam National Parks. The fruit of Ramin is largish (about 4.5 cm/1.77 in), and red and fleshy. Squirrels and flying foxes can be seen foraging and removing the seeds from the fruiting trees, thus acting as seed dispersers for the plant. Some small Ramin trees can be seen at Maludam; they are part of one of the botanical trials set up in the early 2000s.

Access

There are various ways to get to the park, ranging from a sea journey from Kuching and being dropped off at sea to await a smaller boat that then takes you to Maludam town, to the more current method, a road journey. The town is now linked to other rural towns such as Pantu, Pusa, Beladin and Kampung Triso. The boat journey is open during the dry season and is hazardous during the wet monsoon. It is because of the precarious nature of this journey that a road was constructed to link the town to the main Sarawak coastal trunk road. The boat journey takes almost three hours, and there is now a major discussion by the company about ceasing the 'sea drop-off' as visitor numbers have dwindled. The road journey takes six hours.

*Above: Horse-tailed Squirrel (*Sundasciurus hippurus pryeri*). This Near Threatened species can often be seen in the lower branches of trees and sometimes descends to the ground.*

Opposite: Flat-headed Cats can sometimes be seen on the banks of the Maludam River at night. They do dive underwater.

Resources

Acknowledgements

Geoffrey Davison wishes to thank past and present colleagues in the National Parks Board (Singapore) and WWF Malaysia, as well as the Malaysian Nature Society. Lim Li Ching was a useful source of information on the Terengganu coast and islands, Saharin Yusoff on Batu Caves, and Ruth Kiew on Fraser's Hill.

Melvin Gumal would like to thank Daniel Kong for his images shown in the Sarawak section; Sylvia Ng for checking on details on locations, maps and compiling images; Sarawak Forestry Corporation's Abang Arbi and Oswald Braken for providing some details and helping with field trips that resulted in some of the images for Daniel Kong; the Wildlife Conservation Society, Christina, Katherine, Emily, Argus and Caleb for supporting the initiative.

Junaidi Payne would like to thank the following who are some of the many people who played a role in the establishment of the conservation areas described in this book: The late Patrick Mahedi Andau, Datuk Chin Kui Bee, Dr Glyn Davies, Tan Sri Datuk Seri Panglima Harris bin Mohd Salleh, Datuk Wilfred Lingham and Yeo Boon Hai and staff of the Ministry of Tourism and Environmental Development (1988-94), the late Dr Clive Marsh, Datuk Panglima K M Mastan, Datuk Sam Mannan, Dr Robert Ong and staff of Sabah Forestry Department, Datuk Matius Sator (as District Officer, Kinabatangan, 1988-94), Datuk Seri Panglima Musa Haji Aman, Datuk Seri Salleh Said Keruak, Dr Waidi Sinun and staff of Yayasan Sabah, Dr Elizabeth Wood and Datuk Seri Yong Teck Lee.

The authors and the publisher express their appreciation to Ken Scriven for his continued role in the planning and execution of this title.

Bibliography

Bennett, E.L and Gombek, F. (1993). *Proboscis Monkeys of Borneo*. Natural History Publications (Borneo). & Koktas Sabah, Ranau, Sabah, Malaysia.

Bennett, E.L. (1998). *The Natural History of Orang-utan*. Natural History Publications (Borneo).

Corlett, R.T. (2009). *The Ecology of Tropical East Asia.* Oxford University Press.

Das, I. (2010). *A Field Guide to the Reptiles of South-East Asia.* New Holland Publishers.

Das, I. (2012). *A Naturalist's Guide to the Snakes of Southeast Asia.* John Beaufoy Publishing.

Das, I. (2004). *Lizards of Borneo*. Natural History Publications (Borneo).

Davison, G.W.H. and Yeap, C.A. (2012). *A Naturalist's Guide to the Birds of Malaysia*. 2nd ed. John Beaufoy Publishing.

Hazebroek, H.P. and Kashim bin Abang Morshidi, A. (2000). *National Parks of Sarawak*. Natural History Publications (Borneo).

Francis, C.M. (2008). *A Field Guide to the Mammals of South-East Asia.* New Holland Publishers.

Hazebroek, H., Adlin, T.Z.A. and Waidi Sinun (2012). *Danum Valley. The Rain Forest*. Natural History Publications (Borneo).

Hazebroek, H., Adlin, T.Z.A. and Waidi Sinun. (2004). *Maliau Basin: Sabah's Lost World*. Natural History Publications (Borneo).

Hutton, W. (2008). *Tabin: Sabah's Greatest Wildlife Sanctuary*. Tabin Wildlife Holidays.

Inger, R.F. and Stuebing, R.B. (1997). *A Field Guide to the Frogs of Borneo*. Natural History Publications (Borneo) in association with Science and Technology Unit, Sabah.

IUCN. (2013). *The IUCN Red List of Threatened Species*. Version 2013.2. http://www.iucnredlist.org.

Kathirithamby-Wells, J. (2005). *Nature and Nation. Forests and Development in Peninsular Malaysia.* NIAS Press.

Kirton, L. (2013). *A Naturalist's Guide to the Butterflies of Peninsular Malaysia, Singapore and Thailand.* John Beaufoy Publishing.

Myers, S. (2009). *A Field Guide to the Birds of Borneo*. Talisman Publishing.

Payne, J. (1994). *This is Borneo*. New Holland (Publishers) Ltd. Produced in association with WWF Malaysia.

Payne, J. (2010). *Wild Sabah*. John Beaufoy Publishing.

Payne, J., Francis, C.M. and Phillipps, K. (1985). *A Field Guide to the Mammals of Borneo*. The Sabah Society with WWF Malaysia.

Phillipps, Q. and Phillips, K. (2011). *Phillipps' Field Guide to the Birds of Borneo: Sabah, Sarawak, Brunei and Kalimantan*. 3rd ed. John Beaufoy Publishing.

Robson, C. (2008). *A Field Guide to the Birds of South-East Asia.* New Holland Publishers.

Roth, H.L. (1896). *The Natives of Sarawak and British North Borneo. Vols. 1, 2.* Truslove & Hanson.

Seidenfaden, G. & Wood, J.J. (1992). *The Orchids of Peninsular Malaysia and Singapore.* Olsen & Olsen.

Shepherd, C.R. and L.A.S. (2012). *A Naturalist's Guide to Mammals of Southeast Asia.* John Beaufoy Publishing.

Smythies, B.E. & Davison, G.W.H. (1999). *The Birds of Borneo.* 4th ed. Natural History Publications (Borneo).

Sullivan, A. & Leong, C. (1981). *Commemorative History of Sabah.* Sabah State Government.

Warren, J. F. (2008). *The Sulu Zone, 1768-1898: The Dynamics of External Trade, Slavery, and Ethnicity in the Transformation of a Southeast-Asian Maritime State*. University of Hawai'i Press.

Wong, K.M. and Phillipps, A. (eds). (1996). *Kinabalu: Summit of Borneo*. Natural History Publications (Borneo).

Wells, D.R. (1999). *Birds of the Thai-Malay Peninsula. Vol. 1. Non-Passerines*. Academic Press.

Wells, D.R. (2007). *Birds of the Thai-Malay Peninsula. Vol. 2. Passerines.* A. & C. Black.

Whitmore, T.C. (1984). *Tropical Rain Forests of the Far East*. Clarendon Press.

Wong, T.S. (2013). *A Naturalist's Guide to the Birds of Borneo*. John Beaufoy Publishing.

Index

Photo credits

First published in the United Kingdom in 2014 by
John Beaufoy Publishing,
11 Blenheim Court, 316 Woodstock Road,
Oxford OX2 7NS, UK.
www.johnbeaufoy.com

10 9 8 7 6 5 4 3 2 1

ISBN 978-1-909612-25-9

Edited and indexed by Krystyna Mayer
Designed by Glyn Bridgewater
Cartography by William Smuts
Project management by Rosemary Wilkinson

Printed and bound in Singapore by Tien Wah Press (Pte) Ltd.